All Fired Up!

All Fired Up!

250 Fresh and Flavorful Grilling Recipes

2ND EDITION, REVISED AND EXPANDED

Margaret Howard

FIREFLY BOOKS

A FIREFLY BOOK

Published by Firefly Books Ltd. 2010

First printing

Publisher Cataloging-in-Publication Data (U.S.)

Howard, Margaret.
    All fired up! : 250 fresh and flavorful grilling recipes /
Margaret Howard.
2nd ed.
[ ] p. : col. photos. ; cm.
Includes index.
Summary: A collection of over 250 recipes for grilled food and grilled food accompaniments. Contains menu suggestions, grilling tips, and up-to-date information on equipment, health and safety.
ISBN-13: 978-1-55407-597-3
ISBN-10: 1-55407-597-1
1. Barbecue cookery. I. Title.
641.7/ 6 dc22   TX840.B3H693 2010

Library and Archives Canada Cataloguing in Publication

Howard, Margaret, 1930–
    All fired up! : 250 fresh and flavorful grilling recipes /
Margaret Howard. — 2nd ed. rev. and expanded

Includes index.
ISBN-13: 978-1-55407-597-3
ISBN-10: 1-55407-597-1

    1. Barbecue cookery. I. Title.

TX840.B3H68 2009   641.7'6   C2009-905048-X

Published in the United States by
Firefly Books (U.S.) Inc.
P.O. Box 1338, Ellicott Station
Buffalo, New York 14205

Published in Canada by
Firefly Books Ltd.
66 Leek Crescent
Richmond Hill, Ontario L4B 1H1

Cover design: Jacqueline Hope Raynor
Interior design and production: PageWave Graphics Inc.

Printed in China

The Publisher gratefully acknowledges the financial support for our publishing program by the Government of Canada through the Canada Book Fund as administered by the Department of Canadian Heritage.

CONTENTS

INTRODUCTION TO GRILLING

There is a special magic to flame-cooked food, and every recipe in this book has been tested to make your grilling experience simple and fun.

Inside this book you'll find:

Recipes, suggested menus, wine pairings and everything else you need to know about grilling.

Grilling Charts that provide a handy reference for grilling temperatures.

Grilling techniques and safety and health issues.

Icons that signal vegetarian recipes, recipes suitable for indoor grilling, wine suggestions and Marg's favorites (that's like asking me which of my four children I like best!).

| Vegetarian Recipes | Indoor Grilling | Marg's Favorites | Wine Suggestions |

The terms grilling and barbecuing are often used interchangeably, but they are actually not the same thing. Grilling uses relatively high temperatures for fast cooking. True barbecuing uses low temperatures for slow cooking. It is done with a wood fire in the same enclosure, but separate from, the meat being barbecued. Grilling is what we do with the typical backyard "barbecue."

Grilling Methods

There are two types of grilling: direct and indirect. For either method, a gas-fired or charcoal grill can be used.

Direct gas-fired grilling: Cover barbecue and preheat all burners on high for about 10 minutes. Place food on a lightly oiled grill rack that is directly over a heat source; then adjust heat according to the recipe. Usually food is turned once during the cooking. Fast grilling of foods typically takes less than 25 minutes. The grill lid may be open or closed, but closed is more efficient and keeps the grilled side warm after turning.

Indirect gas-fired grilling: After preheating, and just before placing food on the grill, turn off one burner (middle burner if there are three). Place the food on the lightly oiled top grill rack over the cold burner and put a metal pan of water (or other fluid such as beer, wine, broth or fruit juice) under the food, on the lower rack. Hot drippings from the food fall into the liquid and vaporize to automatically baste the food and keep it moist. As well, there are no flare-ups to burn the food, and no turning of the food is necessary. The grill lid is always closed so that heat circulates evenly and the cooking temperature remains stable. Indirect grilling works well for slow grilling of such foods as thick meat cuts, roasts, large chickens or turkeys, game, ham, and some vegetables producing moist tender meat or vegetables with a pleasant crisp exterior.

Direct charcoal grilling: It is important to open grill vents on the bottom of a charcoal grill before you light a chimney starter full of charcoal. When lit, dump coals out across bottom rack, leaving a free space equal to the size of the food to be grilled where food can be moved in case of flare-ups. Coals are at their best for grilling when they are covered with a light ash and there is no evidence of flame. Follow the same procedure as for gas-fired grilling and, as needed, adjust heat by adding or moving coals from under the food.

Indirect charcoal grilling: This method is the same as direct grilling except that a metal pan of water is placed in the middle between the banked coals. The food is placed on a lightly oiled grill rack over the water pan.

Grilling Tips

Propane users should check their fuel supply before starting to grill, particularly if entertaining guests. Many people own two propane tanks so there is always a backup on hand.

Always preheat the grill to the intended grilling temperature before putting food on it. This makes food less likely to stick.

Choose better quality, more tender cuts of marbled meats for the best grilling result. However, marinating less tender cuts before grilling improves tenderness and flavor.

Thicker cuts of meat grill better than thinner cuts. Choose cuts that are at least ¾-inch (2 cm) thick.

Trim excess fat from meat. But do leave some fat if the meat is particularly lean. Nick the outside edges of remaining fat at 2-inch (5 cm) intervals to prevent meat curling during grilling.

Lightly oil the grill rack with vegetable oil before lighting to prevent food sticking to the rack.

Apply bastes partway through grilling, and sauces towards the end. Excess amounts of either can lead to food-scorching flare-ups and a mess on the grill. Sugar in bastes and sauces can caramelize, creating another cleanup chore.

Try to turn steaks and hamburgers only once during cooking. Each turning loses precious juices.

If salt is applied to meat, add only after it is turned or when grilling is completed.

Start to check doneness earlier than indicated in the recipe to ensure food is not overdone.

Factors such as type of grill, cooking temperature, direct sun, wind and ambient temperature affect cooking time.

Wine Pairings

Pairing wine and food is not as mysterious as one might think. Del Rollo, National Director of Hospitality for Vincor Canada, was my invaluable guide for wine selection for this book. There are a few rules that work for most occasions. If you are preparing food that comes from a specific region of the world (Southern Italy, for example) and that region also has vineyards, then generally, the wine being made in that region will go well with the food.

The most food-friendly wines are ones that have good acidity and the alcohol content is not too high, for example, Riesling or Pinot Noir. The other safe choice in most cases is to serve a sparkling wine. The effervescence tends to help cleanse the palate and this wine goes well with almost everything.

As to chill or not to chill red wine, we all know that white should be somewhat chilled, some more than others. But what about red? If your red wines are stored at room temperature, then chances are the bottle needs some chilling in the refrigerator before serving. For lighter reds, like Pinot Noir, some Beaujolais, or Côtes du Rhône, about one hour is beneficial; for a medium-bodied Rioja or Chianti, chill about 45 minutes; and a big Australian Shiraz or California Cabernet Sauvignon or Zinfandel, about 30 minutes.

The choice of wine is really up to you. Del's final words on this subject are "Enjoy and have fun!"

GRILL TEMPERATURE TERMINOLOGY

Cooking times are approximate due to such factors as ambient temperature, wind and differences in grills. Remove meats from the grill when internal temperature is 5°F (2°C) below chart specification. Let stand covered with foil 15 minutes while reserved internal heat brings temperature to specified level.

LOW	MEDIUM–LOW	MEDIUM	MEDIUM–HIGH	HIGH
200°F to 250°F	275°F to 325°F	350°F to 375°F	400°F to 425°F	450°F to 475°F
100°C to 120°C	140°C to 160°C	180°C to 190°C	200°C to 220°C	230°C to 240°C

INDIRECT GRILLING CHART FOR MEATS

CUT	RARE TO MEDIUM–RARE	MEDIUM TO WELL DONE	PREHEAT	GRILL AT
Beef Roasts				
Internal temperatures	145°F (63°C)	160°F to 170°F (71°C to 77°C)		
Grill hours: 2 lb / 1 kg 3 lb / 1.5 kg 4 lb / 2 kg 5½ lb / 2.5 kg Tenderloin	1¾ to 2¼ 2 to 2½ 2¼ to 2¾ 2½ to 3 As above less 30 to 60 minutes	2 to 2½ 2¼ to 2¾ 2½ to 3 2¾ to 3¼ As above less 30 to 60 minutes	High for 10 minutes sear	Medium–low
Veal Roasts Rib, 3 to 5 lb / 1.4 to 2.3 kg				
Internal temperature	N/A	160°F to 170°F (71°C to 77°C)	Medium preheat	Medium
Grill hours	N/A	1¾ to 3		
Veal Roasts Loin, 4 to 6 lb / 1.9 to 2.7 kg				
Internal temperature	N/A	160°F to 170°F (71°C to 77°C)	Medium preheat	Medium–low
Grill hours	N/A	2 to 3		
Pork Boneless loin, 3 to 4 lb / 1.5 to 1.8 kg				
Internal temperature	N/A	160°F (71°C)	High preheat	Medium
Grill minutes per lb / 500 g	N/A	20 to 25		
Pork Boneless shoulder				
Internal temperature	N/A	160°F (71°C)	High preheat	Medium
Grill minutes per lb / 500 g	N/A	30 to 35		
Lamb Roasts Boneless leg, rolled, 4 to 6 lb / 2 to 3 kg				
Internal temperature	140°F (60°C)	150°F to 160°F (65°C to 71°C)	Medium preheat	Medium–low
Grill minutes per lb / 500 g	25 to 30	30 to 40		
Venison Boneless Roasts				
Internal temperature	140°F (60°C) 150°F (65°C)	N/A	Medium–high preheat	Medium–high
Grill minutes per lb / 500 g		25 to 30		

DIRECT GRILLING CHART FOR POULTRY

All grilling times assume the grill lid is closed. Allow additional time if the grill lid is open. Cooking times are approximate due to such factors as ambient temperature, wind and differences in grills.

CUT	FULL COOKING TIME MINUTES	GRILL AT	INTERNAL TEMPERATURE	DONENESS APPEARANCE
Chicken				
Breasts (half) Thighs Legs Drumsticks	15 to 18	Medium	165°F (74°C)	Flesh no longer pink, juices clear
Burgers	12 to 14	Medium	165°F (74°C)	No longer pink, well done
Butterflied	45	Medium	165°F (74°C)	Flesh no longer pink, juices clear
Kebabs	10 to 12	Medium–high	N/A	Flesh no longer pink, juices clear
Turkey				
Thighs up to 1 lb/500 g	30 to 35	Medium	170°F (77°C)	Flesh no longer pink, juices clear
Burgers	8 to 12	Medium	165°F (74°C)	No longer pink, well done
Kebabs	20	Medium–high	N/A	Flesh no longer pink, juices clear
Duck				
Breasts	8 to 10	Medium–high	150°F (65°C)	Slightly pink, juices clear

INDIRECT GRILLING CHART FOR POULTRY

CUT	FULL COOKING TIME HOURS	GRILL AT	INTERNAL TEMPERATURE	DONENESS APPEARANCE
Chicken Whole unstuffed				
3 lb / 1.5 kg 4 lb / 2 kg 5 lb / 2.5 kg	1 to 1½ 1¾ 2	Medium–high	185°F (85°C)	Flesh no longer pink, juices clear
Heavier chickens per lb / 500 g	20 to 25 minutes			
Turkey Whole unstuffed				
6 to 8 lb / 3 to 3.5 kg 8 to 10 lb / 3.5 to 4.5 kg 10 to 12 lb / 4.5 to 5.5 kg	1 to 1¾ 1¼ to 2 1½ to 2¼	Medium	180°F (82°C)	Flesh no longer pink, juices clear
Drumsticks/Thighs	1½ to 1¾			
Cornish Game Hens				
Whole unstuffed	1½	Medium	165°F (74°C)	Flesh no longer pink, juices clear
Quail				
Whole unstuffed	½	Medium	N/A	Flesh no longer pink, juices clear

GRILL TEMPERATURE TERMINOLOGY

All grilling times assume the grill lid is closed. Allow additional time if the grill lid is open. Cooking times are approximate due to such factors as ambient temperature, wind and differences in grills.

LOW	MEDIUM–LOW	MEDIUM	MEDIUM–HIGH	HIGH
200°F to 250°F	275°F to 325°F	350°F to 375°F	400°F to 425°F	450°F to 475°F
100°C to 120°C	140°C to 160°C	180°C to 190°C	200°C to 220°C	230°C to 240°C

DIRECT GRILLING CHART FOR MEATS

CUT	RARE	MEDIUM	WELL DONE	GRILL AT
Beef Steaks				
Internal temperature	145°F (63°C)	160°F (71°C)	170°F (77°C)	
Minutes per side: 　Tender cuts: 　　½ to ¾ inches (1 to 2 cm) 　　1 inch (2.5 cm) 　　1½ inches (4 cm) 　　2 inches (5 cm)	 3 to 4 5 to 6 9 to 10 11 to 14	 4 to 5 6 to 7 10 to 14 14 to 18	 5 to 6 7 to 9 15 to 18 18 to 22	Medium-high
Beef Burgers**				
Internal temperature	N/A	N/A	160°F (71°C)	
Minutes per side	N/A	N/A	5 to 7	Medium-high
Beef Sausage**				
Internal temperature	N/A	N/A	160°F (71°C)	
Total minutes		N/A	20 to 25	Medium-high
Beef Kebabs				
Total minutes	N/A	10		Medium-high
Veal Chops ¾ inch (2 cm)				
Internal temperature	N/A	155°F (68°C)	N/A	
Minutes per side	N/A	5 to 7	N/A	Medium-high
Pork Loin Chops				
Internal temperature	N/A	160°F (71°C)	N/A	
Minutes per side: 　1 inch (2.5 cm) 　1½ inches (3.5 cm)	 N/A N/A	 5 to 6 8 to 9	 N/A N/A	Medium
Pork Tenderloin				
Internal temperature	N/A	160°F (71°C)	N/A	
Minutes per side	N/A	10 to 12	N/A	Medium
Pork Burgers**				
Internal temperature	N/A	N/A	160°F (71°C)	
Minutes per side	N/A	N/A	5 to 7	Medium-high

DIRECT GRILLING CHART FOR MEATS (CONTINUED)

CUT	RARE	MEDIUM	WELL DONE	GRILL AT
Pork Sausage**				
Internal temperature	N/A	N/A	160°F (71°C)	
Total minutes			20 to 25	Medium–high
Pork Kebabs				
Total minutes	N/A	20 until brown	N/A	Medium
Lamb Chops				
Internal temperature	140°F (60°C)	150°F (65°C)	160°F (71°C)	
Minutes per side: 1 inch (2.5 cm)	3 to 4	5 to 6	6 to 7	Medium
Lamb Leg Butterflied				
Internal temperature	140°F (60°C)	150°F (65°C)	160°F (71°C)	
Total minutes	30 to 35	35 to 40	40 to 45	Medium
Lamb Burgers**				
Internal temperature	N/A	N/A	160°F (71°C)	
Minutes per side	N/A	N/A	5 to 7	Medium
Lamb Kebabs				
Total minutes	N/A	10 until some inside pink	N/A	Medium
Venison Steaks				
Internal temperature	145°F (63°C)	150°F (65°C) medium rare	N/A	
Minutes per side: ¾ inch 1½	4 to 5 6 to 7	5 to 6 7 to 8	N/A N/A	High
Venison Tenderloin				
Internal temperature	145°F (63°C)	150°F (65°C) medium rare	N/A	
Minutes per side	4 to 5	5 to 6	N/A	High
Venison Burgers**				
Internal temperature	N/A	160°F (71°C)	N/A	
Minutes per side	N/A	4 to 6	N/A	Medium–high
Venison Kebabs				
Total minutes	N/A	6 to 8 till pink at center	N/A	Medium–high

** All ground meat must be grilled to an internal temperature
of 160°F (71°C) to ensure food safety.

CHAPTER 1
APPETIZERS AND STARTERS

◄ *Chicken Satay with Mexican Cranberry Salsa (page 33)*

Appetizers prepare our palate for the greater and more substantial delights to follow. The recipes in this section have been chosen with that thought in mind. Many are grilled. Others like soups and salsas are not, but match well with grilled main courses.

Appetizers set the theme for a memorable outdoor or indoor feast. If there is room, grill some appetizers along with the main meal. Serve them hot — from grill to guest. Failing this, grill some appetizers beforehand and keep warm in the kitchen oven. Or choose a cold appetizer like Roasted Nuts (page 15), or Grilled Red Pepper and Herb Dip (page 15). They make perfect light preludes with some raw vegetable crudités.

And then there is soup. Think of Chilled Pea and Lettuce Soup (page 31) on a steamy summer evening or a hot Beet Borscht (page 31) for brisker spring or fall occasions. What more could you ask?

Some of the recipes in this section can be used as main courses by simply doubling them or serving larger amounts. Vegetarian Pizza with Provolone (page 28) or Black Bean or Crab-stuffed Quesadillas (pages 22 and 21) all make wonderful main courses.

The fresh flavors of the Versatile Salsas (pages 32–33) enliven grilled meats. So after using for appetizer dipping, have extra salsa on hand to "perk up" a grilled chicken leg or steak. These lively combinations of fresh tastes, colors and textures are magnificent.

Appetizers also form a good basis for tasty luncheon menus. Try Balsamic Onion Confit (page 18) as a filling base for a quiche or Grilled Dilled Scallops with Lime Aioli Dip (page 20) and Rosemary Flatbread (page 29) for your next patio salad luncheon.

GRILLED RED PEPPER AND HERB DIP

The smoky-sweet taste of grilled red peppers is incredible in this yogurt-based dip. Enjoy dipping raw vegetables, corn tortillas or baked chips.

1	large sweet red pepper	1
1	clove garlic	1
¼ cup	plain yogurt or sour cream	50 mL
3 tbsp	light mayonnaise	45 mL
2 tsp	red wine vinegar	10 mL
1 tbsp	chopped fresh oregano or 1 tsp (5 mL) dried	15 mL
⅛ tsp	granulated sugar	0.5 mL
	Salt and freshly ground pepper	

1. Preheat grill on medium. Place red pepper on oiled grill rack. Close lid and cook (use Direct Grilling, page 6) for 8 to 10 minutes or until pepper is streaked with brown and tender when pierced; turn frequently. Place in paper bag until cool enough to handle. Remove any blackened skin, stem and seeds and discard.

2. In blender or food processor, purée red pepper, garlic, yogurt and mayonnaise until smooth. Stir in vinegar, oregano and sugar. Season to taste with salt and pepper. Cover and refrigerate for up to one week. **Makes about 1 cup (250 mL).**

ROASTED NUTS

What more can a grill chef cook on a barbecue? These delicious spicy nuts can be grilled any time there is room on a hot grill.

¼ cup	melted butter or margarine	50 mL
2 tbsp	Worcestershire sauce	25 mL
¼ tsp	hot sauce	1 mL
1 tsp	each: chili powder and garlic powder	5 mL
½ tsp	each: celery seed and cumin	2 mL
4 cups	mixed unsalted nuts	1 L

1. Preheat grill on medium-high. Melt butter, Worcestershire and hot sauce, chili powder, celery seed, garlic powder and cumin in a small saucepan on the grill or on side burner. Add the nuts; stir until evenly coated.

2. Spread nuts on a shallow rimmed baking pan. Place baking pan on grill rack, close lid and roast nuts (use Direct Grilling, page 6) for 15 minutes or until golden brown; stir occasionally. Remove from grill and cool. Store in a tightly covered container. **Makes 4 cups (1 L).**

TAPENADE

Tapenade is a traditional hors d'oeuvre of Provence. Its name comes from Tapeno, the Provençal word for caper, one of the ingredients. Any flavorful black olives can be used, but be sure to buy them in bulk, preferably still sitting in their brine. Serve spooned over chèvre cheese spread on thin slices of baguette or on a cracker.

½ lb	kalamata olives, pitted (about 1 cup/175 mL)	250 g
¼ cup	capers, rinsed and drained	50 mL
¼ cup	anchovy paste	50 mL
2	large cloves garlic	2
2 tbsp	each: olive oil and Cognac or brandy	25 mL
1 tbsp	lemon juice	15 mL
⅛ tsp	each: freshly ground pepper and dry mustard	0.5 mL
1	long baguette, thinly sliced and toasted	1
½ cup	chèvre cheese, softened	125 mL
	Lemon slices	

1. In food processor, process olives, capers, anchovy paste, garlic, olive oil, Cognac and lemon juice with on/off turns until mixture is finely chopped but not smooth. Season to taste with pepper and mustard. Remove to serving bowl and garnish with lemon slices.

2. Arrange toast and cheese on a platter with tapenade bowl in center. **Makes 1½ cups (375 mL).**

Tip: Baguette slices can be toasted quickly on the grill rack while other foods are grilling. Tapenade is a great appetizer to keep on hand, and it can also serve as a sauce for full-flavored grilled fish. It freezes well.

BROCCOLI PESTO

Pesto need not always be the classic basil variety — broccoli pesto is just as delicious. This pesto can serve as the basis of a host of different dishes, a few of which are given below.

3 cups	cut-up broccoli florets and stems	750 mL
2	cloves garlic	2
3 tbsp	olive oil	45 mL
1/3 cup	slivered almonds or walnuts	75 mL
1/4 cup	chopped fresh basil or 4 tsp (20 mL) dried	50 mL
1/3 cup	grated Parmesan cheese	75 mL

1. Cook broccoli in boiling water, for 4 to 5 minutes or until crisp-tender; drain and cool.

2. In food processor, blend broccoli, garlic, oil, almonds and basil until coarsely chopped. Add cheese; process until well mixed. **Makes 2 1/2 cups (625 mL).**

Uses for Broccoli Pesto

Bruschetta: Spread Broccoli Pesto over thick slices of Italian bread. Grill for 3 minutes or until just bubbling and starting to brown. For extra color, add diced tomatoes.

Cream Cheese and Broccoli Pesto Appetizer: Cream 1 pkg (125 g) light cream cheese and 1/2 cup (125 mL) butter or margarine until smooth. Alternately layer one-third cream cheese mixture and one-half Broccoli Pesto in plastic lined bowl, beginning and ending with cheese. Cover and refrigerate until firm. Unmold and serve at room temperature with assorted crackers. Mold smaller amounts in small custard cups and freeze for future use.

Variation: add slivers of sun-dried tomatoes between cheese and pesto layer.

Broccoli Vinaigrette: Prepare a vinaigrette dressing with 1/3 cup (75 mL) extra virgin olive oil, 2 tbsp (25 mL) white wine vinegar and 1 tbsp (15 mL) Broccoli Pesto.

Broccoli Dip: Stir small amount of Broccoli Pesto into sour cream or plain yogurt. Serve with vegetable crudités.

Pasta: Toss small amount of Broccoli Pesto with hot cooked pasta. Sprinkle with extra Parmesan cheese, if desired.

Pesto Tomatoes: Spread Broccoli Pesto on thickly sliced tomatoes. Grill or broil until tomatoes are heated.

ROQUEFORT APPETIZER BREAD

The pungent, somewhat salty taste of Roquefort combines with the rich sharp flavor of Parmesan in this simple, easy-to-make appetizer.

½ cup	Roquefort or blue cheese salad dressing	125 mL
¼ cup	grated Parmesan cheese	50 mL
4	slices sourdough French bread, cut 1-inch (2.5 cm) thick	4
2 tbsp	diced green chilis or sweet green pepper	25 mL
2 tbsp	grated Parmesan cheese	25 mL

1. In small bowl, combine Roquefort dressing and ¼ cup (50 mL) Parmesan cheese; mix well. Grill one side of each bread slice; spread about 2 tbsp (25 mL) of mixture on grilled side; top with green chilis. Sprinkle each slice with additional Parmesan cheese.

2. Preheat grill on high. Place slices on lightly oiled grill rack, cheese side up. Cook, covered (use Direct Grilling, page 6), for 3 to 5 minutes or until lightly browned on under side. Remove from grill and cut into finger-size pieces; serve hot. (To serve as a lunch entrée, leave whole.) **Makes about 2 dozen.**

Tip: Assemble ahead of time, cover with a damp cloth and aluminum foil. Grill just before serving.

BALSAMIC ONION CONFIT

 Confit is a French term referring to the preservation of meats. It seemed appropriate to use this term to describe the rich and mellow flavor of this amazing appetizer.

3 tbsp	butter or margarine	45 mL
1 lb	onions, chopped (about 2 large)	500 g
2 tbsp	granulated sugar	25 mL
1 tsp	salt	5 mL
½ tsp	freshly ground pepper	2 mL
3 tbsp	balsamic vinegar	45 mL

1. Preheat indoor grill on medium-low. Melt butter in heavy saucepan on grill. Add onions, sugar, salt and pepper. Cook, stirring occasionally, until golden brown (approximately one hour).

2. Add vinegar and cook to reduce to syrup-like consistency. The mixture should still be moist and resemble a jam. Delicious served warm or refrigerate and heat just before serving. **Makes 1 cup (250 mL).**

Serving Suggestions: Serve a small spoonful with a wedge of Cheddar cheese on toasted baguette slices. Add to any pizza. Fill small baked phyllo or pastry tarts.

For Outdoor Grilling: Preheat grill on medium–low. Follow procedure as above for Steps 1 and 2. Close lid and cook, checking and stirring frequently.

WARM PINE NUT GOAT CHEESE SPREAD

Warming brings out the lively tart flavor of the goat cheese (chèvre) and the toasty pine pungency of pine nuts. Add a bowl of Tomato Salsa (page 32) and enjoy this simple but elegant appetizer with your favorite summer wine as you wait for dinner to finish grilling.

5 oz	goat cheese	150 g
3 tbsp	pine nuts	45 mL
1	small baguette, thinly sliced	1

1. Place cheese in a small, shallow, oven-proof casserole. Press pine nuts into surface. Preheat grill on medium-high. Place casserole on grill rack (use Direct Grilling, page 6) and heat for 5 to 8 minutes or until cheese is warm and softened.

2. Place cheese dish in center of a serving plate surrounded by baguette slices and a bowl of salsa. To serve, spread bread with warm cheese and pine nuts; top with a spoonful of salsa. **Makes about 24 appetizers.**

GRILLED ROASTED GARLIC

This recipe is so good you may want to do more than one garlic head. Out of the grill season, roast garlic in a moderate oven (375°F/190°C).

1	large head garlic	1
1 tbsp	olive oil	15 mL
	Sliced sourdough bread	

1. Cut the top off the garlic head and place root side down in a small aluminum foil pan. Sprinkle with oil and cover pan with foil.

2. Preheat grill on medium-high. Place pan on grill rack. Close lid and cook (use Direct Grilling, page 6) for about 30 minutes or until garlic is soft. Remove from grill. Cut a thin slice from the top so that the garlic cloves can be scooped out and spread on sliced sourdough bread. **Makes enough roasted garlic to spread on 8 bread slices.**

ONION, NUT AND CHEESE BITES

Create these delicious small appetizer bites from ingredients usually found in your kitchen. They can be prepared beforehand to the end of Step 1, covered with a damp tea towel, then grilled at serving time.

1	large onion, halved and thinly sliced (Vidalia or Spanish preferred)	1
1 tbsp	olive oil	15 mL
¼ cup	chopped pecans, almonds or walnuts	50 mL
1 tsp	granulated sugar	5 mL
1 tbsp	Dijon mustard	15 mL
16	slices (½ inch/ 1 cm thick) French bread stick	16
¾ cup	shredded Cheddar cheese	175 mL

1. In nonstick skillet, cook onion in oil on medium-high heat for about 5 minutes; stir often. Reduce heat, add nuts and sugar; cover and cook for 5 minutes longer or until onion has caramelized and is tender. Stir in mustard. Spoon onion mixture on bread slices and sprinkle with cheese.

2. Preheat grill on medium-high. Place bread on oiled grill rack. Cook, uncovered (use Direct Grilling, page 6), for 3 to 4 minutes or until bread is warm and toasted and cheese has started to melt. Watch carefully to avoid overcooking. **Makes 16 slices.**

GRILLED DILLED SCALLOPS WITH LIME AIOLI DIP

 Grilled scallops offer an amazing start to an outdoor summer meal.

8	large scallops, cut in half	8
1 tbsp	each: canola oil and lemon juice	15 mL
2 tbsp	finely chopped onion	25 mL
1	clove garlic, minced	1
2 tbsp	chopped fresh dill or 2 tsp (10 mL) dried	25 mL
1 cup	diced tomatoes	250 mL
	Salt and pepper	
4	thick slices Italian bread	4
	Chopped fresh dill and lemon wedges	

1. Toss scallop halves with oil, lemon juice, onion, garlic and dill; set aside for 15 minutes. Combine tomatoes, salt and pepper.

2. Preheat grill on medium. Toast bread on grill rack on both sides until golden brown; keep warm.

3. Remove scallops from lemon mixture; place on lightly oiled grill rack. Close lid and grill (use Direct Grilling, page 6) for about 5 minutes or just until opaque; turn once. Remove from grill; top each toast slice with some tomato mixture and 4 scallop halves. Cut each slice into 4 squares and serve with chopped dill and lemon wedges. **Makes 16 squares.**

Dipping Tip: When you want to dip scallops, Lime Aioli Dip is perfect. Combine ½ cup (125 mL) light mayonnaise with 1 tsp (5 mL) grated lime zest, 1 to 2 tbsp (15 to 25 mL) fresh lime juice, 1 tsp (5 mL) Dijon mustard, and a pinch of freshly ground pepper. For a richer flavor, add 1 to 2 tsp (5 to 10 mL) olive oil. This recipe came from my daughter Janice.

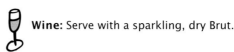 **Wine:** Serve with a sparkling, dry Brut.

CRAB-STUFFED QUESADILLAS

Crabmeat is an interesting departure from the usual meat or refried bean quesadilla filling. Because quesadillas cook so quickly, check the underside frequently. Light grill marks are your clue to doneness.

¼ cup	sun-dried tomatoes (not oil-packed)	50 mL
1	pkg (125 g) light cream cheese, softened	1
½ cup	shredded Monterey Jack or Cheddar cheese	125 mL
1 tbsp	snipped fresh thyme or 1 tsp (5 mL) dried	15 mL
1 tbsp	milk	15 mL
6	7-inch (18-cm) flour tortillas	6
2 tbsp	canola oil	25 mL
½ cup	flaked crabmeat	125 mL
1	green onion, thinly sliced	1

1. In small saucepan, place tomatoes and just enough water to cover; bring to a boil. Reduce heat and simmer for about 2 minutes or until tender; drain and finely chop. Stir together tomatoes, cream cheese, Monterey Jack or Cheddar cheese, thyme and milk in small mixing bowl.

2. Brush one side of three tortillas with some oil. Place tortillas, oil side down, on large baking sheet. Spread cream cheese mixture over each tortilla on baking sheet. Sprinkle each with one-third of crab and green onion; top with remaining tortillas. Lightly brush the top tortillas with remaining oil.

3. Preheat grill on medium. Place quesadillas on lightly oiled grill rack. Close lid and cook (use Direct Grilling, page 6) for about 3 minutes or until cream cheese mixture is heated through and tortillas start to brown; turn once halfway through grilling.

4. To serve, cut each tortilla into 6 wedges. **Makes 4 to 6 servings.**

BLACK BEAN QUESADILLAS

 Mexico's everyday bread, the flour tortilla, is round and flat, resembling a very thin pancake. Quesadillas are tortillas filled with a savory mixture, then either folded in half or sandwiched between 2 tortillas. For an appetizer, cut the quesadillas in bite-sized pieces. For a perfect lunch idea, serve them full size.

1 cup	black beans, drained and rinsed	250 mL
1	medium tomato, diced	1
1	roasted red pepper (see page 178)	1
1	small jalapeño pepper, seeded and diced	1
1	clove garlic, minced	1
½ cup	fresh cilantro, basil or oregano or 2 tbsp (25 mL) dried	125 mL
¼ cup	finely chopped onion	50 mL
1½ cups	shredded Cheddar or mozzarella cheese	375 mL
½ cup	crumbled feta cheese	125 mL
8	8-inch (20 cm) whole wheat flour tortillas	8
	Fresh cilantro, optional	

1. Combine beans, tomato, red and jalapeño peppers, garlic, cilantro and onion. Combine shredded and feta cheese in second container.

2. For each tortilla, layer a small amount of cheese, bean mixture and more cheese on one half of each tortilla. Fold over and brush edges lightly with water to seal. Repeat with remaining tortillas.

3. Preheat grill on medium. Place filled quesadillas on lightly oiled grill rack. Close lid and grill (use Direct Grilling, page 6) for about 3 minutes per side or until tortilla is golden brown and filling is hot.

4. Remove from grill to cutting board and cut each quesadilla in half with a pizza cutter or sharp knife. Garnish with fresh cilantro, if using, and serve. **Makes 16 pieces.**

CROSTINI WITH GRILLED VEGETABLES AND MOZZARELLA

Crostini are like thin bruschetta. Grill crostini on one rack and serve them as appetizers while the main course is cooking on the other rack. If your grill does not have a lid, place foil over the baking pan so that the vegetables stew rather than sauté.

2 tbsp	each: butter or margarine and olive oil	25 mL
2	medium carrots, thinly sliced	2
1	medium onion, thinly sliced	1
1	sweet green pepper, seeded and thinly sliced lengthwise	1
2	large cloves garlic, minced	2
2	yellow squash, thinly sliced on the diagonal	2
4	plum tomatoes, diced	4
½ cup	fresh basil or parsley, minced	125 mL
	Salt and freshly ground pepper	
1 cup	shredded mozzarella cheese	250 mL
1	clove garlic, halved	1
1	loaf French bread, cut into 16 ½-inch (1 cm) slices	1

1. Preheat grill on medium-high. In oblong baking pan, heat butter and oil on grill rack. Add carrots and onion. Close lid and cook (use Direct Grilling, page 6) for about 5 minutes or until onions are softened; stir well. Add green pepper and garlic; close lid and cook for about 3 minutes; stir. Add squash and tomatoes; close lid and cook for about 4 minutes or until all vegetables are just tender.

2. Stir in basil, salt and pepper to taste. Sprinkle with cheese; cover and cook for about 3 minutes or until cheese melts. Remove pan from grill, cover and keep warm.

3. Rub cut sides of garlic over one side of each bread slice. Place bread slices around outer edge of grill rack; toast for 1 minute or until bread is golden; turn once. Transfer bread to serving platter. Top each slice with a portion of grilled vegetables and serve immediately. **Makes 6 to 8 servings.**

PORK SATAY WITH SPICY PEANUT SAUCE

Satay — marinated cubes of meat, fish or poultry threaded on skewers and grilled — is a traditional Indonesian snack, usually served with a spicy peanut sauce. You can serve this satay as an appetizer or a main course, and the peanut sauce is also delicious on a noodle salad with vegetables.

MARINADE

¹/₂ tsp	grated lime peel	2 mL
1 tbsp	each: lime juice, water and liquid honey	15 mL
1 tsp	curry powder	5 mL
1	clove garlic, crushed	1
1 lb	pork tenderloin	500 g
16	soaked wooden skewers	16

PEANUT SAUCE

3 tbsp	smooth peanut butter	45 mL
2 tbsp	each: liquid honey, light soy sauce and water	25 mL
1 tbsp	rice vinegar	15 mL
1 tbsp	minced gingerroot	15 mL
¹/₈ tsp	hot red pepper sauce	0.5 mL

Suggested Menu: Serve the satay as an appetizer with raw vegetables or as a main course with rice pilaf.

Tip: For appetizers, it is best to use wooden or bamboo skewers. Be sure to soak them in water for at least 30 minutes before using to prevent skewers burning. Metal skewers are also good; they are reusable and possibly preferred when the satay is a main course.

1. Trim visible fat from meat and discard. Cut meat into 4 x ¹/₂ inch (10 x 1 cm) strips. (You should have about 16 pieces.)

2. *For marinade:* In small bowl, combine lime peel and juice, water, honey, curry powder and garlic; add pork and toss to coat. Cover and marinate in refrigerator for 1 to 3 hours.

3. *For sauce:* In small bowl, whisk or blend together peanut butter, honey, soy sauce, water, vinegar, gingerroot and hot sauce until smooth. Taste and adjust seasonings if desired.

4. Remove meat from marinade; reserve marinade. Place marinade in small saucepan, bring to a boil, reduce heat and cook for 5 minutes; keep warm. Thread pork on 16 soaked wooden skewers.

5. Preheat grill on medium-high. Place skewers on lightly oiled grill rack. Close lid and cook (use Direct Grilling, page 6) for about 6 minutes per side or until pork is cooked through. Remove pork from skewers and serve with peanut sauce for dipping or drizzled over. **Makes 16 appetizers.**

MUSHROOM BRUSCHETTA

 Bruschetta, known as grilled bread, is very popular. The outdoor grill is a perfect way to cook it for either a luncheon picnic on the deck or an appetizer before dinner. Use different breads such as the commercial and readily available gourmet-style flatbreads or a crusty Italian loaf.

2 tsp	canola or olive oil	10 mL
2	green onions, finely chopped	2
1	clove garlic, minced	1
½ lb	button or portobello mushrooms, sliced (about 4 cups/1 L)	250 g
1 tbsp	each: chopped fresh oregano and tarragon or 1 tsp (5 mL) dried	15 mL
½ tsp	freshly ground pepper	2 mL
pinch	salt	pinch
2 tbsp	chopped fresh parsley	25 mL
½ cup	shredded Cheddar or mozzarella cheese	125 mL
3 tbsp	light cream cheese, softened	45 mL
1	Italian-style plain flatbread (300 g)	1
	Fresh parsley leaves	

1. Heat oil over medium-high in nonstick skillet. Cook onion and garlic for about 2 minutes. Add mushrooms, oregano, tarragon and pepper. Cook for about 8 minutes or until mushroom liquid evaporates. Add salt to taste; stir in parsley and reserve.

2. Blend together cheeses (you may need to add a small amount of milk to have a consistency soft enough for spreading). Spread one side of flatbread with cheese mixture. Top with mushroom mixture.

3. Preheat grill on medium. Place bread on lightly oiled grill rack and grill (use Direct Grilling, page 6) for about 10 minutes or until golden and cheese has started to melt. Remove from grill and cut into thin wedges. Top each with fresh parsley and serve. **Makes 10 to 12 servings.**

Tip: Fresh basil can replace parsley with excellent results.

TOMATO-BASIL BRUSCHETTA

Traditional bruschetta are slices of garlic bread roasted over an open fire and served warm. Today we make a number of variations, but they are still based on a simple, basic theme.

6	thick slices Italian bread	6
2	cloves garlic, halved	2
1	large onion, sliced and separated into rings	1
1 tbsp	olive oil	15 mL
1 tsp	granulated sugar	5 mL
1 tbsp	herb or Dijon mustard	15 mL
2	medium tomatoes, each cut into 6 slices	2
⅓ cup	chopped fresh basil	75 mL
2	green onions, sliced	2
	Salt and freshly ground pepper	
½ cup	grated Parmesan cheese	125 mL
	Fresh basil leaves	

1. Cut each bread slice crosswise in half. Rub one side with cut garlic cloves; mince garlic and reserve. Toast garlic side of bread on preheated grill rack or under the broiler.

2. In heavy, nonstick skillet, cook garlic and onion in hot oil for about 5 minutes or until tender. Add sugar, reduce heat and cook for 5 minutes or until onion has started to caramelize. Stir in mustard. Spoon some of onion onto each half bread slice. Place 1 tomato slice over onion, sprinkle with basil, green onions, salt, pepper and cheese. Allow to stand at room temperature for up to 1 hour.

3. Preheat grill on medium. Place bread slices on oiled grill rack; toast, uncovered, (use Direct Grilling, page 6) for about 2 minutes or until bottom of bread has toasted and tomato is warmed. Garnish with extra basil leaves and serve. **Makes 12 slices.**

Tip: For the most authentic flavor, use Parmigiano-Reggiano cheese from Italy. Buy it by the piece and grate just before using.

VEGETARIAN PIZZA WITH PROVOLONE

For a backyard gathering, prepare lots of vegetables, shredded cheese and seasonings and invite guests to add their own toppings to an Italian-style gourmet flatbread base. Enjoy a glass of red wine while the pizzas are grilling.

1	round or oblong (300 g) Italian-style flatbread	1
1 tbsp	canola oil	15 mL
2 cups	shredded provolone or mozzarella cheese	500 mL
1 cup	roasted sweet green pepper (see page 178) cut into long thin slices	250 mL
1 cup	sliced mushrooms	250 mL
1/4 cup	chopped green onion	50 mL
1/4 cup	grated Parmesan cheese	50 mL
2 tbsp	chopped almonds	25 mL
1 tsp	dried oregano or 1 tbsp (15 mL) chopped fresh	5 mL
pinch	freshly ground pepper	pinch

1. Lightly brush flatbread with oil. Sprinkle with provolone cheese. Top with green pepper, mushrooms, onion, Parmesan cheese, almonds, oregano and pepper.

2. Preheat grill on medium-high. Place pizza directly on lightly oiled grill rack. Close lid and grill (use Indirect Grilling, page 6) for about 20 minutes or until cheese starts to melt and vegetables are hot. Remove flatbread from grill and cut into thin wedges. **Makes 16 servings.**

Variations: Other toppings: red or orange grilled peppers, zucchini, black or green olives, sweet onion, tomatoes, sliced almonds, shiitake or portobello mushrooms and fennel. Mozzarella or Monterey Jack cheese would make an interesting change. And basil or marjoram may be used, as well as prepared pesto.

 Wine: A Cabernet Franc Rosé will match best.

GRILLED POLENTA WITH BASIL AND TOMATOES

Thin slices of cornmeal polenta grilled until golden, then topped with tomato bits and basil, make a tasty nibble.

4 cups	chicken broth	1 L
1⅓ cups	yellow cornmeal	325 mL
3	large tomatoes, finely diced	3
½ cup	chopped fresh basil leaves	125 mL
½ cup	grated Parmesan cheese	125 mL
	Salt and freshly ground pepper	

1. In large saucepan, bring broth to a boil over high heat. Gradually stir in cornmeal until thickened. Reduce heat to low and cook, stirring constantly, for about 10 minutes. Spoon into lightly greased 9 x 5 inch (2 L) loaf pan; cool until firm.

2. Remove polenta from pan onto a cutting board. Slice crosswise into 10 thin slices.

3. Preheat grill on medium-high. Place polenta slices on oiled grill rack. Cook (use Direct Grilling, page 6) until golden brown and crisp; turn once. Remove from grill and cut each slice into 4 squares. Top with tomato, basil and cheese; sprinkle lightly with salt and pepper. Serve warm. **Makes 40 pieces.**

 Wine: An oaked Chardonnay will pair nicely with this appetizer.

ROSEMARY FLATBREAD

Many different variations are made possible by adding toppings to authentic Italian-style plain flatbreads. These simple but elegant versions are comfort foods in your appetizer selections.

2 tbsp	olive, canola or walnut oil	25 mL
2 tbsp	chopped fresh rosemary	25 mL
	Freshly ground pepper	
1	round or oblong (300 g) Italian-style plain flatbread	1

1. Lightly brush flatbread with oil; sprinkle with rosemary and pepper.

2. Preheat grill on medium. Place bread on lightly oiled grill rack. Close lid and grill (use Direct Grilling, page 6) for 2 minutes, rotating bread for even heating. Repeat until bottom of bread is golden brown. Remove flatbread from grill, cut into wedges and serve. **Makes 10 to 12 servings.**

Garlic Flatbread Variation: Crushed garlic can be added to oil, brush bread and follow Step 2 above.

HERBED ITALIAN LOAF

Herbed bread toasted on the grill makes a wonderful appetizer. Cooking appetizers and the main meal on the grill allows you to remain outside with your guests throughout most of the meal preparation.

2 tbsp	each: butter and olive oil	25 mL
¼ cup	finely minced green onion	50 mL
2 tbsp	each: finely minced fresh dill and parsley	25 mL
1	clove garlic, crushed	1
⅛ tsp	crushed red pepper flakes	0.5 mL
1	large crusty Italian loaf	1
⅓ cup	grated Parmesan cheese	75 mL

1. In nonstick skillet, heat butter and oil over medium heat. Cook onion for 2 minutes; add dill, parsley and garlic and cook for 2 minutes or until wilted. Stir in pepper flakes; let cool.

2. Preheat grill on medium. Cut bread in half lengthwise. Toast bread, cut side down, on grill for about 2 minutes or until golden brown. Remove from grill and spread each half with herbed mixture. Sprinkle with cheese, return to grill and heat (use Direct Grilling, page 6) for 3 to 4 minutes or until underside is toasted. Remove and cut crosswise into slices. **Makes 8 to 10 servings.**

GRILLED SOFFRITO BREAD

Soffrito is an Italian sauce made by sautéing onions, green peppers, garlic and sometimes celery in olive oil with herbs until all ingredients are tender and the mixture is thick.

1 cup	chopped sweet red pepper	250 mL
1	small onion, chopped	1
¼ cup	tightly packed fresh cilantro sprigs	50 mL
2	cloves garlic, crushed	2
1 tsp	dried oregano or 1 tbsp (15 mL) fresh	5 mL
½ tsp	cumin seeds or ground cumin	2 mL
1 tbsp	olive oil	15 mL
	Salt and pepper	
12	slices Italian bread, ¼-inch (3 mm) thick and halved	12

1. In blender or food processor, blend red pepper, onion, cilantro, garlic, oregano and cumin until coarsely chopped.

2. In small nonstick skillet, heat oil. Add blended ingredients and cook, stirring frequently for 3 to 5 minutes or until mixture is softened and moisture has evaporated. Season with salt and pepper to taste. (Soffrito may be made 2 days ahead, covered and chilled.)

3. Preheat grill on medium. Spread some soffrito on one side of each bread slice (reserve any remaining sauce for another use). Place on lightly oiled grill rack. Cook, uncovered (use Direct Grilling, page 6), for about 2 minutes or until golden brown.

4. Transfer soffrito bread with tongs to a bread basket and serve warm. **Makes 6 servings.**

BEET BORSCHT

Borscht is the most famous of the Slav soups. Some cooks add horseradish and so do I, as it definitely adds that extra "zing." Borscht is always served with a sour cream garnish and has a most wonderful flavor.

4 cups	beef broth	1 L
3	large beets, peeled and diced	3
1	small onion, finely chopped	1
1 tbsp	each: lemon juice and horseradish	15 mL
½ tsp	salt	2 mL
¼ tsp	freshly ground pepper	1 mL
	Sour cream or plain yogurt	
	Chopped fresh dill	

1. In large saucepan, bring broth to a boil. Add beets, onion, lemon juice, horseradish, salt and pepper. Cook for 20 minutes or until vegetables are tender. Remove from stove and allow to cool for a short time.

2. In food processor, process half of soup until smooth. Return to remaining soup and heat to serving temperature. Taste and adjust seasonings if needed.

3. Garnish each bowl with a large dollop of sour cream or yogurt and sprinkle with chopped fresh dill. **Makes 7 cups (1.75 L), about 6 servings.**

CHILLED PEA AND LETTUCE SOUP

Especially great on steamy hot days, this chilled soup made with either romaine or iceberg lettuce is a fine example of summer cuisine. It can be made in advance of your dinner. Leftovers can be frozen.

2 tbsp	olive oil	25 mL
4	green onions, coarsely chopped	4
12 cups	coarsely chopped lettuce	3 L
3½ cups	chicken broth	825 mL
2 cups	green peas, fresh or frozen	500 mL
1 tsp	granulated sugar	5 mL
½ tsp	salt	2 mL
¼ tsp	freshly ground pepper	1 mL
¾ to 1 cup	buttermilk	175 to 250 mL
2 tbsp	chopped fresh dill	25 mL
	Fresh dill sprigs	

1. Heat oil over medium heat in large saucepan. Cook onion in oil for 5 minutes or until softened. Stir in lettuce, cover and steam for 5 minutes or until wilted; stir occasionally.

2. Add broth, peas, sugar, salt and pepper; bring to a boil. Reduce heat and cook covered for 10 minutes. Remove from heat and partially cool.

3. Purée in batches with buttermilk in food processor or blender until smooth. Pour into large container and refrigerate for 4 hours or overnight.

4. Ladle into bowls and garnish with fresh dill. **Makes 8 cups (2 L).**

VERSATILE SALSAS

FRESH MULTI-VEGETABLE SALSA

1 cup	finely chopped tomatoes	250 mL
¹⁄₂ cup	finely chopped seedless cucumber	125 mL
¹⁄₄ cup	finely chopped sweet green pepper	50 mL
2 tbsp	finely chopped red onion	25 mL
1 to 2 tbsp	chopped fresh cilantro	15 to 25 mL
1	small jalapeño pepper, seeded and minced	1
1	clove garlic, minced	1
1 tsp	each: lemon or lime juice and tomato paste	5 mL
¹⁄₄ tsp	salt	1 mL
¹⁄₄ tsp	each: dried basil and oregano or 1 tsp (5 mL) fresh	1 mL
¹⁄₈ tsp	freshly ground pepper	0.5 mL

1. In medium bowl, combine tomatoes, cucumber, green pepper, onion, cilantro, jalapeño, garlic, lemon juice and tomato paste. Stir in seasonings; cover and let stand at room temperature until serving time. **Makes 1¹⁄₂ cups (375 mL).**

TOMATO SALSA

1¹⁄₂ cups	finely chopped tomato (2 medium)	375 mL
¹⁄₂	jalapeño pepper, seeded and finely chopped	¹⁄₂
¹⁄₄ cup	fresh basil leaves, chopped	50 mL
2 tbsp	finely chopped onion	25 mL
1 tbsp	red wine vinegar	15 mL
1	clove garlic, minced	1
¹⁄₄ tsp	freshly ground pepper	1 mL

1. Combine tomato, jalapeño pepper, basil, onion, vinegar, garlic and pepper. Cover and refrigerate for at least 30 minutes or up to 1 day. **Makes 1¹⁄₂ cups (375 mL).**

Although we suggest using the salsa with a chicken satay, try it wherever you would use cranberry sauce.

MEXICAN CRANBERRY SALSA

2 cups	fresh or frozen cranberries	500 mL
¾ cup	orange juice	175 mL
1	sweet yellow or red pepper, seeded and finely chopped	1
1	hot yellow pepper, seeded and finely chopped	1
1 cup	finely chopped onion (1 large)	250 mL
1	clove garlic, finely chopped	1
¼ cup	each: red wine vinegar and packed brown sugar	50 mL
½ tsp	each: ground cumin and pickling salt	2 mL
½ cup	loosely packed fresh cilantro leaves, coarsely chopped	125 mL

1. Combine cranberries, orange juice, sweet pepper, hot pepper, onion, garlic, vinegar, sugar, cumin and salt in medium saucepan. Bring to a boil, reduce heat and cook, uncovered, for 15 minutes or until mixture thickens and vegetables are tender. Cool salsa before stirring in cilantro. Pour salsa into sealed container; cool slightly before storing in refrigerator. Salsa will keep, refrigerated for up to one month. **Makes 2 cups (500 mL).**

Chicken Satay: Cut ½ lb (250 g) chicken breasts into thin strips. Preheat grill on high. Thread chicken strips on 6 metal or soaked wooden skewers. Place skewers on lightly oiled grill rack. Close lid and cook (use Direct Grilling, page 6) for about 7 minutes or until chicken is golden brown and no longer pink inside; turn often. Beef strips may be a replacement for the chicken with this salsa. **Makes 6 appetizer servings.**

CHAPTER 2
MEATS ON THE GRILL

◀ *Moroccan Lamb Chops (page 54)*

Red meat is a most important part of the grill chef's repertoire. After all, it's what many people think of when they consider grilling. This chapter presents a wide variety of beef, veal, pork and lamb recipes that are sure to enhance your grilling reputation. They range from Marinated Flank Steak (page 47), through Roast Boneless Leg of Lamb with Wine-Mustard Marinade (page 57) and Southern-style Pulled Pork (page 64) to Pecan Veal Roast with Mushroom Brandy Sauce (page 69).

Meat is not tricky to grill, but it is important to understand why meat toughens. All meats are high-protein foods, as are poultry and fish. As proteins cook, the protein molecules draw together squeezing out the water that was originally in them. So, the longer that once-juicy steak cooks, the dryer and tougher it becomes. There will also be shrinkage and weight loss. Quick grilling of tender meats over medium-high heat prevents them from drying out and toughening. Less tender steaks need a tenderizing marinade, but are still most tender when not cooked past medium. Thus, a steak cooked medium-rare will always be more tender and juicier than if well done.

The aspiring grill chef must also understand Direct Grilling and Indirect Grilling methods (both discussed on page 6). And finally, there is the signature of the master grill chef: cross-sear markings on meat off the grill. To get the markings, move the cut of meat a quarter turn halfway through each side of the cooking process.

Each recipe in this chapter describes in greater detail the individual cooking requirements of the particular cut of meat specified. However, let's briefly discuss cooking methods for the major meat categories.

Beef

Steaks: Generally they are cooked rare, medium or well done according to individual preference. To check for doneness, use your finger instead of a knife.

If the steak is soft through to the center, it is rare; if it feels slightly firmer but spongy and bouncy, it is medium; if it is firm when touched, it is well done. Or take an internal temperature reading with an instant-read meat thermometer.

Tender cuts: Rib, rib eye, sirloin, tenderloin, T-bone, strip loin and wing are the more tender steaks and do not require marinating except for flavor addition. Grill them using medium-high heat, turning only once or twice with tongs.

Less tender cuts: Round, sirloin tip and flank steaks require tenderizing by marinating for 12 to 24 hours in the refrigerator (See Chapter 9 for marinade recipes). For maximum tenderness, DO NOT cook a less tender steak past medium, and let it stand for 5 to 10 minutes before serving. During that time, the meat will reabsorb some of its juices, making it more succulent. When serving, slice across the grain.

Lamb and Veal

Treat lamb and veal in much the same way as beef, being careful to not cook it past medium.

Pork

Tender cuts like chops, boneless loin and tenderloin give fabulous results. But never overcook them. Since today's pork is a very lean meat, it gets tough and dry when overcooked. Tougher cuts like spareribs need long, slow cooking to tenderize them. When it comes to grilling them (either side or back ribs), long and slow will produce the most tender and most flavorful result. Low heat, patience and a desire for the best ribs you will have ever eaten may be sufficient reason to use the method we offer in our Smoked Maple-flavored Ribs recipe (page 60). Grill at no higher temperature than 325°F (160°C) always using the Indirect Grilling method with a drip pan of water under the rack the ribs are on.

Spice-crusted Steak with Cilantro Sauce

Be sure to use whole spices in this recipe. Preground spices are too fine to form a crust, and they'll turn bitter during cooking. Crush whole spices by pulsing in a coffee grinder or food processor. The mixture should have a sandy texture — be careful to not turn it into a powder. You can use T-bone, rib, rib eye, strip loin or sirloin steaks in this recipe.

SPICE CRUST

1 tbsp	each: coriander seeds, cumin seeds and fennel seeds	15 mL
1 tsp	coarse salt	5 mL
1/4 tsp	freshly ground pepper	1 mL

STEAK

1 to 2 lb	steak (1 inch/2.5 cm thick)	500 g to 1 kg

CILANTRO SAUCE

1 1/4 cups	plain yogurt	300 mL
3 tbsp	lime juice	45 mL
2	cloves garlic, crushed	2
1 tsp	liquid honey	5 mL
1/4 cup	olive oil	50 mL
1 cup	loosely packed fresh cilantro leaves, coarsely chopped	250 mL
1/8 tsp	each: salt and freshly ground pepper	0.5 mL

1. *For crust:* In a coffee grinder or food processor, pulse coriander, cumin and fennel seeds to a sandy texture. Combine with coarse salt and pepper. Trim excess fat from steak and discard. Press the spices over steak, coating the surface thoroughly to make a crust. Cover with plastic wrap and refrigerate until ready to grill.

2. *For sauce:* Place yogurt in very fine strainer or coffee filter and suspend it over a bowl. Let stand for 20 minutes; discard liquid. In small bowl, combine lime juice, garlic and honey. Beat in olive oil and then mix in drained yogurt until just blended; stir in cilantro. Season to taste with salt and pepper; cover and chill.

3. Preheat grill on medium-high. Place steak on oiled grill rack. Close lid and cook (use Direct Grilling, page 6) to desired stage of doneness (see chart on page 10); turn once. Cover steak with foil for 5 minutes. Slice in serving-size pieces and serve with sauce. **Makes 4 to 6 servings.**

Suggested Menu: If using sirloin steak, slice the steak thinly and nestle it on a bed of crisp lettuce, along with Grilled Red and White Onions (page 184) and Grilled Sweet Potatoes (page 178). Cook the vegetables alongside the steak.

Tip: Well-trimmed steak with not more than 1/4 inch (5 mm) exterior fat reduces smoking and flare-ups.

 Wine: Either a Gewurztraminer or a sweet Pinot Grigio would make an excellent accompaniment.

GREEK GRILLED STEAK

Taste the Mediterranean! Whenever possible, grill other items while the barbecue is hot.

1 lb	flank, blade or inside round steak	500 g
2 tbsp	each: red wine vinegar and olive oil	25 mL
2	small cloves garlic, crushed	2
1 tsp	each: dried oregano and mint or 1 tbsp (15 mL) fresh	5 mL
¼ tsp	freshly ground pepper	1 mL

1. Score meat lightly in a criss-cross pattern on both sides. Place steak in a resealable plastic bag.

2. In bowl, combine vinegar, oil, garlic, oregano, mint and pepper. Pour over steak and marinate in refrigerator for 12 hours or overnight; turn meat occasionally. Remove from marinade; discard marinade.

3. Preheat grill on medium-high. Place steak on oiled grill rack. Close lid and cook (use Direct Grilling, page 6) to desired stage of doneness (see chart on page 10); turn once. (For maximum tenderness, do not cook less tender cuts, such as flank steak, past medium.)

4. Remove meat and cover with foil for 5 minutes. Slice steak in thin strips across the grain and serve. **Makes 3 to 4 servings.**

Suggested Menu: Accompany this steak with Grilled Mediterranean Vegetables (page 189), mashed potatoes beaten with feta cheese and Artichoke Salad (page 206).

Tip: Give heavy–duty plastic milk bags a second life by using them (once only) to marinate meats. Use twist ties or clothes pins to seal the top.

SPICY PEPPERED SIRLOIN STEAK

Rubs are an easy way to add flavor to tender beef cuts that do not need a tenderizing marinade.

SPICE RUB

1 tbsp	chili powder	15 mL
1 tsp	each: ground cumin and freshly ground pepper	5 mL
¼ tsp	each: ground allspice and granulated sugar	1 mL
2	cloves garlic, crushed	2
1 tsp	Worcestershire sauce	5 mL

STEAK

1½ lb	sirloin steak (1 inch/2.5 cm thick)	750 g
	Chopped cilantro	

1. *For rub:* In small bowl, combine chili powder, cumin, pepper, allspice, sugar, garlic and Worcestershire sauce. Trim excess fat from steak and discard. Press spice mixture evenly over both sides of meat. Cover and refrigerate for 2 to 24 hours.

2. Preheat grill on medium-high. Place steak on oiled grill rack. Close lid and cook (use Direct Grilling, page 6) to desired stage of doneness (see chart on page 10); turn once. Remove steak to cutting board, cover with foil for 5 minutes before cutting into serving-size pieces. Sprinkle with cilantro. **Makes 4 servings.**

 Wine: Serve with Shiraz or Zinfandel.

GRILLED STEAK, ARUGULA AND SHAVED PARMESAN

 Grilled steak is popular throughout Tuscany, but Florence claims it as its signature dish, calling it Bistecca alla Fiorentina. Cortona also claims it as their own. No matter where it's from, it's perhaps the most classic and luxurious dish of Tuscany, reflecting how fresh ingredients and simple techniques are keys to Italy's world-famous cuisine.

PASTE

3	large cloves garlic	3
2 tsp	extra virgin olive oil	10 mL
1 tsp	freshly ground pepper	5 mL
1	porterhouse steak (2½ lb /1.125 kg) (about 2-inch /5 cm thick)	1
1	large wedge Parmesan cheese	1
6 cups	loosely packed arugula	1.5 L
	Extras: Salt, freshly ground pepper, extra virgin olive oil, lemon wedges	

1. *For paste:* Blend garlic, oil and pepper in small food processor (or mash by hand with back of a fork) to form a paste. Pat meat dry with paper towel. Rub paste evenly over all surfaces of meat. Let stand at room temperature for 30 minutes or cover and refrigerate for up to 8 hours.

2. Preheat grill on medium-high. Place meat in center of lightly oiled grill rack; sear all sides until grill marks appear. Close lid, and grill (use Direct Grilling, page 6) to desired stage of doneness (see chart on page 10). Turn several times (see Tip).

3. Transfer meat to cutting board and cover loosely with foil; let stand for 10 minutes before cutting into fairly thick slices.

4. Meanwhile, using a coarse grater, shave Parmesan into strips. Arrange arugula on a large platter, top with sliced meat, pour any juices over meat and sprinkle with salt and pepper. A drizzle of olive oil, a liberal sprinkle of cheese strips and a squeeze of fresh lemon juice completes this wonderful meal. **Makes about 8 servings.**

Tip: The way to grill really thick steak differs from thinner ones. Whereas most steaks do best when you don't fiddle with them, these thick ones will need to be moved every few minutes on the grill.

Suggested Menu: Insalata Caprese (page 208) is the perfect partner to this marvelous steak.

 Wine: Try a Chianti or a Montepulciano from Tuscany.

STEAK WITH HORSERADISH MARINADE

T-Bone, porterhouse, rib or strip loin steaks may be used in this recipe. The spiciness of the marinade adds a subtle flavor to the meat.

4	steaks (1 inch/2.5 cm thick)	4
MARINADE		
2 tbsp	red wine vinegar	25 mL
4 tsp	each: horseradish and canola oil	20 mL
1	clove garlic, crushed	1
½ tsp	each: dried thyme and hot pepper sauce	2 mL

1. *For marinade:* In small bowl, combine vinegar, horseradish, oil, garlic, thyme and hot sauce. Trim excess fat from steak and discard. Place in resealable plastic bag; pour marinade over steak and turn to coat. Refrigerate for 12 hours or up to 24; turn steak occasionally.

2. Remove steak from marinade; discard marinade. Preheat grill on medium-high. Place steak on oiled grill rack. Close lid and cook (use Direct Grilling, page 6) to desired stage of doneness (see chart on page 10); turn once. **Makes 4 servings.**

Suggested Menu: For a fabulous backyard grill steak feast, serve with Potatoes and Onions in a Pouch (page 201) and Warm Spinach and Radicchio Salad (page 215).

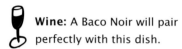 **Wine:** A Baco Noir will pair perfectly with this dish.

SHERRY-MARINATED SIRLOIN STEAK

The sherry marinade with Caribbean spices turns this sirloin into a spicy meal to remember.

1 1/2 lb	sirloin steak (1 inch/2.5 cm thick)	750 g

SHERRY MARINADE

2	cloves garlic, crushed	2
1/2 tsp	each: ground cinnamon, cloves, hot red pepper flakes	2 mL
1/4 tsp	each: salt and pickling spice	1 mL
1/4 cup	dry sherry	50 mL
	Thinly sliced green onions	

1. Trim excess fat from steak and discard. Place meat in a resealable plastic bag.

2. *For marinade:* In bowl, combine garlic, cinnamon, cloves, pepper flakes, salt and pickling spice. Stir in sherry, pour over steak, turn to coat, cover and refrigerate for 2 to 4 hours; turn occasionally.

3. Remove steak from marinade. Place marinade in small saucepan, bring to a boil, reduce heat and cook for 5 minutes; keep warm.

4. Preheat grill on medium-high. Place steak on oiled grill rack, close lid and cook (use Direct Grilling, page 6) to desired degree of doneness (see chart on page 10). Turn steak once, brushing occasionally with warm marinade. Remove from grill, cover with foil for 5 minutes before cutting into serving-size pieces. Garnish with green onions. **Makes 4 servings.**

Suggested Menu: Accompany this steak with steamed green beans and broccoli and cellophane noodles garnished with slivers of green onions.

GRILLED STEAK WITH BOK CHOY

Bok choy provides an attractive and comfortable, tasty bed for grilled steak. It requires a very short cooking time and is also delicious added at the last moment to stir-fries and soups.

1½ lb	sirloin steak (1 inch/2.5 cm thick)	750 g
2 tsp	sesame oil	10 mL
½ tsp	each: garlic powder, salt and freshly ground pepper	2 mL
1 lb	bok choy, washed	500 g
1 tbsp	oyster or fish sauce	15 mL

1. Remove excess fat from beef and discard. Brush beef lightly on each side with oil; season to taste with garlic powder, salt and pepper.

2. Preheat grill on medium-high. Place beef on lightly oiled grill rack. Close lid and cook (use Direct Grilling, page 6) to desired stage of doneness (see chart on page 10); turn once.

3. Meanwhile, in large saucepan, blanch bok choy in boiling water for 2 minutes; drain well. Arrange bok choy on warm serving platter. Slice beef in 1-inch (2.5 cm) thick slices across the grain. Arrange beef on bok choy, drizzle with oyster sauce and serve. **Makes 4 servings.**

Suggested Menu: Serve with basmati rice or cellophane noodles tossed with a small amount of sesame oil and soy sauce.

STEAK AU POIVRE

Dramatic, particularly when prepared as dusk falls, this classic flamed dish can be done outside on the grill rack during good weather or on the stove top anytime.

2 lb	sirloin steak (2 inches/5 cm thick)	1 kg
1 tbsp	freshly ground pepper	15 mL
2 tsp	seasoned salt	10 mL
2 tbsp	each: butter or margarine and olive oil	25 mL
2 tbsp	beef broth	25 mL
⅓ cup	dry red wine	75 mL
¼ cup	brandy or Cognac	50 mL

1. Trim excess fat from steak and discard. Press pepper and seasoned salt into both sides of steak.

2. In large heavy skillet, heat butter and olive oil over medium-high heat on grill rack. Add steak and cook (use Direct Grilling, page 6) to desired degree of doneness (see chart on page 10); turn once.

3. Remove meat from pan to carving board, cover with foil for 5 minutes. Slice meat in thin strips across the grain. Add broth and wine to skillet; heat gently until bubbling. Pour in brandy; set mixture aflame. Pour flaming sauce over steak and serve. **Makes 4 to 6 servings.**

Suggested Menu: Serve with Orzo Spinach Pilaf (page 198) and Zucchini Fingers (page 182).

ZESTY GINGERED STEAK

The paste rubbed over the steak gives an attractive extra zesty ginger flavor to these modest cuts of meat. It's also excellent on lamb and pork.

2 lb	round or flank steak	1 kg
PASTE		
½ cup	finely minced onion	125 mL
3 tbsp	fresh lemon juice	45 mL
2 tbsp	finely minced gingerroot	25 mL
2	cloves garlic, crushed	2
1 tsp	each: ground cumin and crushed green peppercorns	5 mL
½ tsp	brown sugar	2 mL
4	drops hot pepper sauce	4
1 tsp	canola oil	5 mL

1. Trim excess fat from meat and discard.

2. *For paste:* Blend onion, lemon juice, gingerroot, garlic, cumin, peppercorns, sugar, hot sauce and oil in a small food processor (or mash by hand with back of a fork) to form a paste. Pat meat dry with paper towel. Rub paste evenly over all surfaces of meat. Let stand at room temperature for 30 minutes or cover and refrigerate for several hours.

3. Preheat indoor grill on high for 5 minutes. Place meat on lightly oiled grill rack; sear on each side. Cover loosely with foil, reduce heat to medium, grill to desired stage of doneness (see chart on page 10); turn once. (For maximum tenderness, do not cook less tender cuts, such as round or flank steak, past medium). **Makes 4 to 6 servings.**

Suggested Menu: Serve with Potatoes and Onions in a Pouch (page 201) cooked on the grill, but since this recipe needs longer to cook, start it before the meat. Add a large, tossed green salad dressed with zippy tasting Fresh Tomato Vinaigrette (page 220).

For Outdoor Grilling:

Follow procedure as above for Steps 1 and 2.

Step 3: Preheat grill on medium-high. Place meat on lightly oiled grill rack; sear on each side. Close lid and grill (use Direct Grilling, page 6) to desired stage of doneness (see chart on page 10); turn once. (For maximum tenderness, do not cook less tender cuts, such as flank steak, past medium).

Asian-marinated Steak

Use this Thai-inspired marinade for less tender beef cuts such as flank, blade and round steaks.

2 lb	inside round, blade, sirloin tip or flank steak (1 inch/2.5 cm thick)	1 kg

ASIAN MARINADE

	Juice and peel of 1 lime	
¼ cup	chopped fresh mint	50 mL
¼ cup	light soy sauce	50 mL
1	piece gingerroot (1 inch/2.5 cm), minced	1
½	jalapeño pepper, seeded and finely chopped	½
2	cloves garlic, crushed	2
1 tsp	sesame oil	5 mL

1. Trim excess fat from steak and discard. Place steak in resealable plastic bag or shallow nonreactive dish.

2. *For marinade:* In bowl, combine lime juice and peel, mint, soy sauce, gingerroot, jalapeño pepper, garlic and oil. Pour over steak; turn to coat. Refrigerate for 12 to 24 hours; turn steak occasionally. Remove steak from marinade; reserve marinade. Place marinade in small saucepan, bring to a boil, reduce heat and cook for 5 minutes; keep warm.

3. Preheat grill on medium-high. Place steak on lightly oiled grill rack. Close lid and cook (use Direct Grilling, page 6) to desired stage of doneness (see chart on page 10). Brush occasionally with warm marinade. (For maximum tenderness, do not cook less tender cuts, such as flank steak, past medium.)

4. Remove steak from grill; cover with foil for 10 minutes before carving. Cut steak into thin slices across the grain and serve. **Makes 4 to 5 servings.**

Suggested Menu: Prepare Grilled Basil Tomatoes (page 193) toward the end of the cooking time for the steak. Basmati rice, a green salad and crunchy rolls complete the meal.

Tip: Use steak leftovers in a salad the next day. Cut steak into slivers and toss with torn romaine lettuce, bean sprouts, strips of sweet red pepper and a zesty oil and vinegar dressing.

Peeling Gingerroot: Gently peel the thin beige skin from gingerroot. The flesh beneath the skin is the most flavorful. Unpeeled gingerroot may be kept in the refrigerator for two weeks. Peeled gingerroot can be placed in a jar of sherry and kept refrigerated for up to three months.

THICK SIRLOIN WITH CREAMY MUSHROOM SAUCE

Steak needs no seasoning when served with this amazing mushroom and mustard sauce.

MUSHROOM SAUCE

2	large shallots, minced	2
1 tbsp	canola oil	15 mL
8	medium mushrooms, thinly sliced	8
½ cup	vermouth or dry white wine	125 mL
½ cup	heavy cream	125 mL
1 tsp	dried thyme or 1 tbsp (15 mL) chopped fresh	5 mL
1 tbsp	coarse-grained mustard	15 mL
	Salt and freshly ground pepper	
1½ lb	sirloin steak (1-inch/2.5 cm thick)	750 g

1. *For sauce:* In nonstick skillet, sauté shallots in oil over medium-high heat until softened. Add mushrooms; cook until all mushroom liquid has evaporated; stir often. Add vermouth; cook until liquid is reduced to half. Stir in cream, thyme, mustard, salt and pepper to taste; cook gently until sauce has thickened; keep warm.

2. Trim excess fat from steak and discard. Preheat grill on medium-high. Place steak on oiled grill rack. Close lid and cook (use Direct Grilling, page 6) until desired degree of doneness is reached (see chart on page 10). Turn steak once. Remove steak from grill; cover with foil for 5 minutes before serving.

3. Serve each portion with warm mushroom sauce. **Makes 4 servings.**

Suggested Menu: Potatoes and Onions in a Pouch (page 201), Grilled Zucchini (page 178) and a large green salad with Poppy Seed Vinaigrette (page 220) are the best companions for this steak.

 Wine: Pinot Noir would be an ideal match. Alternatively, try a big Burgundian Chardonnay.

Marinated Flank Steak

A flavorful marinade gives flank steak a different personality. It turns lean flank into a succulent lean-meat meal.

1½ lb	flank steak, 1-inch (2.5 cm) thick	750 g
MARINADE		
¼ cup	canola or olive oil	50 mL
¼ cup	each: red wine vinegar and soy sauce	50 mL
2 tbsp	fresh lemon juice	25 mL
1 tbsp	Dijon mustard	15 mL
1½ tsp	Worcestershire sauce	7 mL
2	cloves garlic, minced	2
	Freshly ground pepper	

1. *For meat:* Score meat lightly in a criss-cross pattern on both sides. Place in resealable plastic bag.

2. *For marinade:* Combine oil, vinegar, soy sauce, lemon juice, mustard, Worcestershire sauce, garlic and pepper. Pour over meat; turn to coat, cover and refrigerate for 12 hours or overnight; turn occasionally.

3. Remove meat from marinade; discard marinade. Preheat grill on medium-high. Place meat on lightly oiled grill rack. Close lid and grill (use Direct Grilling, page 6) to desired stage of doneness (see chart on page 10); turn once. Transfer to cutting board, cover loosely with foil; let stand for 10 minutes before thinly slicing across the grain. **Makes 4 to 6 servings.**

Bayou Steak

The zesty hot-pepper flavors of Louisiana come through in this marinade for less tender steaks. Use it to tenderize and flavor any of the more economical beef cuts.

2 lb	inside round, sirloin tip or blade steak (2 inches/5 cm thick)	1 kg
ZESTY MARINADE		
½ cup	beef broth	125 mL
3 tbsp	Worcestershire sauce	45 mL
3 tbsp	cider vinegar	45 mL
1 tbsp	canola oil	15 mL
½ tsp	each: dry mustard, chili powder and paprika	2 mL
½ to 1 tsp	hot pepper sauce	2 to 5 mL
1	bay leaf	1
2	cloves garlic, minced	2
dash	freshly ground pepper	dash

1. Trim excess fat from meat and discard. Pierce meat several times with a fork. Place in a resealable plastic bag or shallow nonreactive dish.

2. *For marinade:* In small saucepan, combine broth, Worcestershire sauce, vinegar, oil, mustard, chili powder, paprika, pepper sauce, bay leaf, garlic and pepper. Bring to a boil over high heat; reduce heat and simmer for 10 minutes, stirring occasionally. Cool before pouring over meat. Refrigerate for 12 to 24 hours; turn meat occasionally.

3. Remove meat from marinade; discard bay leaf and reserve marinade. Place marinade in small saucepan, bring to a boil, reduce heat and cook for 5 minutes; keep warm.

4. Preheat grill on medium-high. Place meat on lightly oiled grill rack. Close lid and cook (use Direct Grilling, page 6) to desired degree of doneness (see chart on page 10). Brush occasionally with warm marinade. (For maximum tenderness, do not cook less tender cuts past medium.)

5. Cover steak with foil for 10 minutes before carving. Slice steak in thin strips across the grain. **Makes 4 to 5 servings.**

MUSHROOM DRESSED BEEF TENDERLOIN

 Recently, our entire family celebrated a special get-together, and 20 of us gathered at a lodge in British Columbia. Each family had its own dwelling, but every evening we met in one location for fun and frivolity and dinner. One evening, we enjoyed this beef tenderloin recipe stuffed with an amazing mushroom filling, and barely a morsel was left. Other family members filled in with salads, couscous, breads and appetizers and "a good time was had by all" as the expression goes.

MUSHROOM STUFFING

½ cup	dried mushrooms (any type)	125 mL
1	large onion, finely chopped	1
3	cloves garlic, minced	3
2 tbsp	melted butter or margarine	25 mL
1 cup	finely chopped fresh mushrooms	250 mL
¼ cup	dry red wine	50 mL
1 tbsp	chopped fresh thyme or 1 tsp (5 mL) dried	15 mL
¼ tsp	each: salt and freshly ground pepper	2 mL
¼ cup	each: chopped fresh parsley and freshly grated Parmesan cheese	50 mL

BEEF

4 to 5 lb	beef tenderloin roast	2 to 2.5 kg
⅔ cup	Basic Red Wine Marinade (page 225)	150 mL
2 tbsp	Dijon mustard	25 mL

1. *For stuffing:* Cover dried mushrooms with boiling water; let stand for 20 minutes or until softened. Meanwhile, sauté onion and garlic in butter in nonstick skillet on medium-high for 5 minutes. Squeeze moisture out of soaked mushrooms; discard liquid. Add soaked and fresh mushrooms, wine, thyme, salt and pepper to onion mixture. Cook until moisture has evaporated. Remove from heat and stir in parsley and cheese. Cool before stuffing meat.

2. *For beef:* Trim excess fat from meat and discard. Make a narrow hole from one end to the other with the handle of a wooden spoon. Press mushroom mixture though hole, again using spoon handle.

3. *To tie the meat:* To give a neat look, tie meat the professional way. Take a long piece of kitchen twine; tie one end of it into a knot around the end of the roast. Wrap the twine nearest the knot around your hand and slip your fingers into the loop that forms. Stretch the loop around the meat and pull securely. Continue wrapping the twine around the meat until the roast is secure, usually 4 to 6 times. When the last loop is completed, take the remaining twine and run it underneath the roast and tie it to the other end.

4. Place meat in a resealable plastic bag. Pour marinade over meat, cover and refrigerate for 6 hours or overnight; turn occasionally.

5. Remove meat from marinade; reserve marinade. Place marinade in a small saucepan, bring to a boil, reduce heat and cook for 5 minutes; keep warm.

6. Rub meat with mustard, preheat grill on medium-high. Place meat in center of lightly oiled grill rack; sear all sides until grill marks appear. Close lid, reduce heat to medium-low and grill (use Indirect Grilling, page 6) to desired stage of doneness (see chart on page 8). Brush occasionally with reserved marinade.

7. Remove meat to cutting board and cover loosely with foil. Let stand for 10 minutes, cut strings and carve meat. **Makes about 20 servings.**

Grilling Tip: Many butchers are willing to make the hole through the tenderloin for you.

Suggested Menu: Slow-roasted Tomatoes (page 193), Black Olive, Rice and Spinach Salad (page 203), and Herbed Italian Loaf (page 30) along with a tossed green salad makes for the perfect outdoor summer dinner.

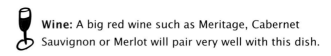 **Wine:** A big red wine such as Meritage, Cabernet Sauvignon or Merlot will pair very well with this dish.

DEEP SOUTH BEEF BRISKET BBQ

In this version, the initial long slow-cooking is done on an outdoor grill using indirect grilling. The second cooking in tomato sauce is done on the stove top, so as to free up the grill for other uses. We think the results are up to the real thing. In fact, it makes the best "beef on a bun" we have ever tasted!

4 to 5 lb	lean beef brisket	2 to 2.5 kg

BARBECUE SAUCE

1 tbsp	canola oil, divided	15 mL
1	large onion, coarsely chopped	1
1	bottle (375 mL) ketchup	1
1	bottle (285 mL) chili sauce	1
¼ cup	each: cider vinegar and dark molasses	50 mL
1 to 2 tbsp	each: hot pepper sauce, prepared mustard and Worcestershire sauce	15 to 25 mL
1½ tsp	black pepper	7 mL
1½ cups	water	375 mL
2 tbsp	lime or lemon juice	25 mL
12 to 16	Kaiser or hamburger buns, toasted	12 to 16

1. Preheat grill on high; brush lightly with oil. Place brisket on grill rack; sear on all sides until brown. Remove meat briefly and lower heat to medium-low; if your grill has a thermometer, this would be about 350°F/180°C. Return meat to grill rack. Close lid and cook (use Indirect Grilling, page 6) for 4 to 5 hours or until meat is fork tender and beef registers 170°F (77°C) on meat thermometer. (During this long cooking time, check water in pan below meat and replenish if necessary.)

2. *For sauce:* Meanwhile, heat remaining oil on medium-high in large heavy saucepan or Dutch oven; add onion and cook for 5 minutes or until softened. Add ketchup, chili sauce, vinegar, molasses, hot pepper sauce, mustard, Worcestershire sauce, black pepper and water. Bring to a boil, reduce heat and simmer for about 20 minutes, stirring occasionally. Remove from heat; stir in lime juice.

3. When meat is done and cool enough to handle, gently pull or slice into strands. Cut into 2-inch (5 cm) pieces and add to sauce. Cover and cook gently for about 1 hour, stirring occasionally. Add more water (or pan drippings) during cooking if needed. Serve meat on toasted buns. **Makes 12 to 16 servings.**

Suggested Menu: For a beef-on-a-bun meal, serve with potato and coleslaw salads, lots of pickles, raw celery and carrot sticks, sliced tomatoes and probably several fruit pies for dessert.

 Wine: Serve with a big Zinfandel from Sonoma.

Beef Prime Rib with Herbes de Provence

Marinated in red wine and herbes de Provence and roasted on the grill, this most exotic beef cut becomes a mouth-watering experience. Herbes de Provence is a blend of herbs usually containing equal parts of basil, fennel, sage, summer savory and thyme. You can buy it at specialty or gourmet food shops or kitchen supply stores, or you can prepare your own mixture at home.

6 lb	prime rib of beef	3 kg
RUB		
2 tbsp	each: olive oil and red wine	25 mL
½ cup	herbes de Provence	125 mL
1 tsp	freshly ground pepper	5 mL
1	clove garlic, crushed	1

1. Trim excess fat from meat and discard.

2. *For rub:* In small bowl, stir together oil, wine, herbes de Provence, pepper and garlic. Rub over entire surface of roast. Cover meat with plastic wrap and refrigerate for 4 hours or overnight.

3. Preheat grill on medium-high. Unwrap meat, and place meat in center of oiled grill rack; sear all sides until grill marks appear. Close lid, reduce heat to medium-low and cook (use Indirect Grilling, page 6) to degree of doneness desired (see chart on page 8). During the final 30 minutes of cooking, add flavored wood chips to coals if desired.

4. Remove roast to cutting board when about 5°F (2°C) below desired degree of doneness. Cover with foil; allow to stand for 15 minutes before carving thinly across the grain. **Makes 8 servings.**

Serving Suggestion: Roasted Horseradish Beets (see recipe) are a marvelous accompaniment.

 Wine: A Meritage or Bordeaux would pair well with this dish.

Roasted Horseradish Beets: While the beef is roasting, place a foil package of 4 medium beets on the rack beside the meat. They will require about 1 hour to become tender. When tender, remove from grill, unwrap and allow to cool; peel and dice. In nonstick skillet, sauté 1 cup (250 mL) chopped red onion in 3 tbsp (45 mL) olive oil; add 2 tbsp (25 mL) balsamic vinegar, 1 tsp (5 mL) coarse salt and ¼ tsp (1 mL) freshly ground pepper. Stir in beets and ¼ cup (50 mL) horseradish. Reheat to serving temperature.

GRILLED SMOKED MEATLOAF

It's as easy as making any meatloaf, but with a kiss of smoke. Brushing with a beer marinade keeps the loaf moist during grilling. Or, if you like a crisp surface, sprinkle lightly with All-purpose Salt-free Rub (page 227). Using smoke is optional.

FOR MEATLOAF

1 lb	ground beef	500 g
²/₃ cup	rolled oats	150 mL
¹/₄ cup	finely chopped onion	50 mL
2 tbsp	chopped fresh oregano or 2 tsp (10 mL) dried	25 mL
¹/₄ cup	ketchup	50 mL
1	egg, lightly beaten	1
2 tsp	horseradish	10 mL
¹/₄ tsp	each: salt and freshly ground pepper	1 mL
	Non-stick grill topper	
	Smoke box	
	Soaked wood chips	

MARINADE

¹/₄ cup	beer or red wine	50 mL
1 tbsp	each: canola oil and ketchup	15 mL

Suggested Menu: While the meatloaf is grilling on Indirect, Potatoes and Onions in a Pouch (page 201) can be cooking by Direct Grilling over the burner providing the heat. Indirect and Direct Grilling at the same time!

1. *For meatloaf:* Combine beef, rolled oats, onion and oregano. Stir together ketchup, egg, horseradish, salt and pepper. Lightly combine with beef mixture and shape into a loaf.

2. *For marinade:* Heat wine, oil and ketchup in small saucepan until it thickens and is reduced in half; set aside.

3. Place a shallow pan of water under the grill rack. Place the smoke box containing soaked chips over flame source. Preheat grill on medium-high. Move meatloaf onto lightly oiled grill topper; place on rack above water pan. Close lid, reduce heat to medium and grill (use Indirect Grilling, page 6) for about 1 to 1¹/₄ hours or until an instant-read meat thermometer inserted into center of meatloaf reads 160°F (71°C). Baste occasionally with marinade. Replace the wood chips as needed.

4. Remove meat from grill, cover with foil and let stand for about 10 minutes before slicing. **Makes 4 to 6 servings.**

SPICY BEEF FAJITAS

1 lb	flank or round steak	500 g
1 cup	shredded lettuce	250 mL
8	12-inch (30 cm) flour tortillas	8

MARINADE

2 tbsp	soy sauce	25 mL
1 tbsp	each: lime juice and liquid honey	15 mL
1	clove garlic, crushed	1
1/2	small jalapeño pepper, seeded and finely diced	1/2
1	medium onion, sliced	1
1/2	sweet red pepper, sliced	1/2
2 tsp	canola oil	10 mL

GUACAMOLE

1	medium avocado, peeled	1
1 tbsp	lime juice	15 mL
1	medium tomato, peeled and diced	1
1/2 cup	onion, finely chopped	125 mL
1 tbsp	fresh cilantro, chopped	15 mL
dash	hot pepper sauce	dash

Variation: Chicken strips may replace beef.

Tip: Placing an avocado pit in the avocado mixture helps to prevent it from turning brown.

Serving: Wrap tortillas in dampened paper towel; microwave on high (100%) for 3 minutes to soften. Place portions of the steak, cooked vegetable mixture and lettuce on each warm tortilla and top with Guacamole. Roll tortillas tightly around filling. Makes 8 servings.

1. Trim excess fat from steak and discard. Score meat lightly in a criss-cross pattern on both sides. Place steak in a resealable plastic bag.

2. *For marinade:* In bowl, combine soy sauce, lime juice, honey, garlic and jalapeño pepper. Pour over steak, turn to coat. Refrigerate for 12 hours or overnight; turn steak occasionally. Remove steak from marinade; reserve marinade. Place marinade in small saucepan, bring to a boil, reduce heat and cook for 5 minutes; keep warm.

3. Preheat grill on medium-high. Place steak on oiled grill rack. Close lid and cook (use Direct Grilling, page 6) to desired stage of doneness (see chart on page 10), brushing often with warm marinade. (For maximum tenderness, do not cook less tender cuts, such as flank steak, past medium.) Remove from grill; cover with foil for 5 minutes before slicing. Slice steak across the grain into thin strips.

4. Meanwhile, sauté onion and red pepper in nonstick skillet in hot oil for 10 minutes or until tender.

5. *For guacamole:* In a bowl, mash avocado. Stir in lime juice, tomato, onion, cilantro and dash hot pepper sauce. **Makes about 1 1/2 cups (375 mL).**

MOROCCAN LAMB CHOPS

Moroccan seasonings are a savory blend of spices, garlic, orange or lemon juice and often their peel. These flavors are becoming increasingly popular in North American home cooking due to the growth of restaurants specializing in Moroccan cuisine.

MARINADE

½ cup	plain yogurt	125 mL
3 tbsp	orange juice concentrate	45 mL
2	cloves garlic, minced	2
1 tsp	each: ground coriander and grated orange peel	5 mL
½ tsp	each: salt, ground cumin and cinnamon	2 mL
¼ tsp	each: ground cloves and ginger	1 mL

LAMB

6	lamb steaks or chops (¾ inch/2 cm thick)	6

CUCUMBER TOMATO SAUCE

¾ cup	diced cucumber	175 mL
½ cup	chopped tomato	125 mL
⅓ cup	finely chopped onion	75 mL
½ cup	plain yogurt	125 mL
	Salt and freshly ground pepper	

1. *For marinade:* In small bowl, combine yogurt, juice, garlic and seasonings; stir well.

2. *For lamb chops:* Trim excess fat and discard. Place lamb in shallow nonreactive dish or resealable plastic bag. Pour marinade over lamb; turn to coat. Cover and refrigerate for at least 4 hours or overnight; turn chops occasionally.

3. Remove lamb from marinade; reserve marinade. Place marinade in small saucepan, bring to a boil, reduce heat and cook for 5 minutes; keep warm.

4. Preheat grill on medium. Place lamb on oiled grill rack. Close lid and cook (use Direct Grilling, page 6) to desired stage of doneness (see chart on page 11); turn once. Baste often with warm marinade.

5. *For sauce:* Meanwhile, in small bowl, combine cucumber, tomato, onion and yogurt. Season to taste with salt and pepper. Serve sauce with lamb steaks. **Makes 6 servings.**

Suggested Menu: Serve with grilled new potatoes (page 178) and artichokes (see page 206) along with a green salad.

 Wine: Serve with Sangiovese or a white Semillon.

GRILLED ROSEMARY LAMB CHOPS

Rosemary is the herb most often associated with lamb. When you taste these lamb chops, you'll know why! We found marinating the lamb no less than four hours developed the best herb flavors.

MARINADE

⅓ cup	wine (white, rosé or red)	75 mL
2 tbsp	olive oil	25 mL
1 tbsp	lemon juice	15 mL
2	bay leaves, broken in half	2
1 tsp	each: dried thyme and rosemary or 1 tbsp (15 mL) chopped fresh	5 mL
½ tsp	freshly ground pepper	2 mL

LAMB

8 to 12	lean loin lamb chops (1 inch/2.5 cm thick)	8 to 12

1. *For marinade:* In nonreactive shallow dish or resealable plastic bag, combine wine, oil, lemon juice, bay leaves, thyme, rosemary and pepper.

2. *For lamb chops:* Trim excess fat and discard. Place lamb in marinade; turn to coat. Cover and refrigerate for at least 4 hours or overnight; turn chops occasionally.

3. Remove lamb chops from marinade; reserve marinade, discard bay leaves. Place marinade in small saucepan, bring to a boil, reduce heat and cook for 5 minutes; keep warm.

4. Preheat grill on medium-high. Place lamb chops on lightly oiled grill rack. Close lid and cook (use Direct Grilling, page 6) to desired stage of doneness (see chart, page 11); turn once, basting often with warm marinade. **Makes 4 to 6 servings, 2 chops per person.**

Suggested Menu: Add a few chopped kalamata olives to mashed potatoes and top with minced fresh parsley to complement the rosemary–lamb flavors. Complete the meal with crunchy multigrain dinner rolls and, in the springtime, tender asparagus spears and steamed carrot sticks.

LEG OF LAMB PERSILLADE

Persil is the French word for parsley, and the combination of parsley with chopped garlic is called persillade — a mixture that always gives a fabulous flavor to lamb.

PERSILLADE

⅓ cup	packed parsley leaves, divided	75 mL
¼ cup	olive oil, divided	50 mL
4	cloves garlic, divided	4
1 tsp	grated lemon peel	5 mL
½ tsp	salt	2 mL
¼ tsp	freshly ground pepper	1 mL
3 tbsp	lemon juice	45 mL
4 to 6 lb	boneless rolled leg of lamb	2 to 3 kg

1. *For persillade:* In blender or food processor, process 3 tbsp (45 mL) parsley, 2 tbsp (25 mL) oil, 2 cloves garlic, lemon peel, salt and pepper to a smooth paste; set aside.

2. Slice remaining 2 garlic cloves into thin slices and chop remaining parsley. Unroll lamb, sprinkle with garlic and parsley, reroll and tie with kitchen cord. Press persillade mixture over outside of lamb.

3. Preheat grill on medium. Place lamb in center of oiled grill rack. Close lid and cook (use Indirect Grilling, page 6) for about 1¼ hours or until well browned but still pink in the center (see chart on page 8). Combine lemon juice and remaining oil. Baste lamb occasionally during cooking with lemon and oil mixture.

4. Transfer meat to cutting board, cover with foil and let stand for 10 minutes before carving. Cut strings and carve meat. **Makes 8 servings.**

Serving Suggestions: Grilled lemon slices and Tuscan Garlic Bread (see recipe below) are an interesting addition to the roast.

Tuscan Garlic Bread: Lightly grill thick slices of French bread on both sides. Rub one side with a cut clove of garlic. Drizzle some fruity olive oil over the bread and season with salt and freshly ground pepper. Bon appétit!

 Wine: A medium-bodied red wine such as a Merlot is a good choice because its sweet tannins do not overpower the delicate lamb flavors.

ROAST BONELESS LEG OF LAMB WITH WINE-MUSTARD MARINADE

The succulence of grilled lamb is so evident in this classic recipe.

MARINADE

½ cup	dry red wine	125 mL
2 tbsp	grainy mustard	25 mL
1 tbsp	finely chopped fresh rosemary	15 mL
2	cloves garlic, minced	2
1 tbsp	finely chopped gingerroot	15 mL
1 tbsp	olive oil	15 mL
¼ tsp	freshly ground pepper	1 mL
4 to 6 lb	boneless leg of lamb, rolled and tied	2 to 3 kg

1. *For marinade:* Combine wine, mustard, rosemary, garlic, gingerroot, oil and pepper.

2. Trim excess fat from meat and discard. Place lamb in a large plastic resealable bag or large container. Pour marinade over, cover and refrigerate for 4 hours or overnight.

3. Remove lamb from marinade; reserve marinade. Place marinade in a small saucepan, bring to a boil, reduce heat and cook for 5 minutes; keep warm.

4. Preheat grill on medium. Place lamb in center of lightly oiled grill rack. Reduce heat to medium-low, close lid and grill (use Indirect Grilling, page 6) for about 1¼ hours to desired degree of doneness (see chart on page 8); turn once. Brush lamb occasionally with warm marinade.

5. Transfer meat to cutting board, cover loosely with foil; let stand for 10 minutes before carving. Cut strings and carve lamb. **Makes 8 servings.**

Menu Suggestion: Grilled Beet and Minted Orange Salad (page 202) is an excellent accompaniment, along with Pine Nut Couscous (page 199). Bon appétit!

 Wine: Pinot Noir or Syrah are both perfect matches.

HAM STEAK WITH CITRUS SALSA

Citrus Salsa with grilled ham is an interesting change from more traditional pineapple. The complementary collection of flavors is quite outstanding.

CITRUS SALSA

2	oranges, peeled and diced	2
½	lemon, peeled and diced	½
½	pink grapefruit, peeled and diced	½
2 tbsp	each: chopped fresh cilantro and diced red onion	25 mL
1	jalapeño pepper, seeded and finely chopped	1
1 tsp	olive oil	5 mL
⅛ tsp	each: salt, freshly ground pepper and dried thyme	0.5 mL

HAM

4	ham steak slices (½ inch/1 cm thick)	4
1 tsp	Dijon mustard	5 mL

1. *For salsa:* In bowl, combine oranges, lemon, grapefruit, cilantro, onion, jalapeño pepper, oil and seasonings; stir to combine. Cover and refrigerate until ready to serve.

2. *For ham:* Preheat grill on medium-high. Place ham steaks on oiled grill. Close lid and cook (use Direct Grilling, page 6) for 4 minutes per side; just before turning, brush lightly with mustard. Serve ham with Citrus Salsa. **Makes 4 servings and 2 cups (500 mL) salsa.**

 **Wine:** A medium-dry Riesling would be the best match.

ZESTY BARBECUED PORK RIBS

Everyone enjoys a good feed of ribs. This family recipe has been enjoyed for many years, either grilled on the barbecue or baked in the oven.

BARBECUE SAUCE

1 cup	ketchup or chili sauce	250 mL
⅓ cup	cider vinegar	75 mL
⅓ cup	brown sugar, lightly packed	75 mL
2 tsp	prepared mustard	10 mL
1	small onion, finely chopped	1
2 tbsp	Worcestershire sauce	25 mL
1 tbsp	vegetable oil	15 mL
2	cloves garlic, crushed	2
⅛ tsp	each: salt, hot pepper sauce and freshly ground pepper	0.5 mL
4 lb	pork spareribs (side or back)	2 kg

1. In medium saucepan, combine ketchup, vinegar, sugar, mustard, onion, Worcestershire sauce, oil, garlic, salt, hot pepper sauce and pepper. Simmer, uncovered, for 20 minutes; stir occasionally. Remove from heat and cool slightly.

2. *To precook ribs:* Remove the thick, tough membrane from the underside of ribs (or ask the butcher to do this for you). Place ribs in large saucepan. Add enough water to cover, bring to a boil, reduce heat and cook gently for about 45 minutes or until tender; drain and discard cooking liquid. Place ribs in shallow dish. Pour sauce over ribs, cover and refrigerate for several hours.

3. Preheat grill on medium. Remove ribs from sauce; reserve sauce. Place ribs on lightly oiled grill rack. Close lid and cook (use Direct Grilling, page 6) for about 20 minutes, turning and brushing with sauce once. (Watch closely to prevent burning.)

4. Remove ribs from grill; cover with foil for 10 minutes before serving. **Makes 6 servings and about 1½ cups (375 mL) sauce.**

Suggested Menu: Ribs are often served with a potato salad or baked potatoes, cabbage or tossed green salad and apple pie for dessert. If you are looking for a change, serve these ribs with Zucchini Fingers (page 182), Grilled Corn on the Cob with Herb Butter (page 191) and crusty Italian bread. The zesty glaze suggests a full-flavored beer that won't get lost between bites.

Tips:

Any unused basting sauce can be covered and refrigerated for another use. It is excellent brushed on chicken during grilling. Be sure to boil sauce before using.

Have your butcher crack the ribs for easy serving. Precooking pork back and side ribs in liquid before grilling has a number of advantages: it helps the meat stay moist and tender, it shortens the grilling time, and it cooks out some of the excess fat.

SMOKED MAPLE-FLAVORED RIBS

The way to great grilled ribs is "slow and low." Soaked wood chips smoldering on the grill give the ribs a nice touch of smoke. The plus is maple syrup in this marinade for that extra zip!

MARINADE

⅔ cup	maple syrup	150 mL
2 tbsp	frozen orange juice concentrate, thawed	25 mL
2 tbsp	chili sauce or ketchup	25 mL
1 tbsp	each: Dijon mustard and soy sauce	15 mL
2 tsp	Worcestershire sauce	10 mL
1½ tsp	curry powder	7 mL
2	cloves garlic, minced	2

RIBS

3 lb	back or pork side ribs	1.5 kg
	Smoke box	
	Soaked wood chips	

1. *For marinade:* Cook maple syrup, orange juice, chili sauce, mustard, soy and Worcestershire sauce, curry powder and garlic until hot. Cool slightly.

2. *For ribs:* Remove the thick tough membrane from the underside of ribs (or ask the butcher to do that for you). The marinade has a better chance of being absorbed. Place ribs in a resealable plastic bag or shallow nonreactive dish; pour marinade over ribs. Refrigerate for at least 4 hours or overnight.

3. Remove ribs from marinade; reserve marinade. Place marinade in a small saucepan, bring to a boil, reduce heat and cook for 5 minutes; keep warm.

4. Preheat grill on medium-low. Place soaked wood chips over the fire source. Place a pan of water on cold side of grill. Place ribs, meaty side up, on lightly oiled grill rack over water pan. For extra moisture, add a pan of water over the heat source. Close lid and grill (use Indirect Grilling, page 6) for about 3 hours. Replenish wood chips as needed with freshly soaked chips during grilling for maximum smoke flavor.

5. After 3 hours, brush the ribs with warm marinade; grill for 10 minutes; then tightly wrap ribs with foil so they will steam in their own moisture for about another hour or until meat is very tender and has pulled back from the bones. Side ribs will take considerably longer than back ribs.

6. Remove ribs from grill; set aside for 10 minutes before opening the foil; cut into serving size pieces. **Makes 6 servings.**

Suggested Menu: Classic Coleslaw (page 217), the creamy variation, would be the perfect salad to serve with the ribs. Then add a steamed green vegetable and new baby potatoes.

Variation: Dry-rubbed Ribs: For a simpler preparation that does not require a marinating time, press a rub of about 1 tbsp (15 mL) of Pork and Rib Rub (page 228) per pound of ribs over all surfaces of the ribs. Grill as above. The ribs can be grilled immediately, although if they are refrigerated for a few hours, you will have a more intense flavor.

 Wine: An off-dry Riesling or a Shiraz will match beautifully with grilled ribs.

Herb-rubbed Pork Tenderloin with Red Pepper Coulis

The culinary term coulis refers to a thick purée or sauce. The coulis in this recipe provides a colorful background to the cumin- and garlic-flavored tenderloin. Both the coulis and the rub can also be used with other cuts of pork and beef.

RED PEPPER COULIS

2	sweet red peppers, grilled (see page 178)	2
1 tbsp	olive or canola oil	15 mL
	Salt, freshly ground pepper	
	Hot pepper sauce	

RUB

1/2 tsp	each: salt, brown sugar, paprika and freshly ground pepper	2 mL
1/4 tsp	each: ground cumin, onion powder and garlic powder	1 mL
pinch	cayenne pepper	pinch
1	pork tenderloin (about 1 lb/500 g)	1
	Fresh parsley	

1. *For coulis:* Cut roasted peppers in half and remove seeds. In blender or food processor, purée peppers, oil and a small amount of water to allow peppers to form a smooth paste. Remove and season to taste with salt, pepper and hot sauce. Set aside; reheat at serving time.

2. *For rub:* Combine salt, sugar, paprika, pepper, cumin, onion and garlic powder and cayenne.

3. Trim excess fat from meat and discard. Score meat crosswise and place in a shallow nonreactive dish. Press rub mixture evenly over all meat surfaces. Cover and refrigerate for 30 minutes or longer.

4. Preheat indoor grill on high for 5 minutes. Place meat on lightly oiled grill rack; sear meat on each side. Cover meat loosely with foil, reduce heat to medium and cook for 10 minutes per side (see chart on page 8); turn once. Remove meat from grill, cover with foil and let stand for 10 minutes before slicing.

5. Place a small amount of warm coulis on each dinner plate. Slice pork crosswise into thin slices and fan slices over coulis; garnish with parsley and serve. **Makes 3 to 4 servings and about 1 cup (250 mL) coulis.**

For Outdoor Grilling:

Follow procedure as above for Steps 1, 2, 3 and 5.

Step 4: Preheat grill on medium–high. Place meat on lightly oiled grill rack; sear meat on each side. Close lid, reduce heat to medium and grill (use Direct Grilling, page 6) for about for 10 minutes per side (see chart on page 10); turn once. Remove meat from grill, cover loosely with foil and let stand for 10 minutes before slicing.

PUNGENT PORK TENDERLOIN MEDALLIONS

This pungent sweet and sour apricot marinade adds moisture and great flavor to lean pork tenderloin.

1 lb	pork tenderloin	500 g
APRICOT MARINADE		
1/3 cup	each: white wine and strained apricot preserves	75 mL
1/4 cup	white wine vinegar	50 mL
1 tbsp	each: cornstarch and granulated sugar	15 mL
1 tbsp	each: dry sherry and light soy sauce	15 mL
1	clove garlic, minced	1
	Chopped fresh parsley	

1. Cut pork tenderloin crosswise into 12 pieces, each approximately 1 inch (2.5 cm) thick. Place each piece, cut side down, on flat surface, between 2 sheets of waxed paper. Pound meat evenly over all surfaces with the flat side of a meat mallet or large knife to 1/4 inch (6 mm) thick.

2. *For marinade:* In small bowl, combine wine, preserves, vinegar, cornstarch, sugar, sherry, soy sauce and garlic. Place meat in shallow nonreactive dish or resealable plastic bag. Pour mixture over meat, turn to coat and refrigerate for 2 to 6 hours.

3. Remove pork from marinade; reserve marinade. Place marinade in small saucepan, bring to a boil, reduce heat and cook for 5 minutes; keep warm.

4. Preheat grill on medium. Place meat on oiled grill rack. Close lid and cook (use Direct Grilling, page 6) to desired stage of doneness (see chart on page 10); turn once and brush frequently with warm marinade. Remove to platter; pour remaining marinade over pork and serve sprinkled with parsley. **Makes 4 servings.**

Suggested Menu: Prepare Orange-sauced Roasted Beets (page 192) beforehand and keep warm while the pork and Grilled Sweet Potatoes (page 178) are cooking. Add crusty rolls and a green salad.

CIDER-SOAKED PORK TENDERLOIN

Simple and simply delicious! The cider "soaking," enhances the moistness of the pork.

RUB

1 tbsp	chopped fresh rosemary or 1 tsp (5 mL) dried	15 mL
½ tsp	each: dried thyme and winter savory	2 mL
	Freshly ground pepper	

MEAT

1	pork tenderloin (about 1 lb/500 g)	1
1½ cups	hard apple cider or apple juice	375 mL
	Smoke box and soaked wood chips (optional)	

1. *For rub:* Combine rosemary, thyme, savory and pepper.

2. *For meat:* Trim excess fat from meat and discard. Pat meat dry with paper towel. Press rub into meat; score meat crosswise and place in resealable plastic bag. Pour cider over meat until completely submerged. Cover and refrigerate for 8 hours or overnight. Remove meat from liquid; discard liquid.

3. Place soaked wood chips in smoke box, if using; place box over the fire source. Preheat grill on medium-high. Place meat on lightly oiled grill rack; sear meat on each side. Close lid, reduce heat to medium and grill (use Direct Grilling, page 6) for 10 to 12 minutes per side (see chart on page 10); turn once. Remove meat from grill, cover loosely with foil and let stand for 10 minutes before slicing. **Makes 4 servings.**

MAPLE LEMON PORK TENDERLOIN

The tang of lemon juice combined with the sweet flavor of maple syrup adds a marvelous taste and glaze to grilled pork.

1 lb	pork tenderloin	500 g

MARINADE

2 tbsp	maple syrup	25 mL
1 tbsp	each: Dijon mustard, oil and lemon juice	15 mL
1 tsp	grated lemon peel	5 mL
1	clove garlic, crushed	1
1 tsp	dried thyme	5 mL
¼ tsp	freshly ground pepper	1 mL

1. Trim excess fat from meat and discard. Score meat crosswise and place in shallow nonreactive dish or resealable plastic bag.

2. *For marinade:* In small bowl, combine maple syrup, mustard, oil, lemon juice and peel, garlic and seasonings. Pour over meat, turn to coat and refrigerate for several hours.

3. Remove meat from marinade; reserve marinade. In small saucepan, bring marinade to a boil, reduce heat and cook for 5 minutes; keep warm.

4. Preheat grill on medium. Place meat on lightly oiled grill rack. Close lid and cook (use Direct Grilling, page 6) to desired degree of doneness (see chart on page 10), turning once; brush occasionally with warm marinade. Remove meat from grill, cover with foil and let stand for 5 minutes before slicing. **Makes 3 to 4 servings.**

SOUTHERN-STYLE PULLED PORK

From its origins in the southern United States, pulled pork is becoming a favorite outdoor meal throughout North America.

MEAT

4 to 5 lb	pork shoulder roast, boneless	2 to 2.5 kg
1½ cups	hard or soft cider or apple juice	375 mL
1 tbsp	mustard seeds	15 mL
1	large onion, sliced	1
6	cloves garlic, halved	6

RUB

2 tbsp	coarse or kosher salt	25 mL
1 tbsp	each: freshly ground pepper and chili powder	15 mL
1 tsp	each: sweet paprika and brown sugar	5 mL
½ tsp	garlic powder	2 mL
pinch	cayenne pepper	pinch
	Smoke box	
	Soaked wood chips	

SAUCE

1¼ cups	cider vinegar	300 mL
⅔ cup	ketchup	150 mL
¼ cup	lightly packed brown sugar	50 mL
1	small onion, chopped	1
2 tbsp	dry mustard	25 mL
2 tbsp	each: fresh lemon juice and Worcestershire sauce	25 mL
1 tbsp	each: crushed red chili pepper flakes and garlic powder	15 mL
6 to 7	drops hot sauce, optional	6 to 7

1. *For meat:* Place meat in a large container. Combine cider, mustard seeds, onion and garlic; pour over meat. Cover and marinate in the refrigerator overnight or up to 2 days. Turn meat occasionally.

2. *For rub:* Combine salt, pepper, chili powder, paprika, sugar, garlic powder and cayenne pepper. Set aside.

3. Remove meat from marinade; strain and discard liquid and solids. Pat dry with paper towel and press rub over all meat surfaces. Preheat grill on medium-high. Place soaked wood chips in smoke box directly over the fire source. Place meat on unlit side of lightly oiled grill rack with pan of water below. A second pan of water over the heat source will provide extra moisture to keep the meat from becoming too dry. Close lid, reduce heat to medium-low and grill (use Indirect Grilling, page 6) for about 4 hours or until an instant-read meat thermometer inserted into center of roast reads 170°F (74°C). Replenish the soaked chips as needed.

4. Remove meat from grill. Place in a large roasting pan, fat side up; cover and roast in 250°F (120°C) oven for 2 hours or until an instant-read thermometer reads 180°F (82°C) (higher for pulled pork due to the longer cooking time allowing meat to become so very tender it is ready to fall apart and can be easily "pulled"). Remove from oven; cover with foil until meat is cool enough to handle. Reserve extra liquid to add to the sauce.

5. *For sauce:* In saucepan, combine vinegar, ketchup, sugar, onion, mustard, lemon juice, Worcestershire sauce, crushed chili flakes and garlic powder. Bring to a boil, reduce heat and cook until sugar is dissolved; stir occasionally; add reserved liquid. Simmer sauce until reduced and thickened.

6. Remove some fat from meat, thinly slice and shred with hands or pull apart with two forks. Place meat in a roasting pan or slow cooker pot, pour sauce over, cover and keep warm until ready to serve. Test for spice level and if desired add a few drops of hot sauce before serving. **Makes about 16 to 20 servings.**

GRILLED CINNAMON PORK ROAST

Cinnamon's "welcome home aroma" is the highlight of this amazing pork roast. The spice is also high in antioxidants, which as we all know, are good for our health.

PASTE

2 tbsp	each: ground cinnamon and granulated sugar	25 mL
1 tbsp	soy sauce	15 mL
1	medium onion, finely chopped	1
5	cloves garlic, minced	5
1/2 tsp	each salt and freshly ground pepper	2 mL
4 lb	boneless pork loin roast (center cut)	2 kg

1. *For paste:* Combine cinnamon, sugar, soy sauce, onion, garlic, salt and pepper.

2. *For pork:* Trim excess fat from meat and discard. Rub paste mixture evenly over surface of pork. Wrap meat in plastic wrap and refrigerate for 8 hours or overnight.

3. Preheat grill on high. Place meat on lightly oiled grill rack. Reduce heat to medium, close lid and grill (use Indirect Grilling, page 6) to desired stage of doneness (see chart on page 8). Remove meat from grill, cover loosely with foil and let stand for 15 minutes before carving into thin slices. **Serves 10 to 14.**

Orange-spiced Pork Chops

The citrus spice-flavored marinade does exotic things to any cut of pork, but it particularly shines with these chops. Add a fresh Watercress and Bean Sprout Salad (page 211) and dinner is almost on the table.

4	pork loin or rib chops, 1-inch (2.5 cm) thick	4
MARINADE		
1 tsp	grated orange peel	5 mL
½ cup	orange juice	125 mL
1 tbsp	liquid honey	15 mL
½ tsp	ground cinnamon	2 mL
¼ tsp	each: ground ginger and mace	1 mL
⅛ tsp	white pepper	0.5 mL
2	small cloves garlic, crushed	2

Grilling Tip: If the pork chops are 1½-inches (3.5 cm) thick, the cooking time will increase.

 Wine: Pair with a Syrah or Pinot Gris.

1. Trim excess fat from chops and discard.

2. *For marinade:* Combine orange peel and juice, honey, cinnamon, ginger, mace, pepper and garlic; pour into a resealable plastic bag. Place meat in bag; turn bag to coat meat. Refrigerate for 6 to 24 hours; turn bag occasionally.

3. Drain meat; reserve marinade. Place marinade in a small saucepan, bring to a boil, reduce heat and cook for 5 minutes; keep warm.

4. Preheat grill on medium-high. Place meat on lightly oiled grill rack; reduce heat to medium. Close lid and grill (use Direct Grilling, page 6) to desired stage of doneness (see chart on page 10); turn once, brushing occasionally with warm marinade. **Makes 4 servings.**

SOY HONEY-GLAZED PORK CHOPS

Use low-sodium soy sauce and dark sesame oil to create very flavorful meat. Brush soy mixture on the chops after they have been turned.

4	pork loin or rib chops, 1-inch (2.5 cm) thick	4
GLAZE		
¼ cup	each: low-sodium soy sauce and liquid honey	50 mL
2 tbsp	fresh lemon juice	25 mL
1 tbsp	grainy mustard	15 mL
1 tsp	dark sesame oil	5 mL
1	clove garlic, crushed	1
	Salt and freshly ground pepper	

1. Trim excess fat from chops and discard.

2. *For glaze:* In small saucepan, combine soy sauce, honey, lemon juice, mustard, sesame oil and garlic. Bring to a boil, reduce heat and simmer for about 3 minutes or until thickened; keep warm. Reserve one-half of glaze; use other half to brush on meat during grilling.

3. Preheat grill on medium. Place meat on lightly oiled grill rack. Close lid and grill (use Direct Grilling, page 6) to desired stage of doneness (see chart on page 10); brush with warm glaze when meat has been turned. Serve meat with reserved glaze. **Makes 4 servings.**

APRICOT-GLAZED VEAL CUTLETS

Served on a nest of thinly sliced green onions, these sweet and spicy veal cutlets are a treat to the eye and the palate.

6	veal cutlets, ¾-inch (2 cm) thick	6
GLAZE		
½ cup	apricot jam	125 mL
1 tbsp	Dijon mustard	15 mL
2 tsp	lemon juice	10 mL
1 tsp	dried thyme or 1 tbsp (15 mL) fresh	5 mL
1	bunch thinly sliced green onions	1

1. Trim excess fat from veal and discard.

2. In bowl, combine jam, mustard, lemon juice and thyme. Spread over each side of veal; cover with plastic wrap and refrigerate for several hours.

3. Preheat grill on medium. Place veal on oiled grill rack. Close lid and cook (use Direct Grilling, page 6) to desired stage of doneness (see chart on page 10); the center will be slightly pink.

4. Serve veal over a nest of green onions. **Makes 6 servings.**

 Wine: A Sancerre–style Sauvignon Blanc would be the ideal choice.

PECAN VEAL ROAST WITH MUSHROOM BRANDY SAUCE

The flavor of wild mushrooms in the sauce, with the "stuffed" marbling of the veal roast, creates an elegant meal for guests. To facilitate carving this roast, have your butcher crack between the rib bones.

PECAN VEAL ROAST

4 to 6 lb	veal rib roast	2 to 3 kg
3	cloves garlic, slivered	3
¼ cup	chopped pecans	50 mL
½ cup	Armagnac or other brandy, divided	125 mL
	Salt and freshly ground pepper	
1 cup	dry white wine	250 mL

MUSHROOM BRANDY SAUCE

1 oz	dried wild mushrooms	30 g
¼ cup	butter or margarine, divided	50 mL
1	clove garlic, minced	1
1 lb	fresh mushrooms, thinly sliced	500 g
1 tbsp	Armagnac or other brandy	15 mL

1. *For roast:* Remove excess fat and discard. With a sharp knife, make many small evenly-spaced slits on surface of roast. Insert garlic slivers and pecans into slits. Brush roast with ¼ cup (50 mL) brandy; sprinkle lightly with salt and pepper and let stand for 30 minutes.

2. Preheat grill on medium. Place pan with wine and 2 cups (500 mL) water below where roast will be placed; place roast on oiled grill rack. Reduce heat to medium-low, close lid and cook (use Indirect Grilling, page 6) for 2½ hours (see chart, page 8). Baste roast occasionally with remaining brandy during last 30 minutes of cooking.

3. Meanwhile, in bowl, soak dried wild mushrooms in ½ cup (125 mL) hot water for 15 minutes or until softened. Drain and discard liquid; set mushrooms aside.

4. Remove meat to cutting board and cover with foil; allow to stand for 10 minutes before carving. Reserve ½ cup (125 mL) pan juices.

5. *For sauce:* In saucepan, over medium-high heat, melt 2 tbsp (25 mL) butter; add garlic and both types of mushrooms and sauté for 10 minutes or until softened. Add brandy and reserved pan juices and bring to boil. Reduce heat and whisk in remaining butter, 1 tbsp (15 mL) at a time. Season to taste with salt and pepper. Cut strings and carve veal; serve with sauce. **Makes 8 servings.**

Suggested Menu: Basil Ratatouille Kebabs (page 182) and Potatoes and Onions in a Pouch (page 201) are very appropriate with this roast. They can be grilled on the rack towards the end of the veal cooking time.

 Wine: Serve with Pinot Noir.

CHAPTER 3

Burgers, Hot Dogs and Sausages on the Grill

◀ *The Great Hamburger World Tour (page 75)*

Hot dogs, hamburgers and sausages are probably North America's ultimate fast comfort foods.

The hot dog — or frankfurter — is usually made of pork, beef or sometimes "veggies." These easy-to-prepare crowd pleasers vary by spicing, size and the toppings added. Why not surprise guests with a new twist on an old favorite? Hot Dog Roll Ups (page 73) are especially popular with kids, and TexMex Hot Dogs (page 73) are always a zesty treat.

Homemade hamburgers are surprisingly simple to make and, like hot dogs, offer variety that's limited only by your imagination. The traditional hamburger uses a beef patty, but chicken, turkey, lamb, pork, salmon and tuna make great protein-packed alternatives. For vegetarians, grill Portobello Mushroom Burgers (page 87); even non-vegetarians would be hard-pressed to know it's not meat. As for toppings and buns, anything goes! See The Great Hamburger World Tour (page 75) for some exciting new options.

It is essential for food safety that burgers and sausages are grilled until a temperature of 160°F (71°C) is reached on a meat thermometer inserted sideways into the meat. Poultry is the exception — the temperature should read 165°F (74°C). See grilling charts on pages 9–11.

Grilling the Perfect Sausage

Too often, grilled sausages turn out to be dry and flavorless due to incorrect and careless grilling, or just plain overcooking. Mind you, because a sausage is a ground-meat product, it does need to be cooked thoroughly. But it should not be incinerated. It should be grilled to an interior temperature of 160°F (71°C) and no more. Be aware our discussion refers to the large country-style or farmer's sausage, not the small breakfast ones.

Never grill sausages over direct heat. It brings their interior juices to a boil causing the casings to split and the loss of precious juices to the fire, where it also causes troublesome flare-ups. Better to use Indirect Grilling (page 6), which is both the best and easiest method for cooking these backyard treats. Since sausages come in different thickness with different ingredients, a cooking time for all sausage is difficult to recommend. The final arbiter is the instant-read digital thermometer.

Follow this simple procedure for grilling the perfect sausage:

Preheat grill on medium-high for about 5 minutes. Place sausages on lightly oiled grill rack and grill for 2 minutes per side or until grill marks and light browning is achieved (but not so long that sausage casings split). Reduce heat to medium on one side of the grill and turn off the other burners. If you're using a charcoal grill, shove coals to one side and move sausages to the side of the grill without direct heat. Continue to grill at medium until an instant-read thermometer registers an interior temperature of 160°F (71°C), but no higher. It should take about 35 minutes or so, depending on the nature of the sausage and the distance from the grilling flame.

Hot Dog Roll Ups

Cheesy and easy! These fast dogs will be easy enough for some children to make themselves. And non-pickle lovers can just leave it out.

1	large dill pickle	1
8	thin wedges Cheddar or Colby cheese, ½ inch (1 cm) thick	8
8	wieners	8
1 tbsp	prepared or Dijon mustard	15 mL
8	strips bacon	8
8	hot dog buns	8

1. Cut pickle lengthwise into 8 thin slices. Cut wieners in half lengthwise, but not completely through. Spread cut surfaces of wiener with mustard. Place one pickle slice and one cheese wedge on each wiener. Repeat until all wieners are filled.

2. Insert toothpick through one bacon slice at one end of each wiener. Wrap securely around the wiener to other end and again secure with a toothpick.

3. Preheat grill on medium, place Hot Dog Roll Ups on grill and grill (see Direct Grilling, page 6) for 8 minutes or until bacon is crisp and wiener is heated; turn occasionally. Discard toothpicks and serve in buns. **Makes 8 servings.**

TexMex Hot Dogs

Plain hot dogs become TexMex! These stuffed dogs were given a high approval rating by an expert panel of several grandchildren.

CHEESE FILLING

1 cup	finely shredded Monterey Jack cheese	250 mL
½ cup	crushed tortilla crumbs	125 mL
3 tbsp	salsa, mild, medium or hot	45 mL
2	green onions, chopped	2
2 tbsp	light mayonnaise	25 mL
½ to 1 tsp	chili powder	2 to 5 mL
10	wieners	10
10	hot dog buns or plain tortillas	10

1. *For filling:* Combine cheese, crumbs, salsa, onion, mayonnaise and chili powder.

2. *For wieners:* Cut a slit lengthwise in each wiener. Spoon about 2 tbsp (25 mL) cheese mixture into slit.

3. Preheat grill on medium-high. Arrange filled wieners on grill rack and grill (use Direct Grilling, page 6) for about 5 minutes or until cheese is melted. At the same time, heat buns or tortillas on top rack of grill. Serve in buns or wrap into plain tortillas. **Makes 10 servings.**

Farmer's Sausage with Fresh Fruit Salsa

The salsa's tropical and fresh mint flavors beautifully complement grilled sausages. Salsa pairs equally well with pork chops, pork tenderloin and chicken.

SALSA

1	kiwifruit, peeled and diced	1
¹⁄₂	mango, peeled and diced	¹⁄₂
¹⁄₂	papaya, peeled, seeded and chopped	¹⁄₂
¹⁄₂ cup	quartered strawberries	125 mL
¹⁄₂ cup	diced cantaloupe	125 mL
¹⁄₂	jalapeño chili pepper, seeded and finely chopped	¹⁄₂
2 tbsp	finely chopped fresh mint leaves	25 mL
1 tbsp	each: lime juice and granulated sugar	15 mL
6	large farmer's sausages or bratwurst	6

1. *For salsa:* Combine kiwifruit, mango, papaya, strawberries, cantaloupe and jalapeño pepper. Add mint, lime juice and sugar; stir to blend. Refrigerate for about 30 minutes to allow for flavor development.

2. *For sausage:* In a covered skillet, poach sausages in gently simmering (but not boiling) water for about 8 minutes; drain and discard liquid. Reserve sausages.

3. Preheat grill on medium-high. Place sausages on lightly oiled grill rack. Close lid and grill (use Direct Grilling, page 6) to desired degree of doneness (see chart on page 11); turn sausages several times. **Makes 6 servings and 3 cups (750 mL) salsa.**

Variation: If you want more intense smoke flavor, tuck a smoke box beside the heat source. In view of the short exposure time for effective smoking, consider loading the smoke box with dry rather than water soaked chips for a short but intense smoke. See comments on smoking in the Appendix (page 246).

The finishing touch to this "perfect sausage" is of course great crusty buns, sauerkraut, a variety of mustards, chopped onion, tomatoes and anything else you fancy.

Tips: Extra salsa may be refrigerated for up to 3 days. Try it on a fruit salad or cottage cheese.

 Wine: A sweeter style Chenin Blanc or a Riesling–Gewurztaminer make excellent choices.

THE GREAT HAMBURGER WORLD TOUR

Forget fuss and formality. Nothing beats a juicy burger, and this basic recipe can be used to prepare a quantity of them. Start with the Basic Burger and take it from there with our international suggestions. You may want to replace ground beef with pork or use a combination of both.

BASIC BURGER

1 lb	lean ground beef	500 g
1	small onion, finely minced	1
1	clove garlic, crushed, optional	1
1	egg, beaten	1
1/3 cup	rolled oats	75 mL
2 tbsp	milk	25 mL
	Salt and freshly ground pepper	

1. Lightly combine beef, onion, garlic (if using), egg, rolled oats, milk, salt and pepper. Gently form into 4 to 6 evenly shaped patties, about 3/4-inch (2 cm) thick. Chill patties for at least 1 hour before grilling.

2. Preheat grill on medium-high. Place patties on lightly oiled grill rack. Close lid and grill (use Direct Grilling, page 6) for 5 to 7 minutes per side or until an instant-read thermometer inserted sidewise into center of each patty reads 160°F (71°C).

3. Serve with World Tour Fixings from the wide variety of pickles, relishes, sauces and extras suggested below. **Makes 4 to 6 patties.**

WORLD TOUR FIXINGS

NAME	BREAD	TYPE OF PICKLE OR RELISH	EXTRAS
Canadian	hamburger buns	hamburger relish and sliced dill pickles	sliced tomatoes, grated old Cheddar cheese, mustard and onion slices
French	baguette slices	Dijon mustard	crumbled Roquefort cheese
Italian	thick Italian bread slices	savory tomato relish	sprinkle with oregano and basil; top with shredded romaine lettuce and sliced Mozzarella cheese; add a dollop of pesto
German	sliced rye or pumpernickel	sauerkraut and onion relish	sprinkle with caraway seeds; top with shredded Muenster cheese
Oriental	sesame seed buns	sweet mixed pickles	drizzle patties with soy sauce before grilling; top with bean sprouts
Hawaiian	cheese buns	sliced sweet pickles	add a pineapple slice during cooking and sprouts as a garnish
Mexican	flour tortillas	hot pepper rings and salsa	shredded lettuce, sliced avocado, finely chopped jalapeño peppers, grated Cheddar or Monterey Jack cheese
California	thick sliced whole wheat bread	baby dill pickles	alfalfa sprouts, tomato slices, light mayonnaise
Greek	halved pita bread	sweet green relish	plain yogurt or tzatziki, tomato, crumbled feta cheese, black olives
Indian	naan	hummus, ground cumin, sesame oil	sliced tomatoes, plain yogurt, chopped green onions

TURKISH SKEWERED BURGERS

Mediterranean flavors predominate in these burgers wrapped in an oval shape around skewers. The oval shape fits a pita pocket better than the usual round shape. Skewers help to retain the oval shape during grilling and then serve as a handle. A light rather than firm touch when shaping patties will keep the patties moister during cooking.

BURGERS

1 lb	lean ground beef	500 g
½ cup	rolled oats	125 mL
½ cup	finely chopped onion	125 mL
1	egg	1
¼ cup	plain yogurt	50 mL
½ tsp	each: dried thyme and oregano or 2 tsp (10 mL) chopped fresh	2 mL
¼ tsp	each: salt and freshly ground pepper	1 mL
dash	hot pepper sauce	dash
3	cloves garlic, minced	3

CUCUMBER SAUCE

½ cup	grated cucumber	125 mL
½ cup	plain yogurt	125 mL
¼ cup	light mayonnaise	50 mL
4	pita pockets, halved	4

 Wine: Opt for a Fumé Blanc.

1. *For burgers:* Combine beef, rolled oats, onion, egg, yogurt, seasonings, hot sauce and garlic. Divide into 8 portions. Shape mixture lightly around 8 short metal skewers making a 4-inch (10 cm) oval.

2. Preheat grill on medium-high. Place skewers on lightly oiled grill rack. Close lid and grill (use Direct Grilling, page 6) for 5 to 7 minutes per side or until an instant-read thermometer inserted into center of meat reads 160°F (71°C); turn once.

3. *For sauce:* In a small bowl, combine cucumber, yogurt and mayonnaise; season to taste with salt and pepper. Serve oval burgers in halved pita pockets with a spoonful of sauce. **Makes 8 burgers, 4 servings of 2 burgers each.**

CUMIN TURKEY BURGERS

Full of spice flavors, these burgers smell absolutely amazing when grilling. Ground chicken works well as a replacement for turkey. Fruit chutney is just the right topping for these burgers.

1 lb	lean ground turkey	500 g
¼ cup	finely chopped onion	50 mL
¼ cup	dried bread crumbs	75 mL
2	cloves garlic, minced	2
1	egg	1
½ to 1 tsp	each: cumin and oregano	2 to 5 mL
½ tsp	each: dried mustard powder and paprika	2 mL
¼ tsp	each salt and freshly ground pepper	1 mL
4 to 6	toasted whole wheat buns	4 to 6

TOPPINGS

Fruit chutney,
shredded lettuce,
sliced onions, optional

1. Lightly combine turkey, onion, bread crumbs, garlic, egg, cumin, oregano, mustard, paprika, salt and pepper. Gently form into 4 to 6 evenly shaped patties, about ¾-inch (2 cm) thick. Refrigerate patties for at least 1 hour before grilling (see Tip).

2. Preheat grill on medium. Place patties on lightly oiled grill rack. Close lid and grill (use Direct Grilling, page 6) for 6 to 7 minutes per side or until an instant-read thermometer inserted sidewise into center of each patty reads 165°F (74°C).

3. Serve on toasted buns with the suggested toppings, if using. **Makes 4 to 6 servings.**

Tip: Patties hold together best if covered and refrigerated for about 1 hour before cooking.

Safety Tips: A little care for your ground turkey (or ground chicken) is in order. After handling these raw meats, wash your hands and all utensils with hot soapy water and rinse well.

After grilling, always place cooked burgers on a clean plate. Never use a plate that held the raw burgers.

CHICKEN MUSHROOM BURGERS

These burgers are a real hit with all ages. A 12-year-old granddaughter, who is particularly suspicious about eating anything different, asks for these whenever she visits.

1 lb	lean ground chicken	500 g
1½ cups	finely chopped mushrooms	375 mL
2	green onions, chopped	2
1 to 2	cloves garlic, minced	1 to 2
¼ cup	oat bran	50 mL
1¼ tsp	dried tarragon or 1 tbsp (15 mL) fresh	6 mL
½ tsp	salt	2 mL
⅛ tsp	freshly ground pepper	0.5 mL
6	whole wheat buns, halved	6

TOPPINGS

Tomato slices, alfalfa sprouts or leaf lettuce, cranberry sauce or mustard, light mayonnaise

1. Lightly combine chicken, mushrooms, onions, garlic, oat bran, tarragon, salt and pepper. Gently form into 6 evenly shaped patties, about ¾-inch (2 cm) thick. Refrigerate patties for at least 1 hour before grilling (see Tip).

2. Preheat grill on medium. Place patties on lightly oiled grill rack. Close lid and grill (use Direct Grilling, page 6) for 6 to 7 minutes per side or until an instant-read thermometer inserted sidewise into center of each patty reads 165°F (74°C); turn once.

3. During last few minutes of cooking, place buns on top rack of grill to warm. Fill each bun with a cooked patty; top with choice of garnishes. **Makes 6 servings.**

Suggested Menu: Serve with Grilled Asparagus (page 177), crinkle cut potatoes with a garnish of chopped fresh mint, and iced mineral water with lemon.

Tip: Patties hold together best if covered and refrigerated for about 1 hour before cooking.

Safety Tips: A little care for your chicken is in order. After handling raw chicken, wash your hands and all utensils with hot soapy water and rinse well.

After grilling, always put burgers on a clean plate. Never use a plate that held the raw burgers.

 Wine: Try either a Pinot Noir or Gamay Noir.

MOROCCAN CHICKEN BURGERS

Curry, cumin and coriander flavors permeate these burgers and their matching yogurt sauce.

YOGURT SAUCE

2 cups	plain yogurt	500 mL
2	small onions, coarsely chopped	2
2 tbsp	olive oil	25 mL
4	cloves garlic	4
1 cup	loosely packed parsley	250 mL
1 tsp	each: coriander seeds and ground cumin	5 mL
½ tsp	crushed red pepper flakes	2 mL
	Salt and freshly ground pepper	

CHICKEN BURGERS

1 lb	lean ground chicken or turkey	500 g
1	egg, beaten	1
¼ cup	dry bread crumbs	50 mL
2	green onions, thinly sliced	2
2 tbsp	finely chopped fresh mint or 2 tsp (10 mL) dried	25 mL
1	clove garlic, minced	1
½ tsp	each: ground cinnamon and salt	2 mL
¼ tsp	freshly ground pepper	1 mL
6	whole wheat sesame burger buns, split	6

TOPPINGS

Chopped lettuce, onion, banana peppers

1. *For sauce:* Blend yogurt, onions, oil, garlic, parsley, coriander, cumin and pepper flakes in a food processor until almost smooth; add salt and pepper to taste. Cover and refrigerate.

2. *For burgers:* Lightly combine chicken, egg, bread crumbs, onions, mint, garlic, cinnamon, salt and pepper. Gently form into 6 evenly shaped patties, about ¾-inch (2 cm) thick. Refrigerate patties for at least 1 hour before grilling (see Tip).

3. Preheat grill on medium. Place patties on lightly oiled grill rack. Close lid and grill (use Direct Grilling, page 6) for 6 to 7 minutes per side or until an instant-read thermometer inserted sidewise into center of each patty reads 165°F (74°C); turn once.

4. During last few minutes of cooking, place buns on top rack of grill to warm. Fill each bun with a cooked patty, top with lettuce, onion, banana peppers and Yogurt Sauce. **Makes 6 servings.**

Tip: Patties hold together best if covered and refrigerated for about 1 hour before cooking.

 Wine: A white Zinfandel would be the best choice.

STUFFED LAMB BURGERS

Lamb, mint, feta cheese, olives and yogurt, all flavors of Greece, make these nicely seasoned grilled burgers a hit with lamb lovers.

1 lb	lean ground lamb	500 g
3	cloves garlic, crushed	3
½ cup	soft bread crumbs	125 mL
3 tbsp	minced fresh mint or 1 tbsp (15 mL) dried	45 mL
½ tsp	each: salt and ground cinnamon	2 mL
¼ tsp	each: freshly ground pepper and hot red pepper flakes	1 mL
½ cup	crumbled feta cheese	125 mL
2	whole wheat or plain pita breads, halved	2

TOPPINGS

Sliced black olives, sliced tomatoes, plain yogurt, chopped cucumber

Suggested Menu: Serve with a traditional Greek salad: cucumbers, tomatoes, black olives, crumbled feta cheese, drizzled with olive oil and lemon juice and generously sprinkled with oregano and pepper.

1. Lightly combine lamb, garlic, bread crumbs, mint, salt, cinnamon, pepper and hot pepper flakes. Gently form into 8 evenly shaped thin patties. Evenly divide feta cheese over 4 patties. Top each with remaining patties; press gently to seal.

2. Preheat grill on medium-high. Place patties on lightly oiled grill rack. Close lid and grill (use Direct Grilling, page 6) for about 6 to 7 minutes per side or until an instant-read thermometer inserted sidewise into center of each patty reads 160°F (71°C). During the final few minutes of cooking, warm pitas until they are golden brown.

3. Serve each patty in half an open pita pocket with your choice of garnishes. **Makes 4 burgers.**

Tasty Tuna Burgers

The price of tuna makes this an expensive recipe unless you find it on sale. However, it makes an elegant burger for an informal but special occasion. Tuna can be replaced with less expensive tilapia or canned tuna.

1 lb	ahi or albacore tuna steak	500 g
2	green onions	2
1	slice gingerroot, optional	1
½ cup	dry bread crumbs	125 mL
2 tbsp	each: dry sherry and soy sauce	25 mL
1	egg	1
1	clove garlic, crushed	1
¼ tsp	salt	1 mL
	Freshly ground pepper	
4	whole wheat buns, split	4

TOPPINGS

Leaf lettuce, mango salsa

1. Pulse tuna, onions and gingerroot, if using, in a food processor until coarsely chopped. Add bread crumbs, sherry, soy sauce, egg, garlic, salt and pepper. Pulse to blend just until ingredients are mixed (do not over blend).

2. Remove to bowl, gently shape into 4 patties, about 1-inch (2.5 cm) thick. Place on plate, cover and refrigerate for 30 minutes or longer.

3. Preheat grill on medium-high. Place patties on lightly oiled grill rack. Close lid and grill (use Direct Grilling, page 6), for 5 to 6 minutes per side turning once or until burgers are crisp on the outside and tuna is opaque and cooked through.

4. Serve on buns with lettuce and fresh mango salsa, if desired. **Makes 4 servings.**

 Wine: Try a white Zinfandel or a Rosé.

Game Burgers

Since game meats are very lean, care must be taken to not overcook them, while keeping in mind that all ground meats should be cooked to well done. This is a modification of my daughter Janice's recipe.

1 lb	ground venison, bison or elk	500 g
½ cup	salsa, preferably mild	125 mL
⅓ cup	rolled oats	75 mL
1	egg	1
¼ tsp	salt	1 mL
pinch	freshly ground pepper	pinch
4 to 6	crusty rolls, halved	4 to 6

1. Lightly combine meat, salsa, oats, egg, salt and pepper. Depending on how wet the salsa is, you may need to add more oats to hold the burgers together. Gently form into 4 to 6 evenly shaped patties, about ¾-inch (2 cm) thick. Chill patties for at least 1 hour before grilling.

2. Preheat grill on medium-high. Place patties on lightly oiled grill rack. Close lid and grill (use Direct Grilling, page 6) for 4 to 6 minutes per side or until an instant-read thermometer inserted sidewise into center of each patty reads 160°F (71°C).

3. Fill each bun with a cooked patty, and top with your choice of toppings much as you would beef burgers. **Makes 4 to 6 servings.**

MIDDLE EASTERN LAMB BURGERS

Black kalamata olives, sweet dried apricots and, of course, cumin and oregano spicing give this burger its significant Middle Eastern flavor. For extra zest, serve with Lime Aioli Dip (page 21).

1 lb	lean ground lamb	500 g
¼ cup	pitted black olives, finely chopped	50 mL
¼ cup	dried bread crumbs	75 mL
2 tbsp	finely chopped dried apricots	25 mL
1	egg	1
½ tsp	each: cumin and oregano	2 mL
¼ tsp	each: salt and freshly ground pepper	1 mL
4 to 6	halved pita pockets	4 to 6

1. Lightly combine lamb, olives, bread crumbs, apricots, egg, cumin, oregano, salt and pepper. Gently form into 4 to 6 evenly shaped patties, about ¾-inch (2 cm) thick. Chill patties for at least 1 hour before grilling.

2. Preheat grill on medium. Place patties on lightly oiled grill rack. Close lid and grill (use Direct Grilling, page 6) for 5 to 6 minutes per side or until an instant-read thermometer inserted sidewise into center of each patty reads 160°F (71°C). **Makes 4 to 6 servings.**

SCRUMPTIOUS SALMON BURGERS

These patties deliver all those wonderful fresh flavors so remindful of "summer at the shore" dinners. Delicious served with Cucumber Raita (page 85).

1 lb	skinless, boneless salmon fillet	500 g
1	egg, beaten	1
½ cup	cracker crumbs	125 mL
2 tbsp	finely chopped red onion	25 mL
1 tbsp	chopped fresh dill	15 mL
1 tsp	grated lemon rind	5 mL
1 tbsp	fresh lemon juice	15 mL
	Salt and pepper	
6	whole wheat rolls or onion buns, split	6

TOPPINGS

Leaf lettuce and sliced tomatoes

1. Pulse salmon in food processor or coarsely chop by hand. Add egg, cracker crumbs, onion, dill, lemon rind and juice, salt and pepper. Pulse to blend just until ingredients are mixed (do not over blend).

2. Remove to bowl, gently shape into 6 patties, about 1-inch (2.5 cm) thick. Place on plate, cover and refrigerate for 30 minutes or longer.

3. Preheat grill on medium-high. Place patties on lightly oiled grill rack. Close lid and grill (use Direct Grilling, page 6), for 5 to 6 minutes per side, turning once or until patties are crisp on the outside and salmon is opaque and cooked through.

4. Serve patties on onion buns with lettuce, sliced tomato and Cucumber Raita (page 85). **Makes 6 servings.**

BULGUR BLACK BEAN BURGERS

This vegetarian-style burger will satisfy any vegetarian's taste buds as well as supplying the necessary protein requirements. Non-vegetarians will find them to be a tasty change from meat. Shape them in the size best suited for your family's appetites.

BURGERS

1 cup	water	250 mL
½ cup	bulgur	125 mL
1	can (19 oz/598 mL) sodium-reduced black beans	1
2	chopped green onions	2
2 tbsp	plain yogurt	25 mL
¼ tsp	each: allspice, cinnamon and cumin	1 mL
	cornmeal (for sprinkling)	

YOGURT VEGETABLE SAUCE

⅔ cup	plain yogurt	150 mL
½ cup	finely shredded carrot	125 mL
½ cup	finely shredded cucumber	125 mL
6	whole wheat buns	6
	Sliced tomato and shredded lettuce	

1. *For burgers:* Bring water to a boil in a small saucepan; add bulgur, cover and reduce heat and cook for 10 minutes or until water is absorbed and bulgur is tender. Set aside.

2. Drain and rinse beans. Mash beans with 2 tbsp (25 mL) yogurt until almost smooth. Stir in bulgur, onion, allspice, cinnamon and cumin. Gently form mixture into 6 evenly shaped patties and place on a plate. Cover and refrigerate until ready to cook.

3. Lightly sprinkle patties with cornmeal. Spray each side with non-stick cooking spray. Preheat grill on medium heat. Place patties on lightly oiled grill rack, close lid and grill for 4 minutes per side or until golden brown and heated through; turn once.

4. *For sauce:* Combine yogurt, shredded carrot and cucumber. Place patty on bun, top with yogurt sauce, sliced tomato and lettuce. **Makes 6 servings and 1 cup (250 mL) sauce.**

VEGETABLE LENTIL BURGERS

 This Indian-style lentil burger is chock-a-block with vegetables — carrots, broccoli and cauliflower. Great for you and great tasting too!

¹⁄₂ cup	dried green lentils	125 mL
2	medium potatoes, peeled and cubed	2
¹⁄₂ cup	each: chopped broccoli, cauliflower and carrots	125 mL
	Salt and freshly ground pepper	
2 tsp	canola oil	10 mL
1	small onion, chopped	1
1	clove garlic, minced	1
¹⁄₂ tsp	each: ground cumin, ginger, mustard seeds and hot red pepper flakes	2 mL
2 tbsp	chopped fresh cilantro	25 mL
²⁄₃ cup	dry bread crumbs, divided	150 mL
¹⁄₂ cup	finely chopped walnuts	125 mL
1	egg, beaten	1
6	whole wheat pita pockets	6

TOPPINGS

Cucumber Raita, sliced tomatoes, alfalfa sprouts

1. Cover lentils and potatoes with water; bring to a boil and cook for 10 minutes. Add broccoli, cauliflower and carrots and return to boil; cook until tender; drain well. (Watch this mixture does not boil dry as lentils absorb water during their cooking). Add salt and pepper to taste.

2. Heat oil over medium in nonstick skillet until hot. Add onion and garlic; sauté for 5 minutes. Add cumin, ginger, mustard seeds and red pepper flakes. Remove from heat; stir in cilantro.

3. Stir onion mixture into lentil mixture along with ¹⁄₂ cup (125 mL) bread crumbs, walnuts and egg; stir gently. With floured hands, divide mixture into 6 equal portions. Shape into 6 patties; dredge with remaining bread crumbs.

4. Preheat grill on medium. Carefully place patties on well-oiled grill rack. Close lid and grill (use Direct Grilling, page 6) for about 5 minutes per side. If desired, brush cooked side with a barbecue sauce. Heat pita pockets during last part of grilling.

5. Open pita and place one patty in each pocket. Garnish with choice of toppings as desired. **Makes 6 servings.**

Tip: Chilling the patties on foil is a handy technique that makes them easier to remove to the grill.

Cucumber Raita: Combine 1 cup (250 mL) plain yogurt, 1 tbsp (15 mL) each: lime juice and chopped fresh mint, 1 tsp (5 mL) ground cumin, 1 medium seedless cucumber, peeled and diced, and salt and freshly ground pepper to taste. **Makes about 1¹⁄₂ cups (375 mL).** Use any leftover sauce as a dip.

MEXICAN BEAN BURGERS

 Start with beans, the foundation of Mexican cuisine. Add the Mexican spice flavors — cumin, garlic and coriander. Top it all with avocado, sour cream and shredded cheese. You end up with the wonderful taste of Mexico in a vegetarian burger.

2	cans (14 oz/398 mL) pinto beans, drained	2
1 tbsp	canola oil	15 mL
¾ cup	finely chopped onion	175 mL
3	cloves garlic, minced	3
2 tbsp	ground coriander	25 mL
4 tsp	each: all purpose flour and ground cumin	20 mL
½ tsp	each: salt and freshly ground pepper	2 mL
6	hamburger or sesame seed buns	6

TOPPINGS

Sliced avocado, sour cream, shredded Monterey Jack cheese, mild or medium salsa

1. Mash pinto beans with a fork or a potato masher; set aside.

2. Heat oil on medium-high in nonstick skillet; cook onions and garlic for 5 minutes or until tender. Add coriander, flour, cumin, salt and pepper; cook, stirring constantly, for 1 minute. Add onion mixture to pinto beans; stir well.

3. Cut 6 squares of waxed paper. Divide bean mixture into 6 equal amounts; shape into patties on each waxed paper square.

4. Preheat grill on medium. Carefully place patties on well-oiled grill rack. Close lid and grill (use Direct Grilling, page 6) for 4 minutes per side. Heat buns during last part of grilling.

5. Place a patty in each warmed bun and serve with choice of toppings. **Makes 6 servings.**

Suggested Menu: Serve a tossed green salad with orange slices and a zesty vinaigrette dressing along with one of the grilled desserts in Chapter 10 for a meat-alternative meal to remember.

 Wine: A big California Merlot or even a Cabernet Sauvignon would be ideal.

PORTOBELLO MUSHROOM BURGERS

 These large, dark brown mushrooms are simply a fully mature crimini (a small brown mushroom). They acquired the more romantic name "portobello" in the 1980s as part of a marketing activity to make this rather ugly fungi more attractive to consumers. Because they are so large, some of the mushroom liquid has evaporated, making them denser and thus ideal for grilling. Their intense meaty flavor and robust texture make them a great substitute for meat. In fact, they are often compared to a tender steak.

4	portobello mushroom caps	4
2 tbsp	each: balsamic vinegar and olive or canola oil	25 mL
1 tsp	each: dried basil and oregano or 1 tbsp (15 mL) chopped fresh	5 mL
1	clove garlic, minced	1
¼ tsp	each: salt and freshly ground pepper	1 mL
4	toasted split buns or ciabatta bread	4

TOPPINGS

Sliced tomatoes, relish, salsa, mustard, shredded lettuce, sliced red or white onion, sliced cheese, mayonnaise

 Wine: A Chianti or Cabernet Sauvignon will match best.

1. Place mushroom caps in a shallow dish. Combine vinegar, oil, basil, oregano and garlic. Drizzle over caps; let stand for about 15 minutes. Sprinkle lightly with salt and pepper.

2. Preheat grill on medium-high. Place mushrooms on lightly oiled grill rack and grill (use Direct Grilling, page 6) for about 12 minutes or until hot and bubbly.

3. Serve with any of the toppings, much as you would for beef burgers. **Makes 4 servings.**

CHAPTER 4
POULTRY ON THE GRILL

◄ *Duck Breasts with Mango Orange Sauce (page 111)*

Chicken, turkey, duck and Rock Cornish hens are all wonderfully flavorful when grilled. This chapter offers many interesting approaches to grilling these tasty birds that will open doors to new taste experiences.

One of these is butterflying, also known as spatchcocking. It provides fast, even, moisture-preserving grilling by flattening whole poultry to present a more level grilling surface. A detailed description of the technique is contained in Grilled Butterflied Lemon Rosemary Chicken (page 100).

Boneless and bone-in chicken breasts are all cooked over medium or medium-high heat using Direct Grilling (page 6), whereas legs, thighs and drumsticks are often grilled by Indirect. Also, large whole chickens and turkeys should be grilled by Indirect Grilling (page 6) or by Spit Roasting (page 140). See charts on page 9 for grilling times. It is essential for food safety that all poultry are grilled until no longer pink and juices run clear when meat is pierced and an instant-read meat thermometer reads 165°F (74°C).

Feeling adventurous? Try adding aromatic wood chips like mesquite to the grill for real wood-smoke flavor. See our discussion on "smoking" on page 246. Or try filling the cavity of whole birds with fresh herbs like rosemary or thyme, slices of lemon or orange and black or green olives. All impart exciting new flavors to the bird. If using a marinade, keep marinating time short so you don't overpower poultry's delicate taste. About 2 hours is maximum for a highly seasoned marinade and 4 hours for a mild one.

Turkey cuts are grilled the same way as chicken cuts, except they are cooked at medium heat for a longer time. Since turkey has a less delicate taste than chicken, marinating times can be longer. Turkey breasts grilled with fresh herbs such as thyme, sage, lemongrass, or rosemary tucked under the skin make an exotic meal requiring little attention. Simply loosen the skin, place the fresh herbs underneath, skewer the skin back in place, brush lightly with olive oil and start the grilling. The aroma is enticing, the taste is tantalizing, and you are left with very little cleanup.

Marinating poultry cuts before grilling gives us more than good-tasting poultry. It reduces the potential for cancer-causing carcinogens. For a full discussion of this, see page 248 in the Appendix. Boil any remaining marinade for 5 minutes to destroy any harmful bacteria before using it to brush on during grilling.

As with any other raw meat, proper storage and handling of poultry is important. Keep poultry clean and keep it cold until you cook it. Before marinating or cooking poultry, rinse and pat dry. Wash and dry hands before and after handling the raw meat. Most poultry can be stored in the refrigerator for up to 48 hours, or in the freezer for up to 6 months. Refrigerate leftovers promptly.

WINE-SAUCED STUFFED CHICKEN BREASTS

Mediterranean flavors of olive, oregano, Parmesan and garlic permeate these succulent chicken breasts. Sliced, the breasts display the attractive marbling of the stuffing. Plan for leftovers. These chicken breasts are as good, if not better, served cold, a day later.

STUFFING

1 cup	soft bread crumbs	250 mL
¼ cup	milk	50 mL
¼ cup	finely chopped black olives	50 mL
1	egg	1
¼ cup	grated Parmesan cheese	50 mL
2 tbsp	chopped fresh parsley	25 mL
1½ tsp	dried oregano or 2 tbsp (25 mL) fresh	7 mL
1	clove garlic, minced	1
	Salt and freshly ground pepper	

CHICKEN

4	boneless, skinless chicken breast halves	4
½ cup	dried bread crumbs	125 mL

WINE SAUCE

1 cup	dry white wine	250 mL
2 tbsp	capers, rinsed and drained	25 mL
1 tbsp	melted butter or margarine	15 mL
½ cup	chicken broth	125 mL
1 tbsp	each: cornstarch and chopped fresh parsley	15 mL

1. *For stuffing:* In small bowl, soak bread in milk for 5 minutes. Stir in olives, egg, cheese, parsley, oregano, garlic, and salt and pepper to taste.

2. *For chicken:* Cut a pocket in the thickest part of each chicken breast, fill with some of the stuffing and close with toothpicks. Coat chicken evenly with dried bread crumbs.

3. Preheat grill on medium. Place chicken breasts on oiled grill rack. Close lid and cook (use Direct Grilling, page 6) for about 10 minutes per side or until brown. Lower heat to medium; continue cooking until meat is no longer pink inside, juices run clear when meat is pierced and an instant-read meat thermometer reads 165°F (74°C); turn once.

4. *For sauce:* Meanwhile, in small saucepan, combine wine, capers and butter. Heat for 5 minutes or until hot. Combine chicken broth, cornstarch and parsley; stir into wine mixture; cook for 5 minutes or until slightly thickened, stirring often.

5. Remove chicken breasts from grill to cutting board. Cover with foil for 5 minutes. Carve each breast crosswise into slices and place on heated serving platter. Pour some warm sauce over chicken and pass extra sauce. **Makes 4 servings.**

Suggested Menu: Serve with buttered cooked noodles, Grilled Eggplant (page 177), and a sliced French baguette.

 Wine: Serve with a crisp, dry Pinot Grigio or Sauvignon Blanc.

GRILLED TURKISH CHICKEN BREASTS

The baste adds Middle East flair to humble chicken breasts. Since this baste is rather strong, we recommend you add it only a couple of hours before grilling.

4	boneless, skinless chicken breasts	4
BASTE		
1 tbsp	olive oil	15 mL
2	cloves garlic, crushed	2
1 tsp	grated lemon peel	5 mL
1 tsp	dried thyme or 1 tbsp (15 mL) chopped fresh	5 mL
1 tsp	ground fennel and cinnamon	5 mL
1/2 tsp	each: paprika and ground coriander	2 mL
1/4 tsp	each: salt and freshly ground pepper	1 mL

1. *For chicken:* Remove excess fat from chicken and discard.

2. *For baste:* Combine oil, garlic, lemon peel, thyme, fennel, cinnamon, paprika, coriander, salt and pepper. Rub mixture evenly over all sides of chicken. Place in a single layer in a shallow nonreactive dish, cover and refrigerate for 1 hour, or no longer than 3 hours.

3. Preheat grill on medium. Place chicken on lightly oiled grill rack. Close lid and grill (use Direct Grilling, page 6) for about 8 minutes per side or until no longer pink and juices run clear when chicken is pierced and an instant-read meat thermometer reads 165°F (74°C); turn once. **Makes 4 servings.**

Suggested Menu: Bulgur Tabbouleh (page 214) and Artichoke Salad (page 206).

 Wine: A Riesling will pair perfectly with this dish.

CREAMY PEPPERCORN CHICKEN BREASTS

The fresh, spicy pepper flavor of the green and black peppercorn sauce gives an exciting lift to grilled chicken breasts.

CREAMY PEPPERCORN SAUCE		
1/4 cup	white wine vinegar	50 mL
1/4 cup	sweet white wine (such as Sauterne)	50 mL
1 tbsp	each: black and dried green peppercorns	15 mL
1 1/4 cups	heavy cream	300 mL
6	boneless, skinless chicken breast halves	6
	Fresh chives	

1. *For sauce:* In heavy saucepan, cook vinegar, wine and peppercorns on medium-high for 10 minutes or until reduced to a glaze. Stir in cream, reduce heat and simmer for 5 minutes or until reduced to about 1 1/4 cups (300 mL); keep warm.

2. Preheat grill on medium-high. Place chicken on oiled grill rack. Close lid and cook (use Direct Grilling, page 6) for 12 to 15 minutes or until meat is no longer pink inside, juices run clear when meat is pierced and an instant-read meat thermometer reads 165°F (74°C); turn once. Remove chicken from grill and serve with warm Creamy Peppercorn Sauce and a garnish of chives. **Makes 6 servings.**

ORIENTAL MARINATED CHICKEN BREASTS

Plum sauce gives an Oriental accent to chicken breasts, a longtime grill favorite. Experiment with different mustards to put a new spin to this simple glaze.

MARINADE

½ cup	plum sauce	125 mL
3 tbsp	soy sauce	45 mL
1	piece gingerroot (1 inch/2.5 cm), minced	1
2 tsp	sesame oil	10 mL
2	cloves garlic, crushed	2
2 tsp	grainy mustard	10 mL
4	boneless, skinless chicken breast halves	4
4	green onion fans	4

1. *For marinade:* In bowl, combine plum and soy sauce, gingerroot, oil, garlic and mustard; stir well.

2. Place chicken breasts in resealable plastic bag; pour plum mixture over chicken and refrigerate for 1 hour or longer depending on depth of flavor desired. Remove chicken from marinade; reserve marinade. Place marinade in small saucepan, bring to a boil, reduce heat and cook for 5 minutes; keep warm.

3. Preheat grill on medium-high. Place chicken on oiled grill rack. Close lid and cook (use Direct Grilling, page 6) for about 15 minutes or until meat is tender and no longer pink inside; juices should run clear when meat is pierced and an instant-read meat thermometer should read 165°F (74°C); turn once. Brush occasionally with warm marinade; turn once. Serve with onion garnish. **Makes 4 servings.**

Suggested Menu: Accompany these chicken breasts with an Oriental–flavored rice, a noodle salad with water chestnuts and snow peas sautéed in sesame and olive oil, or Szechwan Vegetable Salad (page 207).

Tip: If plum sauce is very thick, thin it with 2 tbsp (25 mL) pineapple or orange juice.

CREAMY TARRAGON CHICKEN BREASTS

 It's the sauce, with its anise-tasting tarragon and Dijon mustard, that makes these grilled chicken breasts so delicious — whether grilled indoors or outdoors.

CHICKEN

4	boneless, skinless chicken breasts	4
	Salt and freshly ground pepper	

TARRAGON SAUCE

¼ cup	each: light sour cream and light mayonnaise	50 mL
1 tbsp	Dijon mustard	15 mL
2 tsp	dried tarragon leaves or 2 tbsp (25 mL) fresh	10 mL
1	green onion, finely chopped	1
	Fresh tarragon, optional	

1. Remove excess fat from chicken and discard. Sprinkle lightly with salt and pepper.

2. *For indoor grilling:* Preheat indoor grill on high for 5 minutes. Place chicken on lightly oiled grill rack. Reduce heat to medium, cover chicken with foil and grill for about 8 minutes per side or until chicken is no longer pink and juices run clear when pierced, and an instant-read meat thermometer reads 165°F (74°C); turn once. Remove from grill, cover loosely with foil for 5 minutes before serving.

3. *For sauce:* Combine sour cream, mayonnaise, mustard, tarragon and green onion. Serve a spoonful of sauce with cooked chicken and garnish with fresh tarragon, if using. **Makes 4 servings.**

For Outdoor Grilling: Preheat grill on medium. Place chicken on lightly oiled grill rack. Close lid and grill (use Direct Grilling, page 6) for about 8 minutes per side or until chicken is no longer pink and juices run clear when pierced and an instant-read meat thermometer registers 165°F (74°C); turn once. Remove from grill, cover loosely with foil for 5 minutes before serving.

CHICKEN IN A PITA

Pita pockets and tzatziki sauce make these chicken breasts Greek.

4	boneless, skinless chicken breasts	4
1/2 tsp	grated lemon peel	2 mL
1 tbsp	each: fresh lemon juice and olive oil	15 mL
1 tsp	dried oregano or 1 tbsp (15 mL) chopped fresh	5 mL
1/4 tsp	each: chili powder, salt and pepper	1 mL
4	whole wheat pitas, halved	4
1	large cucumber, sliced	1
	Leaf lettuce, tomato slices, tzatziki sauce	

1. Remove excess fat from chicken and discard. Combine lemon peel and juice, oil, oregano, chili powder, salt and pepper. Press mixture over all sides of chicken until well coated.

2. Preheat grill on medium. Place chicken on lightly oiled grill rack. Close lid and grill (use Direct Grilling, page 6) for about 8 minutes per side or until no longer pink and juices run clear when chicken is pierced and an instant-read meat thermometer reads 165°F (74°C); turn once.

3. Remove chicken from grill; slice lengthwise into strips. Place lettuce, tomatoes, cucumber and chicken in each pita pocket. Top with tzatziki sauce, and serve. **Makes 4 servings.**

ROSEMARY GRILLED CHICKEN BREASTS WITH CITRUS SALSA

The real beauty of boneless, skinless chicken breasts is their simplicity of preparation. They come ready to go. Try marinating them in this simple rosemary-wine mixture and serve with a tangy salsa.

MARINADE

1/2 cup	fresh rosemary sprigs	125 mL
2/3 cup	dry white wine	150 mL
2 tbsp	canola oil	25 mL
1/2 tsp	each: pepper and paprika	2 mL
2	cloves garlic, minced	2
6	boneless, skinless chicken breast halves	6
1 cup	Citrus Salsa (page 58)	250 mL
	Orange twists	

1. *For marinade*: In small bowl, combine rosemary, wine, oil, pepper, paprika and garlic. Place chicken in shallow nonreactive dish in single layer. Pour marinade over chicken; turn to coat. Cover and refrigerate for up to 4 hours.

2. Preheat grill on medium-high. Remove chicken and rosemary from marinade; reserve rosemary sprigs and discard the rest of the marinade. Place chicken on oiled grill rack. Close lid and cook (use Direct Grilling, page 6) for 6 to 8 minutes per side or until chicken is no longer pink inside, juices run clear when meat is pierced and an instant-read meat thermometer reads 165°F (74°C); turn once. After chicken has been turned, sprinkle reserved rosemary on cooked side of chicken.

3. Serve chicken with a spoonful of Citrus Salsa and an orange twist. **Makes 6 servings.**

YUCATAN CHICKEN BREASTS WITH GUACAMOLE

Hot peppers and oregano give these chicken breasts a Mexican flavor. A tomato slice and an oregano sprig are sandwiched within each breast.

3	boneless, skinless whole chicken breasts (about 2 lb/1 kg)	3
CHILI PASTE		
3 tbsp	each: tomato paste and water	45 mL
2 tbsp	chili powder	25 mL
1 tbsp	rice vinegar	15 mL
1 tbsp	minced jalapeño pepper	15 mL
2	cloves garlic, minced and mashed	2
½ tsp	each: dried oregano and salt	2 mL
2	firm medium tomatoes	2
6	fresh oregano sprigs	6
	Jalapeño pepper	
	Red chili pepper	

Suggested Menu: For an authentic "south of the border" taste, serve with crisp corn tortillas, Guacamole (page 53), and Mexican Corn Salad (page 216).

Tip: The longer the marinating time, the more distinctive the depth of spice flavor.

1. Rinse chicken, pat dry and remove excess fat and discard; halve breasts and set aside.

2. *For paste:* In small bowl, stir together tomato paste, water, chili powder, vinegar, jalapeño pepper, garlic, oregano and salt to make a thick paste. Place chicken in shallow nonreactive dish large enough to hold chicken in one layer; coat chicken with chili paste. Cover and refrigerate for at least 3 hours or overnight.

3. With a knife, remove stem end of tomatoes; cut each tomato into three 1-inch (2.5 cm) slices. Arrange 1 tomato slice and 1 oregano sprig on wide end of each chicken breast; fold narrow end over to sandwich tomato and oregano. Thread a skewer through ends of chicken breast and then through folded side, letting pointed end of skewer extend about 2 inches (5 cm) beyond chicken breast. Repeat with remaining tomatoes, oregano and chicken.

4. Preheat grill on medium-high. Place chicken, thick end down, on oiled grill rack. Close lid and cook (use Direct Grilling, page 6) for about 10 minutes; turn and cook on second side until chicken is no longer pink inside, juices run clear when meat is pierced and an instant-read meat thermometer reads 165°F (74°C). Remove chicken and garnish with jalepeño chili peppers and red chili peppers. **Makes 6 servings.**

LEMON CHICKEN DRUMSTICKS

Lemon-flavor highlights come from both the marinade and the sauce. Trimming fat and skin from the drumsticks reduces calories and allows the marinade to be better absorbed by the chicken.

MARINADE

¼ cup	fresh lemon juice, divided	50 mL
3 tbsp	Dijon mustard	45 mL
1	clove garlic, crushed	1
4	chicken drumsticks (about 1 lb/500 g)	4

LEMON SAUCE

2 tbsp	each: low-fat mayonnaise and barbecue sauce	25 mL
1 tsp	chili powder	5 mL
1 tsp	grated lemon peel	5 mL
¾ cup	coarse bread crumbs	175 mL
1 tsp	each: dried oregano and basil	5 mL
	Lemon slices	

1. *For marinade:* Combine 3 tbsp (45 mL) lemon juice, mustard and garlic. Trim and discard skin and excess fat from chicken. Add chicken to marinade and turn to coat evenly. Cover and refrigerate for at least 30 minutes.

2. *For sauce:* Combine remaining lemon juice, mayonnaise, barbecue sauce, chili powder and lemon peel; cover and refrigerate.

3. In shallow pan, combine bread crumbs, oregano and basil. Remove chicken from marinade; discard marinade. Dip chicken in bread crumb mixture.

4. Preheat grill on medium. Place chicken on lightly oiled grill rack. Close lid and grill (use Indirect Grilling, page 6) for about 30 minutes or until chicken is no longer pink, juices run clear when meat is pierced and an instant-read meat thermometer reads 165°F (74°C); turn once. Remove from grill, cover loosely with foil for 5 minutes before serving.

5. Serve chicken with chilled sauce and lemon slices. **Makes 4 servings.**

Kitchen Tip: To remove all skin and fat from poultry, use a sharp knife or poultry shears.

Suggested Menu: The addition of Grilled Rosemary Potato Salad (page 213) and a green salad make a perfect meal.

 Wine: a Pinot Gris or dry Riesling will go well.

BEER BASTED CHICKEN DRUMSTICKS

 Grilled inside or out of doors, it's the rub and the basting sauce that bring unique spice and citrus flavors to the chicken. Any meaty chicken pieces can be used in place of drumsticks.

SPICE RUB

1	clove garlic, minced	1
2 tbsp	packed brown sugar	25 mL
½ tsp	each: lemon peel and dry mustard	2 mL
¼ tsp	each: salt, cayenne and freshly ground pepper	1 mL
6	chicken drumsticks	6

BEER BASTING SAUCE

¼ cup	flat beer or apple juice	50 mL
1 tbsp	each: brown sugar and fresh lemon juice	15 mL
½ tsp	each: dry mustard, salt and freshly ground pepper	2 mL

1. *For rub:* Combine garlic, sugar, peel, mustard, salt, cayenne and pepper. Mash together with back of a spoon. Remove skin and excess fat from chicken and discard. Rub spice mixture evenly over all sides of chicken. Place chicken in a single layer in a shallow nonreactive dish, cover and refrigerate for 6 hours or overnight.

2. *For basting sauce:* Combine beer, sugar, lemon juice, mustard, salt and pepper in a small saucepan. Bring to a boil, reduce heat and simmer for 5 minutes; keep warm.

3. For indoor grilling: Preheat indoor grill on high for 5 minutes. Place chicken on lightly oiled grill rack. Reduce heat to medium, cover chicken with foil and grill for about 30 minutes or until chicken is no longer pink and juices run clear when chicken is pierced and an instant-read meat thermometer reads 165°F (74°C); turn once. Lift foil and brush occasionally with Beer Basting Sauce. Remove from grill, cover loosely with foil for 5 minutes before serving. **Makes 6 servings.**

For Outdoor Grilling: Follow procedure as above for Steps 1 and 2.

Step 3: Preheat grill on medium. Place chicken on lightly oiled grill rack. Close lid and grill (use Direct Grilling, page 6) for about 30 minutes or until chicken is no longer pink and juices run clear when pierced and an instant-read meat thermometer registers 165°F (74°C); turn once. Brush occasionally with Beer Basting Sauce. Remove from grill, cover loosely with foil for 5 minutes before serving.

GRILLED BUTTERFLIED LEMON ROSEMARY CHICKEN

Butterflied or spatchcocked are terms used synonymously to describe a method of flattening a small chicken (or any small fowl). The profile of the flattened bird allows a faster and more even grilling. This reduces cooking time, which in turn produces a juicier result.

Friend Judy, a great cook who lives nearby, served us a roasted version of this recipe. It was so enjoyed we had to adapt the recipe for grilling and include it in our book. Hope you like it! And don't let the butterflying / spatchcocking process described below frighten you. It's really quite easy. A sharp pair of kitchen or poultry shears make short work of a tender broiler-fryer chicken.

1	broiler-fryer chicken, about 2 lbs (1 kg)	1
MARINADE		
	Juice of 1 lemon	
2 tbsp	canola or olive oil	25 mL
3 to 4	garlic cloves, chopped	3 to 4
3	sprigs rosemary	3

1. Cut bird down each side of backbone using sharp kitchen or poultry shears (a very sharp knife works also) and remove bone (save for chicken stock). Turn chicken breast side up; press firmly on breastbone to flatten. Tuck wings behind back. Place chicken in a resealable plastic bag.

2. *For marinade:* Add lemon juice and squeezed lemon, oil, garlic and rosemary to bag. Seal, turn to coat well, and refrigerate for several hours or overnight.

3. Preheat grill on medium-high. Remove chicken from marinade; discard marinade. Place chicken, skin side up, on well-oiled grill rack. Tuck rosemary sprigs between legs and breast, any garlic pieces you can rescue, and top with squeezed lemon halves. Close lid, reduce heat to medium and grill (use Direct Grilling, page 6) for about 50 minutes or until chicken is no longer pink and juices run clear when pierced and an instant-read meat thermometer registers 165°F (74°C). Check occasionally to make sure the chicken is browning well, but not becoming too dark.

4. Remove chicken from grill to cutting board, cover with foil; let stand for 10 minutes before cutting into 4 pieces. **Makes 4 servings.**

 Wine: A Pinot Grigio, Trebbiano or Sauvignon Blanc will provide a nice complement to this dish.

HOISIN-SAUCED CHICKEN THIGHS

Hoisin sauce is a thick, reddish-brown, sweet and spicy sauce that is widely used in Chinese cooking. Soy sauce adds saltiness, and fresh gingerroot provides the heat. And since chicken thighs are more economical than chicken breasts, you have a win-win combination.

6	chicken thighs (about 1 lb/500 g)	6
MARINADE		
3 tbsp	each: hoisin sauce and rice vinegar	45 mL
2 tbsp	each: soy sauce and ketchup	25 mL
1 tbsp	canola oil	15 mL
1 tbsp	granulated sugar	15 mL
1	clove garlic, crushed	1
1 tbsp	minced gingerroot	15 mL

1. *For chicken:* Remove skin and excess fat from chicken and discard.

2. *For marinade:* Combine hoisin sauce, vinegar, soy sauce, ketchup, oil, sugar, garlic and gingerroot. Add chicken and toss to coat evenly. Cover and refrigerate for up to 4 hours.

3. Preheat grill on medium. Remove chicken from marinade; discard marinade. Place chicken on lightly oiled grill rack. Close lid and grill (use Direct Grilling, page 6) for about 15 minutes per side or until no longer pink and juices run clear when chicken is pierced and an instant-read meat thermometer reads 165°F (74°C); turn once. **Makes 6 servings.**

Suggested Menu: Serve with steamed basmati rice and a stir-fry of vegetables or a green salad.

 Wine: Try a Gewurztraminer.

MAPLE CRANBERRY CHICKEN QUARTERS

Maple and cranberry flavors give chicken quarters a special lift. The cranberry theme carries through to the accompanying salsa. Chicken legs or breasts can be substituted for the quarters.

MAPLE CRANBERRY GLAZE

½ cup	maple syrup	125 mL
¼ cup	dried cranberries	50 mL

CHICKEN

2 lb	chicken leg quarters (both thigh and drumstick)	1 kg
1 tbsp	each: canola oil and vinegar	15 mL
	Salt and freshly ground pepper	
1 cup	Mexican Cranberry Salsa (page 33)	250 mL
	Fresh cilantro sprigs	

1. *For glaze:* In small saucepan, cook maple syrup and cranberries for 5 minutes or until fruit is softened. Place mixture in food processor or blender; purée until smooth and set aside.

2. Preheat grill on medium. Combine oil and vinegar; use to brush chicken. Place chicken on oiled grill rack. Close lid and cook (use Indirect Grilling, page 6) on medium for 45 minutes, until juices run clear when meat is pierced and an instant-read meat thermometer reads 165°F (74°C); turn once. Brush often with glaze during last 15 minutes of cooking.

3. Garnish chicken with Mexican Cranberry Salsa and fresh cilantro sprigs. **Makes 4 servings.**

Suggested Menu: Our family enjoys Grilled Sweet Potatoes (page 178) and a green vegetable such as green beans or snow peas. For an easy and fun dessert, try Maple Fruit Pizza (page 244).

Tip: Do not refreeze completely thawed, uncooked chicken. Once chicken is thawed, keep it refrigerated and cook it within 48 hours.

 Wine: Serve with Cabernet Franc Rosé or Pinot Noir Rosé.

Polynesian Honey Turkey Drumsticks

Pineapple juice and gingerroot give an exotic Polynesian twist to ordinary turkey drumsticks.

MARINADE

1/2 cup	pineapple juice	125 mL
1/4 cup	liquid honey	50 mL
3	cloves garlic, crushed	3
3 tbsp	Worcestershire sauce	45 mL
1	piece gingerroot (1 inch/2.5 cm long), finely chopped	1
1/2 tsp	each: salt and paprika	2 mL
1/4 tsp	freshly ground pepper	1 mL
3	turkey drumsticks (about 3/4 lb/375 g each) Snipped fresh chives	3

1. *For marinade:* In small bowl, combine pineapple juice, honey, garlic, Worcestershire sauce, gingerroot, salt, paprika and pepper.

2. Place drumsticks in large resealable plastic bag; pour marinade over drumsticks; turn to coat. Refrigerate for at least 6 hours or overnight. Remove drumsticks from marinade; reserve marinade. Place marinade in small saucepan, bring to a boil, reduce heat and cook for 5 minutes; keep warm.

3. Preheat grill on medium. Place drumsticks on oiled grill rack. Close lid and cook (use Indirect Grilling, page 6) for about 1 1/2 hours or until drumsticks are no longer pink inside, juices run clear when meat is pierced and an instant-read meat thermometer reads 165°F (74°C). Brush occasionally during final 20 minutes with warm marinade.

4. Remove drumsticks from grill; cover with foil and let stand for 10 minutes. Slice meat, arrange on plate and sprinkle with chives. **Makes 4 to 6 servings.**

Tip: Never pierce turkey with a fork to turn. Instead, turn it with a spatula or tongs to retain the juice. Brush on marinade during final 15 to 20 minutes of grilling to prevent burning.

PEPPERED ORANGE TURKEY BREAST

Marinated in Peppered Orange Marinade and slowly grilled on the barbecue, turkey breast is moist and flavorful. Basting with extra marinade during grilling adds more flavor. To enhance the color of this dish, add achiote powder, which is made from the seeds of the annotto tree; it can be found in East Indian, Caribbean and Spanish grocery stores.

PEPPERED ORANGE MARINADE

1	dried chili pepper, seeded and coarsely chopped	1
1 cup	chicken broth	250 mL
1 tbsp	achiote powder (optional)	15 mL
1½ tsp	dried oregano	7 mL
2 cups	orange juice	500 mL
2 tbsp	lime juice	25 mL
1 to 2 tsp	hot pepper sauce	5 to 10 mL
	Salt and freshly ground pepper	

TURKEY

1	whole turkey breast (about 4 lb/2 kg)	1
1 cup	loosely packed fresh cilantro	250 mL
1	medium onion, quartered	1
1	lemon, quartered	1

1. *For marinade:* In small saucepan, combine chili pepper, broth, achiote (if using) and oregano. Simmer for about 30 minutes or until chili pepper starts to soften. Remove from heat and purée. Stir in orange and lime juice, hot pepper sauce, salt and pepper; refrigerate one-half of the marinade.

2. Place turkey breast in a resealable plastic bag or shallow nonreactive dish. Pour remaining marinade over turkey and turn to coat. Refrigerate for 12 hours or overnight; turn occasionally.

3. Remove turkey from marinade; reserve marinade. In small saucepan, bring marinade to a boil, reduce heat and cook for 5 minutes; keep warm. Place cilantro, onion and lemon in breast cavity.

4. Preheat grill on medium. Place breast on oiled grill rack, skin side down; reduce heat to medium-low. Close lid and cook (use Indirect Grilling, page 6) for about 1¾ hours until juices run clear when meat is pierced and an instant-read meat thermometer registers 170°F (77°C); turn several times. Brush turkey occasionally with warm marinade.

5. Remove turkey from grill to carving board; cover with foil for 10 to 15 minutes before slicing. Carve meat on diagonal. Heat refrigerated marinade and serve with turkey. **Makes 6 to 8 servings.**

Suggested Menu: Serve the turkey breast with toasted corn bread, a salad of diced fresh pineapple and other tropical fruits flavored with fresh mint, and perhaps cooked black beans and rice.

Tips: Labels on fresh poultry must give the year, month and day of packaging. Select a fresh turkey breast packaged the day you are in the store. At home, place turkey in refrigerator or freezer immediately.

ROCK CORNISH HENS EN PAPILLOTE

The en papillote cooking method (here, in a foil pouch) provides an interesting transfer of flavors between the hens and the vegetables. Each serving is cooked in a neat package.

HENS

3	Rock Cornish hens, thawed	3
2	cloves garlic, halved	2

STUFFING

2 tbsp	butter or margarine	25 mL
1 cup	chopped onion	250 mL
2 cups	sliced mushrooms	500 mL
1	large tomato, diced	1
1 tbsp	each: dried tarragon and parsley or 3 tbsp (45 mL) chopped fresh	15 mL
1/2 tsp	each: dried thyme and salt	2 mL
1/4 tsp	freshly ground pepper	1 mL
1/4 cup	dried bread crumbs	50 mL

VEGETABLES

1 1/2	medium zucchini, halved lengthwise and crosswise	1 1/2
12	baby carrots, trimmed	12
1	medium red onion, cut into wedges	1
1/2	sweet red pepper, cut into wide strips	1/2
3	medium potatoes, halved	3
1	large stalk celery, cut into 6 pieces	1
	Fresh tarragon	
	Salt and pepper	

1. *For hens:* Wash and dry. Rub cut side of garlic over cavity and outer skin of each hen; crush garlic.

2. *For stuffing:* In skillet, melt butter over medium-high. Add crushed garlic and onion; cook for about 5 minutes. Add mushrooms; cook until mushrooms are softened and liquid has evaporated. Combine mushroom mixture, tomato and seasonings; stir in bread crumbs. Spoon stuffing into cavity of each hen; truss with skewers and kitchen cord. Arrange each hen in center of large piece of foil or in aluminum foil pans.

3. *For vegetables:* Scatter zucchini, carrots, onion, red pepper, potatoes, celery and fresh tarragon around each hen. Sprinkle lightly with salt and pepper. Close foil securely around hen and vegetables.

4. Preheat grill on medium-high. Place foil packages on grill rack. Close lid and cook (use Indirect Grilling, page 6) for about 1 1/2 hours or until juices run clear when meat is pierced and vegetables are tender; meat should no longer be pink inside and an instant-read meat thermometer should read 165°F (74°C).

5. Remove packages from grill. Open foil, split hens down backbone and serve each half with an assortment of vegetables. **Makes 6 servings.**

Wine: Serve with an unoaked Chardonnay.

CORIANDER-SPICED CORNISH HENS

Coriander, in combination with fresh lemon, fennel and a hint of heat, gives these hens a wonderful finish.

2	Rock Cornish hens (1 ½ lb/750 g each)	2
BASTE		
2 tbsp	olive oil	25 mL
2 tbsp	each: grated lemon peel and lemon juice	25 mL
2 tsp	ground coriander	10 mL
1 tsp	each: fennel seeds and salt	5 mL
½ tsp	each: paprika and freshly ground pepper	2 mL
¼ tsp	each: cayenne pepper and ground turmeric	1 mL
2	cloves garlic, crushed	2

1. Rinse and prepare hens for grilling.

2. *For baste:* Combine oil, lemon peel and juice, coriander, fennel seeds, salt, paprika, pepper, cayenne pepper, turmeric and garlic. Brush generously over hens. Cover and refrigerate for up to 3 hours.

3. Preheat grill on medium. Place hens on lightly oiled grill rack, backbone side down. Close lid and grill (use Indirect Grilling, page 6) for about 1 ½ hours or until no longer pink, juices run clear when pierced, and an instant-read meat thermometer reads 165°F (74°C); turn once.

4. Remove hens from grill; cover with foil; let stand for 10 minutes before cutting into halves through the backbone. **Makes 4 servings.**

Suggested Menu: Barley Risotto with Vegetables (page 200) and Grilled Fruits and Pineapple (page 242) complete this easy menu.

 Wine: Shiraz or Rosé would make a lovely accompaniment.

SHERRY-PEACH-GLAZED ROCK CORNISH HENS

Celebrate the summer peach season with this glaze and salsa. They are quite sensational with the grilled Cornish game hens. The salsa also goes well with chicken breasts and chicken burgers.

2	Rock Cornish hens (1 1/2 lb/750 g each)	2
	Canola oil and fresh rosemary sprigs	

SHERRY-PEACH GLAZE

1/3 cup	peach preserves or jam	75 mL
1 tbsp	sherry or lemon juice	15 mL
1 tsp	dried rosemary or 1 tbsp (15 mL) fresh	5 mL

PEACH 'N' PEPPER SALSA

2 cups	chopped peeled peaches (2 medium)	500 mL
1/2 cup	each: chopped sweet red and green pepper	125 mL
1/4 cup	each: finely chopped red onion and chopped fresh cilantro	50 mL
1/2	jalapeño pepper, chopped	1/2
1	clove garlic, crushed	1
1 tbsp	each: lime juice and rice vinegar	15 mL
1 tsp	liquid honey	5 mL
	Fresh rosemary sprigs	

1. Rinse and prepare hens for grilling; brush lightly with oil; sprinkle rosemary in cavity.

2. Preheat grill on medium-high. Place hens in center of oiled grill rack, backbone side down. Close lid and cook (use Indirect Grilling, page 6) for about 1 1/2 hours or until meat is no longer pink inside, juices run clear when meat is pierced and an instant-read meat thermometer reads 165°F (74°C); turn once.

3. *For glaze:* In small saucepan, melt preserves; stir in sherry and rosemary. Brush hens with glaze during last 15 minutes of cooking.

4. *For salsa:* Meanwhile, in medium bowl, combine peaches, sweet peppers, onion, cilantro, jalapeño pepper and garlic. Stir in lime juice, vinegar and honey. Cover and refrigerate.

5. Remove hens from grill, cover with foil for 5 minutes before cutting each in half through backbone.

6. Lay each half on a large warm platter, garnish with rosemary. Serve with salsa.
Makes 4 servings and 3 cups (750 mL) salsa.

Suggested Menu: Accompany Rock Cornish Hens with Thyme-scented Artichoke Kebabs (page 180). Grilled fresh peach halves brushed occasionally with balsamic vinegar provide an exciting garnish along with the salsa.

Tip: Since jalapeño peppers vary greatly in heat levels, add them to taste.

QUAILS WITH LEMON MARINADE

A lemon marinade is ideal for this delicately flavored fowl. Hearty appetites should be able to deal with two of these small birds — hence my suggestion that this recipe makes two to four servings, depending on appetite. It's an easy recipe to double.

4	quails (6 oz/180 g) each	4

LEMON MARINADE

⅓ cup	lemon juice	75 mL
1 tsp	grated lemon peel	5 mL
4 tsp	brown sugar	20 mL
1 tbsp	chopped fresh parsley	15 mL
1 tbsp	olive oil	15 mL
2	cloves garlic, crushed	2
1 tsp	dried oregano or 1 tbsp (15 mL) chopped fresh	5 mL
½ tsp	salt	2 mL
¼ tsp	freshly ground pepper	1 mL

1. Remove backbone and breastbone from quails (or better still, ask the butcher to do this). Rinse and pat dry. Thread soaked wooden skewers through meat to help quail remain flat during grilling.

2. *For marinade:* In bowl, whisk together lemon juice and peel, sugar, parsley, oil, garlic, oregano, salt and pepper. Place quails in a large resealable plastic bag. Pour lemon mixture into bag, turn to coat and reseal. Refrigerate for about 30 minutes; turn bag occasionally.

3. Remove quails from marinade; reserve marinade. Place marinade in small saucepan, bring to a boil, reduce heat and cook for 5 minutes; keep warm.

4. Preheat grill on medium-high. Place quail on oiled grill rack, skin side down. Close lid and cook (use Indirect Grilling, page 6) for 30 minutes (see chart on page 9). Baste often with warm marinade. Remove quails from grill, cover with foil for 5 minutes. **Makes 2 to 4 servings.**

Suggested Menu: Serve on a bed of Warm Spinach and Radicchio Salad (page 215).

Tip: It is wise not to marinate poultry in an acid mixture any longer than 30 minutes since the meat requires flavor enhancement rather than tenderizing. Longer marinating in acids such as citrus juices and vinegar starts to "cook" the meat and changes the texture. This is also true for marinating fish.

DUCK BREASTS WITH MANGO ORANGE SAUCE

Mangos and oranges make a marvelous sauce to grace grilled duck breasts. Duck can be a challenge to cook. The breast may be perfectly done to medium-rare while the legs are still undercooked. The classic solution, taken here, is to cook and serve only the breasts and keep the legs for another occasion.

2	whole boneless duck breasts (12 oz/375 g each)	2

MARINADE

½ cup	dry white wine	125 mL
⅓ cup	orange marmalade	75 mL
1 tbsp	canola oil	15 mL
1	clove garlic, minced	1
1 tsp	ground summer savory	5 mL
¼ tsp	freshly ground pepper	1 mL

MANGO ORANGE SAUCE

1	ripe mango, peeled and sliced	1
½ cup	orange juice	125 mL
¼ cup	liquid honey	50 mL
1 tsp	each: chopped fresh gingerroot and orange peel	5 mL
¼ tsp	salt	1 mL
⅛ tsp	white pepper	0.5 mL
	Mango slices	

1. Place duck in shallow nonreactive dish or resealable plastic bag.
2. *For marinade:* In small bowl, combine wine, marmalade, oil, garlic, savory and pepper. Pour over duck, turn to coat, cover and refrigerate for 4 hours or overnight; turn occasionally.
3. *For sauce:* In small saucepan, combine mango, orange juice, honey, gingerroot, peel, salt and pepper. Bring to boil, reduce heat and cook for about 5 minutes or until fruit is soft. Remove from heat, cool slightly. Place in food processor or blender and purée until smooth. Return to saucepan and keep warm.
4. Remove duck from marinade; reserve marinade. Place marinade in small saucepan; bring to a boil, reduce heat and cook for 5 minutes; keep warm. Score duck skin in crisscross pattern with sharp knife.
5. Preheat grill on medium. Place duck on oiled grill rack. Close lid and cook (use Direct Grilling, page 6) for about 4 minutes per side or until an instant-read meat thermometer reads 150°F (65°C); brush often with warm marinade.
6. Remove duck from grill, remove skin and discard; slice meat thinly. Fan duck slices on warm plates and garnish with a spoonful of Mango Orange Sauce and sliced mango. **Makes 4 servings.**

Wine: Try an Alsatian Gewurztraminer.

Tip: Since duck is high in fat, place a grilling pan with cold water below the grill rack to prevent flare-ups during cooking.

CHAPTER 5

FISH AND SEAFOOD ON THE GRILL

◀ *Halibut with Provençal Sauce (page 124) and Ginger Sesame Salmon Steaks (page 116)*

Fish and shellfish are among the most satisfying foods to cook on the grill. Cooking times are relatively short, and the results can be utterly amazing. Furthermore, they are good for you. All seafood is nutritious and, in most cases, a lower-fat alternative to meat. And the fat content is of the omega-3 fatty acid type, which plays a role in reducing blood cholesterol levels.

The most important thing to know in grilling seafood is what variety to use. Choose a fish that has a firm, meaty texture so it won't fall apart while grilling. Of the ocean's seafood, grouper, tuna, salmon, arctic char, swordfish, halibut, scallops and shrimp are most suitable. Tilapia, a low-fat fish, is one of the less expensive farm-raised fish and is most suitable for grilling. Add to this, freshwater whitefish, lake trout and pickerel (walleye). More delicate textured fish are better grilled "en papillote." See Fish and Mushrooms en Papillote (page 133).

The next important thing to know when grilling fish and shellfish is when they are done. Overcooked, they are tough and tasteless, but you don't want to eat them raw either. Fish and shellfish contain lots of moisture. To ensure they do not dry out and become tough, grill them quickly on medium-high heat. Start checking a few minutes before you think they are done. Fish reaches desired doneness when it is firm to the touch, flakes easily and is opaque, whereas undercooked fish appears shiny and semi-translucent. The rule of cooking developed by the Canadian Department of Fisheries and Oceans (now Fisheries and Oceans Canada) is to measure fish at their thickest part, then cook for 10 minutes per inch (2.5 cm) of thickness at medium-high temperature. Then inspect for doneness. A simple method that is used by a national Canadian magazine suggests fish should cook for the recommended time for its type and size and is done when a knife inserted in the center of fish for 10 seconds comes out warm. Shellfish doneness tends to be unique to the species, so check your recipe.

It's nice to grill fish and shellfish on a grill topper (see Tools page 248). It keeps bits from falling between the openings in the grill racks, and it gives a solid support to fish without sacrificing the barbecue taste. To ensure easy removal of cooked fish, lightly spray or oil the cooking surface before starting to grill. Then make sure the cooking surface is very hot when you put the fish on it. Leave fish for a few minutes before moving. as this will further help prevent sticking. Always be sure the rack is clean, as any residue from a previous meal could interfere with seafood's delicate flavor.

It is best to turn skinless fish steaks and fillets after half the cooking is completed. Don't turn fillets with skin. Cook them skin side down. The flesh is protected from the direct heat and is easily removed from the skin before serving.

Citrus-glazed Planked Salmon (page 115) is a variation of the classic North American Native Peoples' method of cooking salmon on a cedar plank. It is a way to ensure the fish stays very moist while cooking, plus adding flavors from the plank as well as a hint of smoke. Tuna Steaks with Tomato-Basil Coulis (page 126) adds interesting flavors and moisture to a somewhat dry fish. The fabulous Orange-glazed Shrimp (page 137) can be served in smaller amounts as an appetizer, or larger for a main dish. Check out the divine sauce for Fish Steaks with Wine Olive Sauce (page 132) for another dinner.

Grilling fish and shellfish tends to give a maximum of delight for a minimum of effort!

CITRUS-GLAZED PLANKED SALMON

Baking on wooden planks goes back to the North American Native Peoples. Originally, fish were tied to the planks and set upright near hot coals until cooked. Planking fish does wonders to keep it moist, and it is far easier to cook. And for a change, place salmon atop orange slices during the cooking. This method does take longer to cook than if the salmon were directly on the grill rack, but certainly is well worth the effort.

1	Cedar plank	1
	Vegetable oil	

CITRUS-MUSTARD GLAZE

1 tbsp	canola or olive oil	15 mL
1 tbsp	frozen orange juice concentrate, thawed	15 mL
1 tbsp	grainy mustard	15 mL
¼ tsp	each: salt and freshly ground pepper	1 mL

FISH

8	thick orange slices (1 whole orange)	8
4	pieces salmon fillets (about 1½ lb/750 g)	4

1. Soak plank in hot water for one hour or longer. Remove plank from water and dry. Lightly brush top (cooking) side with oil.

2. *For glaze:* Combine oil, orange concentrate, mustard, salt and pepper; mix well. Set aside.

3. Preheat grill on medium-high to 400°F (200°C). Preheat plank on grill rack for about 5 minutes before adding fish. Arrange orange slices on plank. Top with salmon, skin side down; spoon glaze over each fillet.

4. Close lid and grill (use Direct Grilling, page 6) for about 15 minutes or until fish is opaque and flakes easily with a fork. Remove cooked fish by sliding a large spatula between skin and fish. Serve fish with orange slices. **Makes 4 servings.**

Suggested Menu: Serve with Coconut Rice (page 136) and a green salad.

GINGER SESAME SALMON STEAKS

Ginger has a special affinity with grilled salmon. You can substitute any firm-fleshed fish such as grouper, tuna or halibut.

GINGER SESAME BASTE

1 tbsp	sesame seeds, toasted	15 mL
1 tbsp	minced gingerroot	15 mL
2	cloves garlic, crushed	2
4 tsp	sesame oil	20 mL
1 tbsp	soy sauce	15 mL

FISH

4	salmon steaks (1 inch/2.5 cm thick) (about 2 lb/1kg in total)	4
	Salt and lemon pepper	
	Lemon wedges	

1. *For Baste:* In small bowl, combine sesame seeds, gingerroot, garlic, oil and soy sauce; set aside.

2. Season salmon lightly with salt and lemon pepper. Preheat grill on medium-high. Place salmon on oiled grill rack and brush with reserved sesame mixture. Close lid and cook (use Direct Grilling, page 6) for about 10 minutes (10 minutes per inch/2.5 cm of thickness) or until fish is opaque and flakes easily with a fork; turn once. Remove fish from grill and serve with lemon wedges. **Makes 4 servings.**

Wine: A Germanic-style Riesling or Gewurztraminer will pair well with this dish.

ASIAN GRILLED SALMON

 Salmon becomes a springtime feast with asparagus wrapped in a creamy sauce and new boiled potatoes.

ASIAN MARINADE

¼ cup	rye whisky	50 mL
2 tbsp	canola oil	25 mL
2 tbsp	light soy sauce	25 mL
1	clove garlic, crushed	1
¼ tsp	freshly ground pepper	1 mL
2 tsp	brown sugar	10 mL

FISH

4	salmon fillets (about 1½ lb/ 750 g)	4

1. *For marinade:* Combine rye, oil, soy sauce, garlic, pepper and sugar; mix well.

2. Place salmon in resealable plastic bag or nonreactive shallow dish; pour marinade over fish; turn to coat; cover and refrigerate for 2 to 4 hours. Turn salmon occasionally.

3. Remove salmon from marinade; reserve marinade. Place marinade in small saucepan, bring to boil, reduce heat and cook for 5 minutes; keep warm.

4. Preheat grill on medium-high to 400°F (200°C). Place fish, skin side down, on lightly oiled grill rack. Close lid and grill (use Direct Grilling, page 6) for about 10 minutes (10 minutes per inch/2.5 cm of thickness) or until fish is opaque and flakes easily with a fork. Baste occasionally with reserved warm marinade. Remove cooked fish by sliding a large spatula between skin and fish. **Makes 4 servings.**

SALMON STEAKS WITH MUSTARD SAUCE

This exciting combination of a mild and creamy mustard sauce with salmon is perfect.

CREAMY MUSTARD SAUCE

½ cup	low-fat sour cream	125 mL
⅓ cup	light mayonnaise	75 mL
2 tsp	each: Dijon mustard and lemon juice	10 mL
¼ tsp	each: dried thyme and freshly ground pepper	1 mL
2 tbsp	fresh snipped chives	25 mL

FISH

6	salmon steaks (¾ inch/2 cm thick)	6
⅓ cup	sliced toasted almonds	75 mL
	Fresh snipped chives	

1. *For sauce:* In small saucepan, combine sour cream, mayonnaise, mustard, lemon juice, thyme and pepper. Cook on low heat until hot; stir frequently. Stir in chives and keep warm. (Alternatively, microwave sauce in microwaveable container on medium-low [40%] for 2 to 3 minutes; stir occasionally.)

2. Preheat grill on medium-high. Place salmon on oiled grill rack. Close lid and cook (use Direct Grilling, page 6) for about 5 minutes per side or until fish is opaque and flakes easily with a fork (10 minutes per inch/2.5 cm of thickness).

3. To serve, spoon Creamy Mustard Sauce over each salmon steak. Sprinkle with toasted almonds and garnish with extra snipped chives. **Makes 6 servings.**

GRILLED STUFFED RAINBOW TROUT

Spinach stuffing adds a lot of flavor to this classic trout recipe. It also adds moisture to the fish. Consider the same approach with tilapia, whitefish or snapper.

STUFFING

¼ cup	chopped green onions	50 mL
1 tbsp	olive or canola oil	15 mL
2 tbsp	dry sherry	25 mL
2 cups	packed fresh spinach leaves, chopped	500 mL
¼ cup	pine nuts	50 mL
1 cup	soft bread crumbs	250 mL
1 tbsp	fresh lemon juice	15 mL
¼ tsp	each: salt and freshly ground pepper	1 mL

FISH

6	fillets rainbow trout, about ½ lb (250 g) each	6

1. Sauté onions in oil in nonstick skillet on medium-high for 3 minutes or until softened. Add sherry, spinach and pine nuts. Cook for 2 minutes or until spinach wilts. Remove from heat; add bread crumbs, lemon juice, salt and pepper; mix well.

2. Place 3 fish fillets on flat surface. Divide stuffing over each. Top each with remaining fish fillets; tie loosely with kitchen string to secure stuffing.

3. Preheat grill on medium-high to 400°F (200°C). Place stuffed fish on lightly oiled grill rack. Close lid and grill (use Direct Grilling, page 6) for about 20 minutes (10 minutes per inch/2.5 cm of thickness) or until fish is opaque and flakes easily with a fork.

4. To serve, remove cooked fish by sliding a large spatula between skin and fish; cut each stuffed fish in half and serve. **Makes 6 servings.**

STUFFED RAINBOW TROUT WITH DILL SAUCE

The delicate flavors of the crabmeat stuffing and the trout complement each other beautifully, and the lemon gives a gentle zip to both. The foil wrapping keeps the fish moist throughout the grilling and helps to secure the stuffing.

CRAB STUFFING

1	small onion, finely chopped	1
1	stalk celery, finely chopped	1
1 tbsp	butter or margarine	15 mL
1	can (4.5 oz/128 g) crabmeat, drained and coarsely chopped	1
1½ cups	cooked rice	375 mL
1 tbsp	each: lemon juice and finely chopped fresh parsley	15 mL
1 tsp	grated lemon peel	5 mL
	Salt and freshly ground pepper	

FISH

6	rainbow trout fillets (1½ lb/750 g)	6

DILLED MAYONNAISE

½ cup	each: light mayonnaise and plain yogurt	125 mL
2 tsp	lemon juice	10 mL
2 tsp	chopped fresh dill or ½ tsp (2 mL) dried	10 mL
⅛ tsp	each: salt and freshly ground pepper	0.5 mL
	Fresh dill sprigs	

Tip: For a change, replace crabmeat with either chopped baby shrimp or smoked salmon.

1. *For stuffing:* In medium skillet, cook onion and celery in butter over medium-high heat for 5 minutes or until softened. Remove from heat and stir in crabmeat, rice, lemon juice, parsley, peel, and salt and pepper. Divide stuffing over three fish fillets; top with other three. Secure with toothpicks or string. Wrap each stuffed fillet loosely in several layers of aluminum foil and close to form secure packages.

2. *For mayonnaise:* In small bowl, combine mayonnaise, yogurt, lemon juice, dill, salt and pepper; set aside.

3. Preheat grill on medium-high. Place foil packages on grill rack. Close lid and cook (use Indirect Grilling, page 6) for about 30 minutes or until fish is opaque and flakes easily with a fork (10 minutes per inch/2.5 cm of package thickness); turn once.

4. Cut each filled fillet in half. Serve with a spoonful of Dilled Mayonnaise and fresh dill sprigs. **Makes 6 servings.**

TUSCAN-STYLE GRILLED FISH FILLETS

The flavors of Tuscany make a Mediterranean delicacy out of any firm-fleshed fish fillet.

2 tbsp	lemon juice	25 mL
1 tsp	salt	5 mL
2 tbsp	extra virgin olive oil, divided	25 mL
2 tbsp	chopped fresh basil	25 mL
1/8 tsp	freshly ground pepper	0.5 mL

FISH

| 4 | red snapper, sea bass, salmon or perch fillets (1½ lb/750 g) | 4 |

TUSCAN SAUCE

¼ cup	finely chopped onion	50 mL
2	cloves garlic, crushed	2
1	large tomato, cubed	1
2 tsp	capers, drained and rinsed	10 mL
	Freshly ground pepper	

1. In small bowl, stir together lemon juice and salt until salt is dissolved. Add 1 tbsp (15 mL) oil, basil and pepper; set aside.

2. *For sauce:* In nonstick skillet, sauté onion and garlic in remaining oil for about 5 minutes. Stir in tomato, capers and pepper to taste. Cook over low heat until tomatoes have thickened into a sauce-like consistency; keep warm.

3. Preheat grill on medium-high. Drizzle fish with lemon-basil mixture. Place fish on oiled grill rack. Close lid and cook (use Direct Grilling, page 6) for 10 minutes per inch (2.5 cm) of thickness or until fish is opaque and flakes easily with a fork. Serve with Tuscan Sauce. **Makes 4 servings.**

Suggested Menu: A creamy spinach risotto dish would be perfect with this fish recipe. Prepare your favorite risotto recipe and stir in some chopped spinach part way through the cooking. Finish with a generous sprinkling of grated Parmesan cheese.

 Wine: Pinot Grigio or Trebbiano would pair well with this dish.

SHRIMP-STUFFED FISH FILLETS WITH COCONUT SAUCE

Go Polynesian with these attractive and tasty fish roll ups.

SHRIMP RICE FILLING

10	fresh or frozen cooked shrimp, shelled, cleaned and chopped	10
1 cup	cooked long grain rice	250 mL
1/2 cup	shredded unsweetened coconut	125 mL
	Salt and lemon pepper	

FISH

4	sole, turbot, halibut or whitefish fillets (about 1/4 lb/125 g each)	4

COCONUT SAUCE

1/2 cup	coconut milk	125 mL
1/2	small onion, finely chopped	1/2
1	clove garlic, minced	1
2 tsp	each: cornstarch and lime juice	10 mL
1/2 tsp	chili powder	2 mL
	Salt and lemon pepper	
	Flaked coconut	

Suggested Menu: Serve with sautéed snow peas, sweet red pepper strips and enoki mushrooms.

1. *For filling:* In small bowl, combine shrimp, rice, coconut, salt and lemon pepper to taste; set aside.

2. Wipe fish fillets with paper toweling. Place fillets between two sheets of waxed paper; flatten each with a rolling pin. Place some filling along center of each fillet. Roll from narrow end; secure with toothpicks.

3. Preheat grill on medium-high. Place fish rolls on oiled grill rack. Close lid and cook (use Indirect Grilling, page 6) for about 20 minutes (10 minutes per inch/2.5 cm of thickness of rolls), or until fish is opaque and flakes easily with a fork.

4. *For sauce:* Meanwhile, in small saucepan, combine coconut milk, onion and garlic; cook on low heat until onion is tender. Stir in cornstarch, lime juice, chili powder, salt and lemon pepper to taste. Cook until slightly thickened; keep warm.

5. Place fish rolls on warm plates, drizzle with sauce and garnish with extra coconut. **Makes 4 servings.**

BALSAMIC-GLAZED FISH FILLETS

This glaze, featuring balsamic vinegar along with garlic and mustard, changes the dullest fish fillet into a vibrant masterpiece.

BALSAMIC GLAZE

1 tbsp	canola or olive oil	15 mL
2	cloves garlic, minced	2
2 tbsp	grainy Dijon mustard	25 mL
1 tbsp	liquid honey	15 mL
1 tbsp	fresh lemon or lime juice	15 mL
¼ cup	balsamic vinegar	50 mL
	Freshly ground pepper	

FISH

2 lb	fish fillets: salmon, whitefish or halibut	1 kg

1. Heat oil and sauté garlic in small saucepan for 2 minutes or until softened. Add mustard, honey, lemon juice, vinegar and pepper. Simmer, uncovered, for about 3 minutes or until thickened. Allow to cool before brushing on fish. Brush fish, cover and refrigerate for up to one hour before cooking.

2. Preheat grill on medium-high to 400°F (200°C). Place fish, skin side down, on lightly oiled grill rack. Close lid and grill (use Direct Grilling, page 6) for about 10 minutes (10 minutes per inch/2.5 cm of thickness) or until fish is opaque and flakes easily with a fork. Remove cooked fish by sliding a large spatula between skin and fish. **Makes 5 to 6 servings.**

Suggested Menu: Grilled Pepper Gazpacho Salad (page 210) along with Orzo Spinach Pilaf (page 198) or fluffy rice and a tossed green salad.

 Wine: Serve with a Sauvignon Blanc or Riesling.

VERMOUTH-BASTED FISH FILLETS

Think of a cross between a fish and a martini to imagine this recipe. Use to baste almost any fish fillet. We have enjoyed it with whitefish, rainbow trout, perch, sole, snapper and, of course, salmon.

¼ cup	dry vermouth	50 mL
1 tbsp	canola or olive oil	15 mL
¼ tsp	each: salt and freshly ground pepper	1 mL
1 lb	fish fillets	500 g
4	slices lemon	4
	Fresh parsley	

1. Combine vermouth, oil, salt and pepper.

2. Preheat indoor grill on high for 5 minutes. Place fish, skin side down, on lightly oiled grill rack; brush with vermouth mixture. Cover loosely with a tent of foil; grill for about 10 minutes (10 minutes per inch/2.5 cm of thickness) or until fish is opaque and flakes easily with a fork. Remove cooked fish by sliding a large spatula between skin and fish. Serve with lemon slices and parsley. **Makes 4 servings.**

 Wine: Serve with a Sauvignon Blanc or Riesling.

GRILLED MANGO AND CITRUS FISH FILLETS

Citrus flavors and fish are natural partners. Grilled mango slices add taste and eye appeal.

MANGO AND CITRUS MARINADE

⅓ cup	each: orange, lemon and lime juice	75 mL
¼ cup	marmalade	50 mL
½ tsp	granulated sugar	2 mL
½	medium onion, finely chopped	½
1	piece gingerroot (1 inch/2.5 cm), grated	1

FISH

6	salmon, orange roughy, sea bass or halibut fillets (¼ lb/125 g each)	6
½ cup	fresh cilantro, chopped	125 mL
2	mangoes, peeled and sliced	2
	Vegetable oil	

1. *For marinade:* In blender or food processor, process juices and marmalade until well blended. Pour ½ cup (125 mL) juice mixture into a bowl; stir in sugar until dissolved and reserve.

2. Add onion and gingerroot to remaining mixture in blender; process until smooth. Transfer onion mixture to shallow nonreactive dish. Arrange fillets in single layer over mixture; turn to coat; sprinkle with cilantro. Cover and refrigerate for up to 30 minutes.

3. Preheat grill on medium-high. Remove fish from marinade; discard marinade. Place fish on oiled grill rack, skin side down. Close lid and cook (use Direct Grilling, page 6) until fish is opaque and flakes easily with a fork (10 minutes per inch/2.5 cm thickness). At same time, place sliced mango on grill rack, brush lightly with oil and cook until grill marks appear and mango is heated.

4. Remove cooked fish by sliding a metal spatula between skin and fish; transfer to a heated serving platter. Drizzle with reserved juice mixture and serve with mango slices. **Makes 6 servings.**

Suggested Menu: A fluffy aromatic rice (such as Thai or basmati) and asparagus are perfect companions to this fish.

 Wine: Gewurztraminer makes an excellent match for this dish.

GRILLED HALIBUT WITH PROVENÇAL SAUCE

The French certainly have a flair for preparing food, and this recipe is an excellent example of it!

PROVENÇAL SAUCE

1 tbsp	olive oil	15 mL
1	medium onion, chopped	1
3 cups	cubed unpeeled eggplant	750 mL
1	medium zucchini, cubed	1
2	medium tomatoes, cut in large dice	2
1	sweet green pepper, seeded and diced	1
3	cloves garlic, minced	3
½ cup	chopped fresh basil or 2 tbsp (25 mL) dried	125 mL
	Salt and freshly ground pepper	

FISH

2 lb	halibut (1-inch/2.5 cm thick)	1 kg
⅓ cup	plain yogurt	75 mL
3 tbsp	Dijon mustard	45 mL
	Lemon wedges	

1. *For sauce:* Heat oil on medium-high in large nonstick skillet. Cook onion for 5 minutes. Add eggplant, zucchini, tomatoes, green pepper and garlic. Cook, uncovered, for about 30 minutes or until mixture is thickened. Stir in basil, salt and pepper to taste; keep warm.

2. *For fish:* Spread both sides of halibut evenly with a mixture of yogurt and mustard.

3. Preheat grill on medium-high to 400°F (200°C). Place fish on oiled grill rack. Close lid and grill (use Direct Grilling, page 6) for about 10 minutes (10 minutes per inch/2.5 cm of thickness) or until fish is opaque and flakes easily with a fork; turn once. Transfer fish to warmed plates and serve with sauce and a lemon wedge. **Makes 4 servings.**

Suggested Menu: Cooked fresh pasta along with crusty baguette slices complete this exciting meal.

 Wine: Either Pinot Grigio or lightly oaked Chardonnay would be an excellent accompaniment.

Halibut Fillets with Roasted Red Pepper Mayonnaise

The flavor of roasted red peppers complements grilled fish beautifully. Any left? It makes a marvelous dip for crudités. Or, if you prefer, make the Yogurt Mustard Sauce (see recipe below).

RED PEPPER MAYONNAISE

1 cup	bottled roasted red peppers, drained	250 mL
1/3 cup	light mayonnaise	75 mL
2 tbsp	Dijon mustard	25 mL
2	cloves garlic, minced	2
1 tsp	fresh lemon juice	5 mL
	Salt and freshly ground pepper	
1 cup	packed fresh basil leaves, chopped	250 mL

FISH

4	halibut steaks (4 oz/125 g each)	4

1. *For mayonnaise:* Purée red peppers, mayonnaise, mustard, garlic and lemon juice in a food processor until smooth. Add salt and pepper to taste. Reserve 2 tbsp (25 mL) mayonnaise mixture. Stir remaining mixture with basil; set aside.

2. Preheat grill on medium-high to 400°F (200°C). Pat halibut dry with paper towel; spread 2 tbsp (25 mL) mayonnaise mixture on one side of each piece. Place fish, starting with mayonnaise side down, on lightly oiled grill rack. Close lid and grill (use Direct Grilling, page 6) for 5 to 6 minutes. Turn fish and cook for 3 to 4 minutes (10 minutes per inch/2.5 cm of thickness) or until fish is opaque and flakes easily with a fork.

3. Serve halibut with reserved red pepper mayonnaise. **Makes 4 servings.**

Grilling Tip: If preferred, grill your own sweet red peppers (see page 178).

Yogurt Mustard Sauce: Combine 1/3 cup (75 mL) plain yogurt, 2 tbsp (25 mL) light mayonnaise, 2 tsp (10 mL) Dijon mustard and a pinch of salt and freshly ground pepper. Makes about 1/2 cup (125 mL) sauce. Also a great dip for veggies!

Suggested Menu: See Chapter 8 for a rice or pasta accompaniment.

 Wine: Try a Cabernet Franc Rosé.

TUNA STEAKS WITH TOMATO-BASIL COULIS

Grilled tuna steaks are always superb, but a flavorful tomato sauce makes them even more appealing.

TOMATO BASIL COULIS

1 tbsp	olive oil	15 mL
2	medium shallots, finely chopped	2
4	medium tomatoes, peeled and coarsely chopped	4
1/2 cup	light sour cream	125 mL
1 tbsp	all-purpose flour	15 mL
1/2 tsp	salt	2 mL
1/4 tsp	freshly ground pepper	1 mL
1/2 cup	loosely packed fresh basil leaves, chopped	125 mL

FISH

4	tuna steaks (about 1 1/2 lb/750 g)	4
	Fresh basil leaves	

Suggested Menu: Serve with spinach fettuccini, a Caesar salad and crusty rolls. Fresh fruit with Warm Sabayon Sauce (page 238) provides a light finish to a wonderful meal.

1. *For coulis:* In large nonstick skillet, heat oil over medium-high heat. Cook shallots for 2 minutes or until softened. Add tomatoes; reduce heat to low and cook gently, uncovered, for 25 minutes or until tomatoes have thickened into a sauce-like consistency. Combine sour cream and flour and stir gradually into hot mixture. Cook, stirring frequently, until sauce has thickened. Add salt and pepper; cover and keep sauce warm. Just before serving, stir in chopped basil.

2. Meanwhile, preheat grill on medium-high. Place tuna on oiled grill rack. Close lid and cook (use Direct Grilling, page 6) for about 10 minutes (10 minutes per inch/2.5 cm of thickness) or until fish is opaque and flakes easily with a fork; turn once.

3. Spoon a generous amount of sauce on 4 warm plates. Place tuna steaks on sauce, garnish with several leaves of fresh basil and serve. **Makes 4 servings.**

WHOLE FISH WITH ORANGE DILL SAUCE

Whether your whole fish is an ocean swimmer or a freshwater one, the same cooking techniques apply. Cooking times are based on the thickness of the fish. Measure the fish at the thickest part and then cook, covered, for 10 minutes per inch (2.5 cm) of thickness at high heat — 450°F (230°C) — whether over hot coals or at high on a gas barbecue.

ORANGE MARINADE

¾ cup	orange juice	175 mL
2 tbsp	olive oil	25 mL
1 tbsp	minced fresh dill or 1 tsp (5 mL) dried	15 mL
⅛ tsp	freshly ground pepper	0.5 mL

FISH

4 to 6 lb	whole fish (salmon, whitefish, snapper, cod) cleaned and head removed	2 to 3 kg
	Fresh dill sprigs	

ORANGE DILL SAUCE

¼ cup	softened butter or margarine	50 mL
1 tsp	grated orange peel	5 mL
1 tsp	minced fresh dill or ¼ tsp (1 mL) dried	5 mL
¼ tsp	salt	1 mL
⅛ tsp	freshly ground pepper	0.5 mL

1. *For marinade:* In small bowl, combine juice, oil, dill and pepper. Wipe fish with paper toweling; pat dry. Place fish in shallow nonreactive dish. Arrange fresh dill sprigs inside cavity of fish. Pour marinade over fish, turn to completely coat. Cover and refrigerate for several hours depending on size of fish.

2. Preheat grill on medium-high. Remove fish from marinade; discard marinade. Place fish in grill basket or on oiled grill rack. Close lid and cook (use Indirect Grilling, page 6) for about 20 minutes (10 minutes per inch/2.5 cm of thickness) or until fish is opaque and flakes easily with a fork; turn once. Remove skin and backbone and discard. Cut fish into serving pieces.

3. *For sauce:* Meanwhile, combine butter, orange peel, dill, salt and pepper. Spread Orange Dill Sauce over each serving of fish. **Makes 6 to 8 servings.**

Alternate cooking technique: Place fish on heavy-duty foil. Add lemon or orange slices for extra flavor and moisture. Close foil securely and proceed as above.

Suggested Menu: New red-skinned boiled potatoes, steamed snow peas, carrots and multigrain bread complete this wonderful meal.

SWORDFISH STEAK WITH LEMON CAPER SAUCE

This simple, traditional approach is particularly appropriate for the mild flavored yet dense meat-like nature of swordfish, but it could become your favorite for any firm-fleshed fish.

LEMON CAPER SAUCE

1 tsp	salt	5 mL
2 tbsp	lemon juice	25 mL
1 tbsp	chopped fresh oregano or 1 tsp (5 mL) dried	15 mL
3 tbsp	olive oil	45 mL
1 tbsp	capers, drained and washed	15 mL
¼ tsp	freshly ground pepper	1 mL

FISH

4	swordfish steaks (½ inch/1 cm thick, about 2 lb/1 kg)	4

Suggested Menu: Start with Chilled Pea and Lettuce Soup (page 31) and serve Double Cheese–topped Potatoes (page 197) and a green salad with the fish.

1. *For sauce:* Place salt in small bowl; stir in lemon juice until salt has dissolved. Add oregano, then slowly whisk in oil until creamy. Add capers and pepper; set aside.

2. Preheat grill on medium-high. Place fish on oiled grill rack. Close lid and cook (use Direct Grilling, page 6) for about 6 minutes (10 minutes per inch/2.5 cm of thickness) or until fish is opaque and flakes easily with a fork; turn once. Transfer fish to warmed plates. Prick fish with a fork in several places and drizzle with reserved Lemon Caper Sauce. **Makes 4 servings.**

GROUPER WITH GAZPACHO SAUCE

The Gazpacho Sauce makes this recipe. Although it is a bit of extra work, it is well worth the effort. Any firm-fleshed fish can be substituted for grouper.

GAZPACHO SAUCE

¼ cup	finely chopped onion	50 mL
1	clove garlic, minced	1
1 tbsp	olive oil	15 mL
1½ cups	chopped ripe tomatoes (about 3)	375 mL
¼ cup	finely chopped sweet yellow pepper	50 mL
2 cups	tomato juice	500 mL
½ cup	fish stock or vegetable bouillon	125 mL
2 tbsp	balsamic vinegar	25 mL
½ tsp	Worcestershire sauce	2 mL
	Salt and freshly ground pepper	

FISH

6	grouper, sea bass, red snapper or whitefish fillets (about 1½ lb/750 g)	6
	Fresh rosemary sprigs	

1. *For sauce:* In large heavy saucepan, cook onion and garlic in oil over medium-low heat until softened; stir occasionally. Add tomatoes, yellow pepper, tomato juice, stock, vinegar and Worcestershire sauce. Bring to a boil, reduce heat and simmer, uncovered, for 30 to 40 minutes, or until sauce is thickened. Season to taste with salt and pepper. Remove from heat and cool slightly. Taste and stir in additional vinegar and Worcestershire sauce, if needed. (Sauce may be made 1 day ahead, covered and chilled.)

2. Preheat grill on medium-high. Place fish in basket or directly on oiled grill rack. Close lid and cook (use Direct Grilling, page 6) for about 5 minutes per side (10 minutes per inch /2.5 cm of thickness) or until fish is opaque and flakes easily with a fork.

3. Spoon ¼ cup (50 mL) Gazpacho Sauce around edge of each plate, place fish in center and top with rosemary sprigs. **Makes 6 servings.**

Suggested Menu: Serve with Orzo Spinach Pilaf (page 198) and Grilled Zucchini and Yellow Squash (page 178).

Tip: Fish stock is available frozen at seafood stores or specialty foods shops.

 Wine: Serve with a Riesling or Rosé.

LEMON-HERB GRILLED WHITEFISH

Lemon and herbs, an ageless combination with fish, is given a modern twist in this recipe with a touch of vermouth and Dijon mustard. Other firm-fleshed fish such as sea bass, halibut, swordfish, orange roughy and grouper can also be used.

LEMON-HERB MARINADE

2 tbsp	olive or canola oil	25 mL
2 tbsp	dry vermouth or white wine	25 mL
1 tbsp	lemon juice	15 mL
1 tbsp	each: chopped fresh chives and dill or 1 tsp (5 mL) dried	15 mL
2 tsp	grated lemon peel	10 mL
1 tsp	Dijon mustard	5 mL
	Salt and white pepper	

FISH

4	whitefish fillets (about 4 oz/125 g each)	4
8	slices red onion	8
	Fresh dill sprigs and lemon wedges	

Suggested Menu: Serve with Grilled Fennel (page 178) and Grilled Zucchini (page 178) and fluffy rice.

Wine: A Pinot Blanc would be an excellent match.

1. *For marinade:* In small bowl, combine oil, vermouth, lemon juice, chives, dill, lemon peel, mustard, salt and pepper. Place fish and onion in a shallow, nonreactive dish or resealable plastic bag. Pour marinade over fish; turn fish and onion to coat well. Marinate in refrigerator for 30 minutes; turn fish occasionally.

2. Remove onion and fish from marinade; reserve marinade. In small saucepan, bring marinade to a boil; reduce heat and cook for 5 minutes; keep warm.

3. Preheat grill on medium-high. Place onion and fish (skin side down) on oiled grill rack. Close lid and cook (use Direct Grilling, page 6) for about 10 minutes (10 minutes per inch/2.5 cm of thickness) or until fish is opaque and flakes easily with a fork and onion is tender; turn once. Brush occasionally with warm marinade.

4. Remove cooked fish by sliding a metal spatula between skin and fish. Serve fish and onion garnished with fresh dill and lemon wedges. **Makes 4 servings.**

Fish Steaks with Wine Olive Sauce

Tomatoes, basil, oranges and olives — all flavors of the Mediterranean — come through in this superb sauce. Use a firm-fleshed fish such as sea bass, perch, tuna, salmon or snapper.

WINE OLIVE SAUCE

1 tsp	fennel seeds	5 mL
2	cloves garlic, minced	2
1/3 cup	dry white wine	75 mL
1/4 cup	each: sliced green and black kalamata olives	50 mL
1 tbsp	orange juice	15 mL
1 tsp	grated orange peel	5 mL
1/8 tsp	crushed red pepper flakes	0.5 mL
1	medium tomato, diced	1

FISH

4	fish steaks (about 1 lb/500 g, 3/4 inch/2 cm thick)	4
	Salt and freshly ground pepper	
	Fresh basil leaves	

1. *For sauce:* In nonstick skillet, over high heat, sauté fennel and garlic for 3 minutes or until seeds are toasted. Reduce heat to medium; stir in wine, green and black olives, orange juice and peel, and pepper flakes. Cook until liquid is reduced. Allow to cool slightly before stirring in tomato; set aside.

2. Preheat grill on medium-high. Sprinkle fish lightly with salt and pepper. Place fish on oiled grill rack or in fish basket. Close lid and cook (use Direct Grilling, page 6) for about 5 minutes per side or until fish is opaque and flakes easily with a fork (10 minutes per inch/2.5 cm of thickness).

3. Serve fish with Wine Olive Sauce; garnish with fresh basil. **Makes 4 servings and 1 1/4 cups (300 mL) sauce.**

Suggested Menu: These fabulous flavors of Italy belong with Orzo Spinach Pilaf (page 198), a green salad and crusty country bread.

 Wine: Serve with Viognier.

Fish and Mushrooms en Papillote

Use sea bass, red snapper, whitefish, salmon, perch or other firm-fleshed fish for this easy recipe. Grilling en papillote (in a package) assures a moist and juicy as well as tidy result. In this recipe we replace the traditional greased parchment paper with more readily available aluminum foil.

4	fish fillets (about 1 lb/500 g)	4
2	chopped green onions	2
2	large shiitake mushrooms, sliced	2
¼ cup	chopped fresh parsley	50 mL
¼ cup	dry white wine	50 mL
2 tsp	olive oil	10 mL
1	clove garlic, minced	1
¼ tsp	each: dried thyme and salt	1 mL
⅛ tsp	freshly ground pepper	0.5 mL

1. Cut 4 pieces of aluminum foil 2 inches (5 cm) longer than fish fillets and twice as wide. Center one fillet on each piece; divide onions, mushrooms and parsley over fish.

2. In small bowl, combine wine, oil, garlic, thyme, salt and pepper; drizzle over each fillet. Fold foil over fish and seal with double fold; tuck ends under to seal securely.

3. Preheat grill on medium-high. Place each package on grill rack. Close lid and cook (use Indirect Grilling, page 6) for about 15 minutes (10 minutes per inch /2.5 cm of package thickness) or until fish is opaque and flakes easily with a fork and vegetables are tender; turn once. **Makes 4 servings.**

Suggested Menu: Open the fish parcels and serve over fluffy rice. Accompanied with Watercress and Bean Sprout Salad (page 211) and steamed snow peas and red pepper strips, this meal becomes a veritable feast.

LEMON TUNA STEAKS WITH GREMOLATA

Gremolata, made with minced parsley, lemon peel and garlic, is more of a garnish than a sauce. Traditionally, it is used to sprinkle over veal dishes such as osso buco. In this recipe, gremolata adds a wonderful fresh flavor to grilled tuna.

GREMOLATA

½ cup	finely chopped fresh parsley	125 mL
2 tsp	grated lemon zest	10 mL
2	cloves garlic, finely chopped	2

FISH

4	tuna steaks (¾ inch/2 cm thick)	4
	Salt and freshly ground pepper	
	Lemon wedges	

1. *For gremolata:* In small bowl, combine parsley, lemon zest and garlic; mix well and reserve.

2. Preheat grill on medium-high. Sprinkle fish lightly with salt and pepper. Place on oiled grill rack. Close lid and cook (use Direct Grilling, page 6) for about 5 minutes per side (10 minutes per inch/2.5 cm of thickness) or until fish is opaque and flakes easily with a fork.

3. Garnish each steak with gremolata and a lemon wedge. **Makes 4 servings.**

 Wine: Serve with Sauvignon Blanc or an unoaked Chardonnay.

GRILLED ORANGE TUNA PACKETS

This quick and easy tuna packet recipe is a breeze to make! Combining citrus, herbs and plain yogurt enhances albacore's delicate flavor and white color.

1 lb	albacore tuna steak	500 g
¼ cup	each: orange juice and plain yogurt	50 mL
1 tbsp	olive or canola oil	15 mL
2	cloves garlic, minced	2
1 tbsp	chopped fresh parsley	15 mL
1 tsp	granulated sugar	5 mL
¼ tsp	each: salt and freshly ground pepper	1 mL

1. Place fish on large sheet of double thickness aluminum foil.

2. Combine orange juice, yogurt, oil, garlic, parsley, sugar, salt and pepper. Drizzle over fish, close foil edges over to secure packet.

3. Preheat grill on medium-high to 400°F (200°C). Place packet on lightly oiled grill rack. Close lid and grill (use Direct Grilling, page 6) for about 10 minutes (10 minutes per inch/2.5 cm of thickness) or until fish is opaque and flakes easily with a fork. Remove packet from grill, cut foil open to release steam and serve. **Makes 4 servings.**

 Wine: A wine made from Viognier grapes is a perfect choice.

PARMESAN-CRUSTED SHRIMP AND SCALLOPS

This exciting way to coat seafood combines the rich sharpness of Parmesan cheese with the delicate flavors of shrimp and scallops. The coating also seals in the juices of the shrimp and scallops while they grill. Top it all off with a Lemon Basil Sauce.

LEMON BASIL SAUCE

3 tbsp	butter or margarine	45 mL
1 tbsp	lemon juice	15 mL
1 tsp	grated lemon peel	5 mL
1 tbsp	each: snipped fresh chives and basil	15 mL

COATING

½ cup	finely crushed melba toast crumbs	125 mL
4 tsp	grated Parmesan cheese	20 mL
1 tbsp	finely chopped fresh parsley	15 mL
¼ tsp	each: paprika, freshly ground pepper and salt	1 mL

SEAFOOD

1 lb	sea scallops	500 g
12	jumbo shrimp, shells removed	12
2 tbsp	melted butter or margarine	25 mL

1. *For sauce:* In small saucepan, combine butter, lemon juice and peel; heat until butter is melted. Remove from heat and stir in chives and basil; keep warm.

2. *For coating:* In resealable plastic bag, combine toast crumbs, cheese, parsley, paprika, pepper and salt. Brush scallops and shrimp with melted butter. Place in plastic bag; shake to coat.

3. Preheat grill on medium-high. Place seafood on oiled grill rack or in fish basket. Close lid and cook (use Direct Grilling, page 6) for about 6 minutes per side or until shrimp and scallops are opaque and cooked; turn once. Serve with warm Lemon Basil Sauce. **Makes 4 to 6 servings.**

 Wine: Try a Fumé Blanc or white Meritage.

Suggested Menu: Definitely serve with a seasoned cooked rice, a green salad and possibly an olive or herbed focaccia bread.

Tips: Normally shrimp is grilled with the shell on to obtain the juiciest shrimp. However, in this recipe the crumb coating seals in the juices. Leave tail intact when grilling to provide a handle when eating. If buying frozen shrimp, look for bags marked "zipper–backed" for easy peeling.

Tandoori Scallops with Vegetables

The term tandoori refers to an Indian style of cooking using a traditional clay and brick tandoor oven with a rounded top. Before cooking, meat, fish or seafood is marinated in a mixture of such spices as ground ginger, cumin, coriander, turmeric and paprika stirred into plain yogurt. In the following recipe, the tandoor oven is replaced by a covered grill.

TANDOORI MARINADE

½ cup	plain yogurt	125 mL
2 tbsp	lemon juice	25 mL
1 tsp	each: ground cumin, coriander, paprika, turmeric, cayenne and salt	5 mL
1	clove garlic, crushed	1

SEAFOOD

1 lb	sea scallops	500 g
2 tsp	cornstarch	10 mL
½ lb	snow peas, trimmed	250 g
4	carrots, sliced diagonally	4
½ lb	mushrooms	250 g
2 tsp	olive oil	10 mL
	Coconut Rice (recipe follows)	
	Fresh cilantro	

1. *For marinade:* In small bowl, combine yogurt, lemon juice, spices and garlic; mix well and reserve.

2. Wash scallops and pat dry. Coat scallops thoroughly with reserved marinade. Cover and refrigerate for 2 hours.

3. Remove scallops from marinade; reserve marinade. In small saucepan, stir cornstarch into reserved marinade. Cook over low heat until thickened and smooth; keep warm.

4. Steam snow peas and carrots; lightly sauté mushrooms in oil.

5. Meanwhile, preheat grill on medium-high. Thread scallops onto 4 metal or soaked wooden skewers. Place kebabs on oiled grill rack. Close lid and cook (use Direct Grilling, page 6) for 5 to 6 minutes or until scallops are opaque and done; turn once.

6. Remove scallops from skewers. Serve scallops on a bed of cooked Coconut Rice surrounded with vegetables. Drizzle lightly with warm sauce and add a garnish of fresh cilantro. **Makes 4 servings.**

Coconut Rice: Coconut Rice is a great accompaniment to these scallops. Combine 3 cups (750 mL) cooked Asian rice with 2 tbsp (25 mL) grated coconut, 2 tbsp (25 mL) coconut milk, and 1 tbsp (15 mL) minced gingerroot.

ORANGE-GLAZED SHRIMP

Shrimp grilled after marinating in this zesty citrus mixture are absolutely irresistible.

24	cleaned jumbo shrimp	24
3 tbsp	orange juice	45 mL
1 tbsp	chili sauce	15 mL
2	cloves garlic, crushed	2
2 tsp	canola or olive oil	10 mL
1 tbsp	minced gingerroot	15 mL
6	soaked wooden skewers	6

1. Combine shrimp, orange juice, chili sauce, garlic, oil and gingerroot in a container. Cover and refrigerate for several hours.

2. Drain shrimp; discard marinade. Thread 4 shrimp onto each skewer.

3. Preheat grill on medium-high to 400°F (200°C). Place skewers on lightly oiled grill rack. Close lid and grill (use Direct Grilling, page 6) for about 5 minutes or until shrimp are opaque and cooked; turn once. **Makes 6 servings.**

Suggested Menu: Cooked fettucine, steamed green beans and crusty rolls.

 Wine: a Gewurztraminer or Cabernet Franc Rosé will nicely complement the dish.

LOBSTER TAILS WITH CHIVE LEMON SAUCE

Entertaining with style! This is one of the most elegant, yet easiest dinners.

LOBSTER

4	medium frozen or fresh lobster tails (about 6 oz/180 g each)	4
	Juice and peel of 1 lemon	
2 tbsp	olive oil	25 mL
1 tsp	paprika	5 mL

CHIVE LEMON SAUCE

1/2 cup	butter	125 mL
1 tbsp	lemon juice	15 mL
1 tsp	grated lemon peel	5 mL
1 tbsp	snipped fresh chives	15 mL
	Lemon wedges	

1. Thaw lobster if frozen; wash and pat dry with paper toweling. To butterfly the lobster tail (so it will lie flat during grilling), using kitchen scissors, cut lengthwise through centers of hard top shells and meat; do not cut through the undershell. Press tails open.

2. In small bowl, combine lemon juice and peel, oil and paprika; brush on exposed lobster meat.

3. Preheat grill on medium-high. Place tails, meat side down, on oiled grill rack. Close lid and cook (use Direct Grilling, page 6) for 6 to 8 minutes or until lobster is opaque; turn once.

4. For sauce: In small saucepan, melt butter, lemon juice and peel. Remove from heat, add chives and keep warm.

5. Serve lobster tails on individual warmed plates with a lemon wedge and a small dish of sauce for dipping. **Makes 4 servings.**

CHAPTER 6
GOURMET ON THE GRILL

◄ Chicken on a Spit with Chardonnay Glaze (page 163)

Here we look at some of the most interesting areas of grill cooking — kebab and spit grilling — and the many fabulously exciting recipes that go with them. Let's deal first with kebabs, always so easy to grill and so satisfying to share with family and guests.

Kebab Grilling

Kebabs are a method of open-air cooking that traces back to the mountain people of the Caucasus who impaled meat on their swords and roasted it over an open fire. Today, skewers have replaced swords and grills have been substituted for the open fire. It has become a chic style of cooking in North America.

The popularity of kebabs is well deserved. Their festive appearance and their mingling of different flavors turn any meal into a celebration. In spite of their exotic nature, they are an inexpensive way to serve a crowd. Since a kebab consists of small pieces of meat interspersed with vegetables or sometimes fruit, small amounts of meat go a long way. Furthermore, small pieces of meat are ideal for marinating, so economical meat cuts can be used. Kebabs fit right into the smaller meat servings that are part of the current healthy eating culture.

Our kebab recipes are an exciting and eclectic selection of meats, seafood, chicken and vegetarian foods. Meats include chicken, venison, beef, lamb, sausage and pork. Turkey can substitute for chicken in all the chicken kebab recipes. Seafood selections include salmon, tuna, shrimp and scallops. Tofu is the basis for two vegetarian kebabs.

Some representative examples of recipes are: Calvados Pork Kebabs with Vegetables using a wonderful brandy marinade (page 145), Pomegranate-Lemon Lamb Kebabs with Vegetables (page 149), Marinated Tofu and Melon Kebabs (page 161) and a chicken kebab recipe with a Polynesian influence on page 154.

Skewers of some kind are essential for kebab grilling. They come in many sizes in either wood or metal. The wooden ones are great for a crowd. Their modest cost lets everyone have their own skewer. Soaking in warm water ahead of time for about 30 minutes prevents the wood catching on fire and burning the food during grilling. Arranging food so it covers most of the wood reduces the skewers' exposure to charring. Food on metal skewers cooks faster than on wooden ones, since the metal conducts the heat into the middle of the food. While more expensive than wooden ones, they are reusable.

When threading meat on skewers, leave some space between the pieces to ensure even grilling. Less tender cuts of meat require marinating for flavor and tenderness, and then a short grilling to be succulent. Tender cuts only need marinating for a desired flavor. Always grill kebabs by Direct Grilling (see page 6). For cooking times and temperatures, see the charts on pages 9–11. During cooking, turn kebabs several times. Partially precook less tender vegetables (onions, carrots, potatoes and broccoli) before adding to meat on skewers. This ensures they are properly cooked when the meat is done. Other vegetables, like cherry tomatoes, zucchini, sweet peppers and mushrooms, do not require precooking.

Spit Roasting

Roasting on a rotating spit continuously exposes the entire surface of a roast or fowl to the heat source. This allows the meat to cook evenly and to continually self-baste with its own juices resulting in grilled roasts or fowls that are juicy, moist and flavorful. Placing a drip pan of liquid under the roast or poultry to catch drippings keeps the grill clean, prevents flare-ups and adds moisture. Using this pan does assume that grilling is done with a gas back burner (charcoal is dealt with on the next page). The collected juices can be used for making au jus gravy. Always grill with the lid closed for an efficient and even distribution of heat. And it requires little attention compared to other cooking methods. Whole chickens, ducks, Cornish hens and boneless roasts of beef, veal, lamb and pork are all ideal candidates for the spit.

Spit Roasting Tips

For meat: Choose a boneless roast that is tied securely with string, is compact and evenly shaped, and has some fat covering to protect it.

For poultry: Tie with natural fiber string (synthetic string will burn) or wire to keep the shape uniform all around. Wings and legs, once tied securely to the body, may be covered with pieces of foil to prevent over cooking. Never stuff a bird with bread dressing. The temperature within the cavity is not sufficiently high to guarantee food safety of the dressing.

For meat and poultry: Insert the pointed end of the spit rod lengthwise through the center of the roast or poultry. The holding forks at each end of the roast or poultry are inserted into the meat. Tighten them with pliers as they tend to loosen during rotation. Test for balance by rotating the spit rod in your hands. If the spit is not balanced, the rotisserie will not turn properly and undue strain will be placed on the motor. Balance the spit by adjusting the weight device supplied by the manufacturer.

Preheat the grill on high using the back burner only. Place the spit with the meat on it in the rotisserie and turn on the motor. Place the drip pan under the meat (some people use beer, juice, wine or broths instead of water). Close the lid and grill until the surface of the meat has browned. Adjust the back burner heat to medium-high for the rest of the specified time (see chart below). Never allow pan liquids to evaporate. If you are applying a basting sauce, some contents from the drip pan can be added to the sauce for added flavor. Most basting should be done toward the end of the roasting.

If you are spit roasting over charcoal, the same process is used except there is no back burner and the hot coals would have to be arranged to accommodate a drip pan under the meat. Whether this is worth the benefits of the drip pan is a personal judgment.

INDIRECT GRILLING FOR SPIT ROASTING

Preheat grill on high, then reduce heat according to chart below. Remove meat about 5°F (2°C) below desired degree of doneness. Cover meat loosely with foil for 15 minutes before serving.

MEAT CUT	INTERNAL TEMPERATURE	GRILL TEMPERATURE	GRILLING TIME MIN PER LB	GRILLING TIME MIN PER KG
Beef Roasts	rare 145°F (63°C)	Medium-high	18 to 20	40 to 45
	medium 160°F (71°C)	Medium-high	22 to 25	50 to 60
	well done 170°F (77°C)	Medium-high	30	75
Veal Roasts	medium 160°F (71°C)	Medium-high	25	55
	well done 170°F (77°C)	Medium-high	35	80
Lamb Roasts	rare 145°F (65°C)	Medium		
	medium 160°F (71°C)	Medium	about 20	about 40
Pork Roasts	medium 160°F (71°C)	Medium	20 to 30	45 to 75
Whole Turkey	180°F (82°C)	Medium-high	30	75
Whole Chicken	185°F (85°C)	Medium-high	30	75
Cornish Hens	165°F (74°C)	Medium-high	30	75

Gingered Beef Kebabs with Mushrooms and Red Peppers

This recipe was inspired by the Beef Information Bureau Winning Tastes of Beef special issue of Canadian Living magazine. I have taken a few liberties with the recipe. I hope you will enjoy it.

MARINADE

½ cup	soy sauce	125 mL
1	piece gingerroot (1 inch/2.5 cm), minced	1
2	cloves garlic, crushed	2
1½ lb	round or sirloin steak (1 inch/2 cm thick)	750 g
1	medium sweet red pepper, cut into squares	1
24	medium mushrooms, trimmed	24
2 tbsp	liquid honey	25 mL
3 cups	cooked rice (1 cup/250 mL raw)	750 mL
¼ cup	chopped fresh parsley	50 mL
	Salt and freshly ground pepper	
6	metal or soaked wooden skewers	6

Suggested Menu: Here is another menu idea: Make a couscous salad using the recipe for Pine Nut Couscous (page 199) served cold with halved grapes and a sprinkle of fresh thyme to set off the beef and red pepper kebabs.

 Wine: Select a Cabernet Franc Rosé.

1. Remove excess fat from beef and discard. Cut beef into 1-inch (2 cm) cubes and place in resealable plastic bag.

2. *For marinade:* In bowl, combine soy sauce, gingerroot and garlic. Pour over beef; turn to coat and refrigerate for up to 6 hours; turn beef occasionally.

3. Remove beef from marinade; reserve marinade. Thread beef, red pepper and mushrooms alternately onto 6 metal or soaked wooden skewers.

4. In small saucepan, combine marinade and honey; bring to a boil, reduce heat and simmer for 5 minutes; keep warm.

5. Preheat grill on medium. Place kebabs on oiled grill rack. Close lid and cook (use Direct Grilling, page 6) for about 10 minutes or until vegetables are golden brown and meat is medium-rare; turn three times, brushing with warm marinade.

6. Combine cooked rice and parsley, season to taste with salt and pepper. Remove meat and vegetables from skewers and serve over parsley rice. **Makes 6 servings.**

BEEF KEBABS WITH RED PEPPER SAUCE

Dip cooked beef kebabs into this smoky, roasted pepper sauce at serving time. Before grilling, rub beef with herbs for a wonderful and full-flavored meat.

RED PEPPER SAUCE

3	large sweet red peppers	3
1 tbsp	balsamic vinegar	15 mL
1	clove garlic	1
½ tsp	salt	2 mL
¼ tsp	freshly ground pepper	1 mL
2 tbsp	chopped Italian parsley	25 mL

BEEF AND RUB

1½ lb	rib, sirloin, strip loin or tenderloin steak (¾ inch/2 cm thick)	750 g
3	cloves garlic, minced	3
1 to 2 tsp	dried herbs (thyme, basil, oregano or rosemary) or 1 to 2 tbsp (15 to 25 mL) fresh	5 to 10 mL
	Salt and freshly ground pepper	
6	metal or soaked wooden skewers	6

1. *For sauce:* Either cut peppers in half and remove seeds or leave them whole. Preheat grill on medium-high. Place peppers on oiled grill rack. Close lid and cook (use Direct Grilling, page 6) for about 20 minutes or until skins are blistered on all sides; turn often. Place hot peppers in a paper bag to cool for about 15 minutes. Peel away the blackened skin.

2. In food processor, purée peppers, vinegar, garlic, salt and pepper until almost smooth. Stir in parsley. Cover and refrigerate until ready to use.

3. *For beef and rub:* Remove excess fat from beef and discard. Cut beef into ¾-inch (2 cm) cubes and place in shallow nonreactive dish. In small bowl, combine garlic, herbs, salt and pepper; press mixture evenly over all sides of beef. (Rub it in with your fingers, if necessary.)

4. Thread beef cubes onto 6 metal or soaked wooden skewers. Preheat grill on medium. Place kebabs on oiled grill rack. Close lid and cook (use Direct Grilling, page 6) for about 10 minutes or until meat is cooked to desired stage of doneness (see chart on page 10); turn kebabs three times.

5. Remove beef from skewers and serve with Red Pepper Sauce for dipping. **Makes 6 servings and about 1 cup (250 mL) sauce.**

Suggested Menu: Potatoes and Onions in a Pouch (page 201) can be grilled at the same time as the kebabs. Toss a green salad with Creamy Buttermilk Dressing (page 217).

Tip: Store Red Pepper Sauce for up to 3 days in the refrigerator or freeze for longer storage. It is most flavorful when brought to room temperature before serving.

CALVADOS PORK KEBABS WITH VEGETABLES

Apples, apple juice and Calvados (an eau-de-vie distilled from apples), complement pork in this exciting kebab.

1½ lb	boneless pork (shoulder or tenderloin)	750 g

MARINADE

½ cup	apple juice	125 mL
¼ cup	Calvados or brandy	50 mL
2	cloves garlic, crushed	2
1 tsp	ground cinnamon	5 mL
½ tsp	each: ground nutmeg and ginger	2 mL
1	large onion, cut into wedges	1
1 cup	broccoli florets	250 mL
2	medium carrots, cut into 1-inch (2.5 cm) chunks	2
1 tbsp	liquid honey	15 mL
2	firm apples, cored and thickly sliced	2
6	metal or soaked wooden skewers	6

1. Cut pork into 1-inch (2.5 cm) cubes. Remove excess fat and discard. Place in resealable plastic bag.

2. *For marinade:* In bowl, combine apple juice, Calvados, garlic, cinnamon, nutmeg and ginger. Pour over pork, turn to coat; refrigerate for 4 hours or overnight.

3. Partially cook onion, broccoli and carrot pieces individually until barely tender; drain and reserve.

4. Remove pork from marinade; reserve marinade. Place marinade in small saucepan; stir in honey and bring to a boil. Reduce heat and simmer for 5 minutes; keep warm.

5. Preheat grill on medium. Thread pork, apple, onion, broccoli and carrot alternately onto 6 metal or soaked wooden skewers. Place kebabs on oiled grill rack. Close lid and cook (use Direct Grilling, page 6) for about 20 minutes or until vegetables and apples are tender, pork is browned and juices run clear. Turn several times, brushing with warm marinade. **Makes 6 servings.**

Suggested Menu: Since there is such a variety of vegetables on the skewers, boiled new potatoes and a small salad are all that is necessary to complete this menu.

Tip: For variety, replace the apple slices with pineapple and any of the vegetables with sweet red pepper squares and green onion pieces.

 Wine: Pair with a sweeter, off–dry Riesling.

Sweet 'n' Sour Pork Kebabs

The intriguing sweet and sour flavors of the sauce are so right with pork.

SAUCE

1 tbsp	canola or olive oil	15 mL
2	cloves garlic, minced	2
1	can (7 ½ oz/213 mL) tomato sauce	1
3 tbsp	rice vinegar	45 mL
2 tbsp	packed brown sugar	25 mL
2 tbsp	soy sauce	25 mL
1 tsp	sesame oil	5 mL

PORK AND VEGETABLES

1 ½ lb	boneless pork (shoulder or tenderloin)	750 g
1	sweet red pepper, cubed	1
4	green onions, cut into 1½-inch (4 cm) lengths	4
3	slices fresh pineapple, cubed	3
6	metal or soaked wooden skewers	6

1. *For sauce:* Heat oil in a small saucepan over medium heat; cook garlic for 1 minute. Stir in tomato sauce, vinegar, sugar and soy sauce. Bring to a boil, reduce heat and simmer, uncovered, for 8 minutes or until thickened; stir occasionally. Stir in sesame oil. Set aside.

2. *For pork and vegetables:* Cut pork into 1-inch (2.5 cm) cubes; remove excess fat and discard. Alternately thread pork, red pepper, green onions and pineapple onto skewers.

3. Preheat grill on medium-high; reduce heat to medium; place kebabs on lightly oiled grill rack. Brush with one-half of sauce; close lid and grill (use Direct Grilling, page 6) for about 20 minutes or until pork is browned and vegetables are crisp-tender; turn several times. Continue brushing with sauce during last 5 minutes of grilling. **Makes 6 servings.**

Suggested Menu: Fluffy cooked basmati rice and Soused Dessert Kebabs (page 242). Although we repeat the kebabs, this dessert is a perfect complement to the pork entrée.

TROPICAL THAI HAM AND SHRIMP KEBABS

These kebabs can serve as an appetizer or as a main entrée — just vary the quantity.

½ cup	each: light mayonnaise and peanut butter	125 mL
½ cup	pineapple juice	125 mL
¼ cup	each: liquid honey and soy sauce	50 mL
2	cloves garlic, crushed	2
¼ tsp	cayenne pepper	1 mL
1 lb	sliced ham, ¾ inch (2 cm) thick	500 g
12	cleaned jumbo shrimp	12
	Soaked wooden or metal skewers	

1. In bowl, combine mayonnaise, peanut butter, pineapple juice, honey, soy sauce, garlic and cayenne. Stir well to blend; reserve half of the sauce for dipping. Pour remaining sauce into a resealable plastic bag or shallow nonreactive dish. Cut ham into cubes and place in bag, turn to coat and refrigerate for 4 hours or overnight. Add shrimp during last hour of marinating.

2. Remove ham and shrimp from marinade; discard marinade. Thread ham and shrimp alternately onto metal or soaked wooden skewers. (The number of skewers depends on whether the kebabs will be used as an appetizer or a main course.)

3. Preheat grill on medium. Place kebabs on oiled grill rack. Close lid and cook (use Direct Grilling, page 6) for 8 minutes or until ham is golden brown and shrimp is opaque; turn frequently. Remove from skewers and serve with reserved dipping sauce. **Makes 12 appetizer or 4 main course servings.**

Suggested Menu: Zucchini Fingers (page 182) and fluffy rice will complement the kebabs perfectly. If another grilled item is not too much, pineapple and papaya kebabs with Lime Rum Sauce (page 237) can be prepared ahead of time.

 Wine: Serve with Gewurztraminer.

Honey Mustard Sausage Kebabs

Choose your favorite sausage from the ever-increasing varieties available. Precooking in simmering water saves time and gives a firmer sausage for threading on skewers.

HONEY MUSTARD SAUCE

¼ cup	Dijon mustard	50 mL
2 tbsp	each: liquid honey and light mayonnaise	25 mL

SAUSAGE AND VEGETABLES

4	sausages, your favorite ones	4
1	yellow or orange sweet pepper, cut into 12 cubes	1
1	red onion, cut into 12 chunks	1
1	zucchini, cut into 12 chunks	1
	Vegetable oil	
6	metal or soaked wooden skewers	6

1. *For sauce:* Whisk together mustard, honey and mayonnaise. Set aside.

2. *For sausage:* Precook in simmering water for about 10 minutes; drain and cool until easy to handle. See our Grilling the Perfect Sausage (page 72) for more detail. Cut into bite-sized pieces.

3. Alternately thread sausage, pepper cubes, onion and zucchini onto skewers.

4. Preheat grill on medium-high. Brush kebabs lightly with oil. Place on grill rack; reduce heat to medium. Close lid and grill (use Direct Grilling, page 6) for about 15 minutes or until vegetables are golden brown and crisp-tender and sausage is heated through; turn several times. Serve with sauce for dipping. **Makes 6 servings.**

POMEGRANATE-LEMON LAMB KEBABS WITH VEGETABLES

Pomegranate, lemon and lamb say Middle East to us. These kebabs are as easily prepared on an indoor grill as outdoors. It is best to precook potatoes and onion for a few minutes before grilling so they finish with the meat. Naturally, zucchini cooks quickly, making precooking unnecessary.

1 lb	lean boneless lamb (shoulder or leg)	500 g

MARINADE

¼ cup	pure pomegranate juice	50 mL
1 tsp	lemon peel	5 mL
2 tbsp	each: fresh lemon juice and olive oil	25 mL
2	cloves garlic, minced	2
¼ tsp	each: salt and freshly ground pepper	1 mL

VEGETABLES

12	potato chunks	3
1	red onion, cut into 8 wedges	1
12	zucchini chunks	12
	Lemon wedges	
4	metal or soaked wooden skewers	4

1. *For lamb:* Trim excess fat from lamb and discard. Cube meat into 1-inch (2.5 cm) cubes and place in a resealable plastic bag.

2. *For marinade:* Combine pomegranate juice, lemon peel and juice, oil, garlic, salt and pepper. Pour one-half of the marinade over lamb, turn to coat; refrigerate for 2 to 6 hours. Reserve remaining marinade for basting.

3. Cook potatoes in boiling water for about 10 minutes or until almost tender; drain and reserve. Repeat with onion wedges.

4. Remove lamb from marinade; discard used marinade. Thread lamb on 2 skewers. Alternately thread potatoes, onion and zucchini on remaining 2 skewers.

5. *For Indoor Grilling:* Preheat indoor grill on medium-high for 5 minutes. Place skewers on lightly oiled grill rack; grill for about 10 minutes or until meat and vegetables are cooked to desired doneness (see chart on page 11). Turn skewers several times; brush with reserved marinade. Remove lamb and vegetables from skewers and arrange on serving plates with lemon wedges. **Makes 4 servings.**

For Outdoor Grilling: Follow procedure as above for Steps 1, 2, 3 and 4.

Step 5: Preheat grill on medium. Place skewers on lightly oiled grill rack. Close lid and grill (use Direct Grilling, page 6) for about 10 minutes or until meat and vegetables are cooked to desired doneness. Turn skewers several times; brush with reserved marinade.

 Wine: Serve with a Syrah.

Middle Eastern Lamb Kebabs with Couscous

Yogurt is widely used in Middle Eastern cooking. Here, it makes a low-fat marinade that brings a taste of the Middle East to the lamb. Couscous, another staple of the Middle East, is the perfect accompaniment.

YOGURT MARINADE

1 cup	plain yogurt	250 mL
2	cloves garlic, crushed	2
1 tbsp	finely minced onion	15 mL
1 tsp	granulated sugar	5 mL
1 tsp	dried oregano or 1 tbsp (15 mL) fresh	5 mL
$\frac{1}{2}$ tsp	salt	2 mL
$\frac{1}{2}$ tsp	dried thyme or 2 tsp (10 mL) fresh	2 mL
$\frac{1}{4}$ tsp	freshly ground pepper	1 mL
1 lb	lean boneless lamb (leg or shoulder)	500 g
	Pine Nut Couscous (see page 199)	
	Fresh parsley	
	Cherry tomatoes, halved	
6	metal or soaked wooden skewers	6

Suggested Menu: Serve with Grilled Eggplant brushed with olive oil (see page 177) and a sprinkle of chopped fresh mint. Whole wheat pita breads complete this international menu.

1. *For marinade:* In bowl, combine yogurt, garlic, onion, sugar, oregano, thyme, salt and pepper.

2. Trim excess fat from lamb and discard. Cut lamb into 1-inch (2.5 cm) pieces and place in shallow nonreactive dish or resealable plastic bag. Pour marinade over lamb, cover and refrigerate for 2 to 6 hours.

3. Remove lamb from marinade; reserve marinade. Place marinade in small saucepan, bring to a boil, reduce heat and cook for 5 minutes; keep warm. Thread lamb onto 4 metal or soaked wooden skewers.

4. Preheat grill on medium. Place kebabs on oiled grill rack. Close lid and cook (use Direct Grilling, page 6) for about 10 minutes or until meat is cooked to desired stage of doneness; turn twice, brushing with warm marinade.

5. Place foil package of Pine Nut Couscous on grill rack beside kebabs. Grill for about 10 minutes or until heated through; turn frequently.

6. Open package and divide couscous between 4 warm dinner plates. Remove lamb from skewers onto couscous; garnish with parsley and cherry tomatoes. **Makes 4 servings.**

GROUND CHICKEN KEBABS WITH VEGETABLES

Ground chicken (or turkey) is an economical, convenient alternative to more expensive chicken breasts. As with other recipes involving ground meats, these kebabs should be well cooked.

1½ lb	lean ground chicken or turkey	750 g
1 cup	quick rolled oats	250 mL
1	egg, lightly beaten	1
3 tbsp	milk	45 mL
1 tbsp	each: horseradish and Worcestershire sauce	15 mL
½ tsp	salt	2 mL
¼ tsp	freshly ground pepper	1 mL
24	pieces sweet green pepper (2 peppers)	24
16	cherry tomatoes	16
16	large mushrooms, trimmed	16
4	green onions, trimmed and cut into 2 pieces	4
1 cup	barbecue sauce (your choice)	250 mL
8	metal or soaked wooden skewers	8

1. Combine chicken, oats, egg, milk, horseradish, Worcestershire sauce, salt and pepper. Lightly shape into 24 meatballs.

2. Thread 3 meatballs, 3 green pepper pieces, 2 cherry tomatoes, 2 mushrooms and 1 piece of green onion alternately onto 8 metal or soaked wooden skewers. Brush lightly with barbecue sauce.

3. Preheat grill on medium-high. Place kebabs on oiled grill rack. Close lid and cook (use Direct Grilling, page 6) for 8 to 12 minutes or until brown and chicken is no longer pink inside; turn frequently, brushing with extra sauce. **Makes 8 servings.**

Suggested Menu: Slice 8 submarine buns lengthwise and toast on grill. Place contents of 1 skewer in each bun and serve. Possible condiments include mustard, Mexican Cranberry Salsa (page 33), more barbecue sauce and banana peppers.

 Wine: Serve with Rosé, Pinot Grigio or an unoaked Chardonnay.

Tips: Fresh ground chicken should be used within 2 days of purchase or frozen for longer keeping. There are two basic rules for the safe handling of chicken and turkey: keep it clean, and keep it cold until you cook it. Be sure to wash your hands before and after handling raw poultry.

SPICY CHICKEN AND VEGETABLE KEBABS

These chicken kebabs can be as spicy as you wish. It's all in the length of time the chicken stays in the marinade.

SPICY MARINADE

2 tbsp	each: soy sauce and molasses	25 mL
1 tbsp	red wine vinegar	15 mL
1 to 2 tsp	hot pepper sauce	5 to 10 mL
½ tsp	each: ground ginger and cloves	2 tsp
⅛ tsp	each: salt, cayenne and freshly ground pepper	0.5 mL

CHICKEN AND VEGETABLES

1 lb	boneless, skinless chicken breast	500 g
12	medium mushrooms	12
12	pieces sweet green pepper	12
1	large onion, cut into 12 wedges	1
	Green onion fans	
4	metal or soaked wooden skewers	4

1. *For marinade:* In shallow nonreactive dish or resealable plastic bag, combine soy sauce, molasses, vinegar, pepper sauce, ginger, cloves, salt, cayenne and pepper; stir well. Add chicken, turn to coat. Refrigerate for 2 to 4 hours (depending on depth of flavor desired).

2. Remove chicken from marinade; discard marinade. Thread chicken and vegetables alternately onto 4 metal or soaked wooden skewers.

3. Preheat grill on medium-high. Place kebabs on oiled grill rack. Close lid and cook (use Direct Grilling, page 6) for 7 minutes per side or until chicken is no longer pink inside; turn frequently.

4. Remove chicken and vegetables from skewers to warm plates to serve. Garnish each with a green onion fan. **Makes 4 servings.**

Suggested Menu: Black beans and saffron-flavored rice pair well with the sunny and spicy flavors of this dish.

Tip: To make green onion fans, cut onion in thin slices from the stem almost, but not quite, to the green top; fan out on plate as a garnish.

 Wine: Look for a crisp, smooth white wine, such as a Sauvignon Blanc to serve with these chicken kebabs.

POLYNESIAN CHICKEN MANGO KEBABS

Bold herbs and spices teamed with lime and coconut milk make a satisfying marinade for chicken. If you have time, let the chicken marinate overnight.

LIME-COCONUT MARINADE

½ cup	coconut milk	125 mL
2 tbsp	lime juice	25 mL
1 tsp	grated lime peel	5 mL
3	cloves garlic, minced	3
1	green onion, finely chopped	1
1 tsp	coriander seeds, crushed	5 mL
½ tsp	each: ground cumin and paprika	2 mL
¼ tsp	each: salt and freshly ground pepper	1 mL
⅛ tsp	hot pepper sauce	0.5 mL

CHICKEN AND MANGO

4	boneless, skinless chicken breast halves	4
1 tbsp	liquid honey	15 mL
1	large mango, peeled and cubed	1
	Toasted sesame seeds	
4	metal or soaked wooden skewers	4

Suggested Menu: Fluffy rice and Grilled Asparagus (page 177) drizzled with Mint Vinaigrette (see below) make a refreshing accompaniment for this entrée.

Mint Vinaigrette: Combine 1 tbsp (15 mL) water, 1 tbsp (15 mL) olive oil, 2 tsp (10 mL) rice vinegar and 1 tsp (5 mL) minced fresh mint leaves.

1. *For marinade:* In bowl, combine coconut milk, lime juice and peel, garlic, onion, coriander, cumin, paprika, salt, pepper and pepper sauce.

2. Cut chicken into 1-inch (2.5 cm) cubes. Place in shallow nonreactive dish or resealable plastic bag. Pour marinade over chicken, cover and refrigerate for 2 to 4 hours or overnight.

3. Remove chicken from marinade; reserve marinade. Place marinade in small saucepan, stir in honey and bring to a boil. Reduce heat and simmer for 5 minutes; keep warm.

4. Preheat grill on medium-high. Thread chicken cubes and mango alternately onto 4 metal or soaked wooden skewers. Place kebabs on oiled grill rack. Close lid and cook (use Direct Grilling, page 6) for about 10 minutes or until browned and chicken is no longer pink inside; turn three times, brushing with warm marinade. Remove chicken and mango from skewers and sprinkle with sesame seeds. **Makes 4 servings.**

VENISON KEBABS WITH CRANBERRY GRAVY

In culinary terms, "venison" can be meat from elk, deer, moose, antelope or caribou. All have similar grilling characteristics. However, when this meat is offered for sale, the type of animal must be specified on the package label. All are the meat lover's health salvation. It is a red meat that is lean and tender, high in protein, low in fat (about one-half the fat of most beef, lamb and pork cuts). And it is delicious, either simply grilled or with an elaborate sauce.

MARINADE

2 tsp	olive or canola oil	10 mL
2	cloves garlic, minced	2
1	shallot, finely chopped	1
1 cup	dry red wine	250 mL
1 tbsp	balsamic vinegar	15 mL
	Freshly ground pepper	

VENISON

1½ lb	loin of venison	750 g
¼ tsp	freshly ground pepper	1 mL
6	metal or soaked wooden skewers	6

CRANBERRY GRAVY

½ cup	cranberry juice	125 mL
¼ cup	chopped dried cranberries	50 mL
1 tbsp	ketchup or chili sauce	15 mL
	Chopped fresh parsley	

1. *For marinade:* In nonstick skillet, heat oil on medium-high. Cook garlic and shallot for about 4 minutes or until softened. Add wine, vinegar and pepper; cool.

2. *For venison:* Cut venison into ¾-inch (2 cm) cubes and place in resealable plastic bag. Pour cool marinade over meat; turn to coat and refrigerate for 12 hours or overnight. Remove meat from marinade; strain marinade and reserve.

3. Preheat grill on medium-high. Thread meat on skewers. Place kebabs on lightly oiled grill rack. Close lid and grill (use Direct Grilling, page 6) for 6 to 8 minutes for medium-rare or until browned on the outside but still pink in the center; turn several times.

4. *For gravy:* Meanwhile, combine cranberry juice, dried cranberries, ketchup and strained marinade. Bring to a boil, reduce heat and cook until liquid is partially reduced. If desired, thicken gravy with cornstarch and water.

5. Place skewers on warmed plates and serve with Cranberry Gravy and a sprinkle of chopped parsley. **Makes 6 servings.**

Suggested Menu: Serve with Grilled Sweet Potato Slices (page 178) and Grilled Portobello Mushrooms (page 200).

Grilling Tip: Venison should not be cooked beyond the medium–rare stage: 145°F (63°C). Anything beyond that will tend to toughen the meat and it can develop a livery taste.

 Wine: Try a Merlot or Zinfandel.

CURRIED TUNA, SHRIMP AND SCALLOP BROCHETTES

The Sesame Orange Dipping Sauce is a cooling complement to curried multi-seafood kebabs.

SEAFOOD

1 lb	tuna	500 g
8	jumbo shrimp	8
8	large scallops	8

MARINADE

1/4 cup	dry sherry	50 mL
1 tbsp	sesame oil	15 mL
1 tsp	each: curry powder and grated lemon peel	5 mL
dash	cayenne pepper	dash
4	metal or soaked wooden skewers	4

SESAME ORANGE DIPPING SAUCE

1/3 cup	each: chicken broth and orange juice	75 mL
2	green onions, thinly sliced	2
1 tbsp	rice vinegar	15 mL
1 tsp	sesame oil	5 mL

1. *For seafood:* Wipe tuna with paper toweling, remove skin and cut into 1-inch (2.5 cm) pieces. Remove shell and vein from shrimp. Wipe scallops. Place tuna, shrimp and scallops in a resealable plastic bag.

2. *For marinade:* Combine sherry, 1 tbsp (15 mL) sesame oil, curry powder, lemon peel and cayenne. Pour over seafood; close bag and refrigerate for 2 hours or up to 6 hours; turn bag occasionally.

3. Remove fish from marinade; reserve marinade. Place marinade in a small saucepan, bring to a boil, reduce heat and cook for 5 minutes; keep warm. Alternately thread seafood on skewers.

4. Preheat grill on medium-high. Place kebabs on lightly oiled grill rack. Close lid and grill (use Direct Grilling, page 6) for about 10 minutes or until tuna and scallops are opaque and shrimp is pink; turn once or twice, basting occasionally with warm marinade.

5. *For sauce:* In small bowl, combine chicken broth, orange juice, onions, vinegar and 1 tsp (5 mL) sesame oil; mix well. Remove seafood from skewers to each plate. Serve with a small bowl of dipping sauce. **Makes 4 servings.**

Suggested Menu: Serve with Grilled Asparagus (page 177), Szechwan Vegetable Salad (page 207) and fluffy cooked rice.

SCALLOP, SHRIMP AND VEGETABLE KEBABS

These two favorite seafoods grilled with sweet peppers and mushrooms and brushed with Ginger-Sherry Marinade make a succulent entrée.

GINGER-SHERRY MARINADE

¼ cup	dry sherry	50 mL
1 tbsp	sesame oil	15 mL
1 tbsp	grated gingerroot	15 mL
2 tsp	light soy sauce	10 mL
1	large clove garlic, crushed	1

SEAFOOD AND VEGETABLES

16	sea scallops	16
12	jumbo shrimps	12
8	squares each: sweet red and green peppers	8
12	medium mushrooms	12
4	metal or soaked wooden skewers	4

Suggested Menu: Serve with Grilled Zucchini or Yellow Squash (page 169), crusty rolls and cooked jasmine rice.

Wine: The spicy sweet–tart fruit flavors of white Zinfandel will complement the shrimp.

1. *For marinade:* In bowl, combine sherry, oil, gingerroot, soy sauce and garlic. Place scallops and shrimp in shallow nonreactive dish or resealable plastic bag. Pour marinade over, turn to coat; cover and refrigerate for 1 to 2 hours.

2. Blanch pepper cubes in boiling water for 1 minute; drain well.

3. Remove seafood from marinade; reserve marinade. Place marinade in small saucepan, bring to a boil, reduce heat and cook for 5 minutes; keep warm. Thread scallops, shrimp, pepper cubes and mushrooms alternately onto 4 metal or soaked wooden skewers.

4. Preheat grill on medium-high. Place kebabs on oiled grill rack. Close lid and cook (use Direct Grilling, page 6) for about 10 minutes or until shrimp and scallops are opaque; turn once or twice, basting occasionally with warm marinade. **Makes 4 servings.**

Skewered Dilled Salmon with Vegetables

The meaty texture of salmon makes it an ideal fish for kebabs. This dish has become a favorite dinner with our Calgary grandchildren when their parents, mother Margie and father Paul, serve it.

1 lb	salmon, cut into 1-inch (2.5 cm) cubes	500 g

MARINADE

¼ cup	olive or canola oil	50 mL
¼ cup	chopped fresh dill or 1½ tbsp (22 mL) dried	50 mL
½ tsp	grated lemon peel	2 mL
2 tbsp	fresh lemon juice	25 mL
½ tsp	salt	2 mL
¼ tsp	freshly ground pepper	1 mL
dash	hot pepper sauce	dash

VEGETABLES

1	sweet green pepper, cut into 2-inch (5 cm) cubes	1
1	yellow squash or zucchini, cut into 1-inch (2.5 cm) cubes	1
12	cherry tomatoes	12
8	small new potatoes, precooked	8
4	metal or wooden soaked skewers	4

1. Place fish in resealable plastic bag.

2. *For marinade:* Combine oil, dill, lemon peel and juice, salt, pepper and hot sauce. Pour over fish; turn to coat and refrigerate for 15 minutes or up to 1 hour.

3. Remove fish from marinade; reserve marinade. Place marinade in small saucepan, bring to a boil and cook for 5 minutes; keep warm.

4. Preheat grill on medium-high. Alternately thread fish, pepper, squash, tomatoes and potatoes onto skewers. Place kebabs on lightly oiled grill rack. Close lid and grill for about 10 minutes (use Direct Grilling, page 6) or until fish is opaque and flakes easily and vegetables are tender. Turn often and brush with warm marinade. **Makes 4 servings.**

Variations: The following will enjoy the same marinade as salmon:

Lamb with mushrooms, cherry tomatoes and sweet yellow pepper.

Shrimp or scallops with sweet red pepper, green onion chunks and artichoke quarters.

Chicken with snow peas, water chestnuts and sweet red pepper.

 Wine: Opt for a full-bodied Chardonnay or new world Syrah.

MARINATED TOFU AND MELON KEBABS

Vegetarian foods can be bold-flavored and exciting, depending on the extras added and the marinade used. This vegetarian kebab is full of eastern flavors — gingerroot, soy and cilantro.

MINT MARINADE

¼ cup	each: chopped fresh mint and cilantro	50 mL
¼ cup	each: light soy sauce and lime juice	50 mL
1 tbsp	brown sugar	15 mL
1 tbsp	finely chopped gingerroot	15 mL
2 tsp	canola oil	10 mL
1 tsp	curry powder	5 mL
¼ tsp	crushed chili peppers	1 mL
1	clove garlic, minced	1

TOFU, MELON AND ONION

1	pkg (350 g) extra firm tofu, drained	1
3	green onions, cut diagonally in 2-inch (5 cm) pieces	3
12	cantaloupe cubes, about 1 inch (2.5 cm)	12
	Salt and freshly ground pepper to taste	
4	metal or soaked wooden skewers	4

1. *For marinade:* In small bowl, combine mint, cilantro, soy sauce, lime juice, sugar, gingerroot, oil, curry powder, chili peppers and garlic; mix well.

2. Cut tofu into 2-inch (5 cm) cubes; you should have 16 cubes. Place in resealable plastic bag or shallow nonreactive dish. Pour marinade over, turn to coat, and refrigerate for several hours; turn tofu occasionally.

3. Drain tofu, reserve marinade. Thread tofu, onions and cantaloupe alternately onto 4 metal or soaked wooden skewers.

4. Preheat grill on medium-high. Place kebabs on oiled grill. Close lid and cook (use Direct Grilling, page 6) for about 10 minutes or until tofu is crisp and melon and onion are tender. Turn kebabs several times, basting with reserved marinade. Sprinkle lightly with salt and pepper and serve. **Makes 4 servings.**

Suggested Menu: The obvious choice is to serve the kebabs on a bed of cooked rice or noodles, possibly with steamed snow peas and sweet red pepper strips.

VEGETABLE TOFU KEBABS

 This is a vegetarian meal for everyone. Thanks to tofu's ability to take on the flavors of the foods it accompanies — in this case the marinade — even dedicated meat eaters will be sure the tofu is chicken.

MARINADE

¼ cup	light soy sauce	50 mL
2	cloves garlic, minced	2
1 tbsp	minced gingerroot	15 mL
1 tsp	each: lemon juice and olive oil	5 mL
⅛ tsp	freshly ground pepper	0.5 mL

TOFU AND VEGETABLES

1	pkg (350 g) extra firm tofu, drained	1
1	red onion, cut into wedges	1
16	pieces sweet red pepper	16
12	3-inch (7.5 cm) strips zucchini	12
4	metal or soaked wooden skewers	4

Tip: For best results, use firm tofu; the silken variety is too soft to hold on the skewers.

1. *For marinade:* In small bowl, combine soy sauce, garlic, gingerroot, lemon juice, oil and pepper; mix well.

2. Cut tofu into 2-inch (5 cm) cubes; you should have 16 pieces. Place tofu in a resealable plastic bag or shallow nonreactive dish. Pour marinade over, turn to coat, and refrigerate for several hours; turn tofu occasionally.

3. Drain tofu; reserve marinade. Thread tofu, red onion, red pepper and zucchini alternately onto 4 metal or soaked wooden skewers.

4. Preheat grill on medium-high. Place kebabs on oiled grill rack. Close lid and cook (use Direct Grilling, page 6) for about 10 minutes or until tofu is crisp and vegetables are tender. Turn kebabs several times, basting with reserved marinade. **Makes 4 servings.**

CHICKEN ON A SPIT WITH CHARDONNAY GLAZE

On returning from a visit to Sardinia, our daughter Martha told us of the most wonderful chicken she was served in a restaurant. It was roasted with lemons and black or pimento-stuffed green olives placed in the cavity. Since rotisserie poultry should never be bread stuffed, it seemed like a good idea. Brushing a glaze of Chardonnay wine and honey on the chicken gives it a wonderful crisp crust.

CHICKEN

6 to 8 lb	chicken	3 to 4 kg
2	large lemons, cut into chunks	2
1 cup	olives, black or green	250 mL
	Salt and freshly ground pepper	

GLAZE

½ cup	liquid honey	125 mL
½ cup	Chardonnay wine	125 mL
3	fresh rosemary sprigs	3
1 tbsp	cornstarch	15 mL
¼ cup	water	50 mL
	Fresh rosemary sprigs	

1. *For chicken:* Rinse and pat bird dry inside and out with paper toweling. Remove neck and giblets. Skewer neck skin to back. Tuck drumsticks under the band of skin across the tail. Twist wing tips under the back. Place lemons and olives in cavity; sprinkle bird lightly with salt and pepper. Truss bird with string or wire; cover wing tips and drumsticks with foil, if desired.

2. *For glaze:* In small saucepan, while chicken is grilling, bring honey, wine and rosemary to a boil. Whisk together cornstarch and water, stir into hot wine mixture until smooth.

3. Preheat grill on high. Place bird on spit; be careful to balance meat and follow manufacturer's directions. Adjust heat to medium-high, close lid and grill (see Spit Roasting, pages 140–141) for about 2½ hours or until an instant-read meat thermometer registers 165°F (74°C). About 20 minutes before chicken is cooked, start brushing glaze mixture over. Remove bird from spit to carving board; cover loosely with foil for about 10 minutes before carving. Discard lemon-olive mixture. Serve chicken with additional fresh rosemary. **Makes 6 to 8 servings.**

 Wine: Serve with Chardonnay, of course!

PROVENÇAL-STUFFED ROTISSERIE CORNISH HENS

The Provence-style tomato, mushroom and onion stuffing makes these juicy miniature chickens irresistible. Prior to the 19th century, tomatoes were regarded with suspicion by the residents of Provence, but once accepted, tomatoes had a revolutionary effect on the cooking of the region.

2	Cornish hens, thawed	2

PROVENÇAL TOMATO STUFFING

2	cloves garlic, halved	2
2 tbsp	butter or margarine	25 mL
1	medium onion, chopped	1
1½ cups	sliced mushrooms	375 mL
2	large tomatoes, diced	2
3 tbsp	chopped fresh tarragon or 1 tbsp (15 mL) dried	45 mL
1 tbsp	chopped fresh parsley or 1 tsp (5 mL) dried	15 mL
2 tsp	chopped fresh thyme or ½ tsp (2 mL) dried	10 mL
½ tsp	each: salt and freshly ground pepper	2 mL
3 tbsp	dried bread crumbs	45 mL

1. Wash and dry hens.

2. *For stuffing*: Rub cut side of garlic over cavity and outer skin of each hen; crush garlic. In nonstick skillet, melt butter over medium heat. Add garlic and onion and cook for about 5 minutes or until tender. Add mushrooms and tomatoes. Cook for about 10 minutes or until slightly thickened; stir often. Add tarragon, parsley, thyme, salt and pepper. Taste and adjust seasoning; cool slightly; stir in bread crumbs. Spoon stuffing into cavity of each hen. Truss with skewers and kitchen cord.

3. Preheat grill on high. Place hens on spit; be careful to balance hens and follow spit manufacturer's directions. Adjust heat to medium-high and cook (see Spit Roasting, pages 140–141) for about 1¼ hours or until juices run clear and meat thermometer registers 165°F (74°C). Remove hens from spit to carving board, cover loosely with foil for about 10 minutes before cutting in half to serve. **Makes 4 servings.**

Tip: The difference between a Cornish hen and a broiler chicken is mainly the size. The hens weigh less than 1½ pounds (750 g) and are an excellent size for 1 to 2 servings. The all-purpose broiler chicken weighs between 1½ and 4 pounds (750 g and 2 kg) and so serves 2 to 5.

Tip: Use this stuffing for small broiler chickens, or press a small amount into a pocket cut in thick pork or lamb chops.

CHUTNEY-PEPPERED ROTISSERIE OF BEEF

Chutney and pepper flavors permeate the roast through both the marinade and the rub.

RUB

1 tbsp	each: black and green peppercorns	15 mL
1 tsp	each: mustard seeds and celery seeds	5 mL
1/2 tsp	each: garlic powder and salt	2 mL
4 lb	boneless rolled rib or sirloin or tenderloin roast of beef	2 kg

MARINADE

1/2 cup	pineapple juice	125 mL
1/3 cup	each: orange juice and steak sauce	75 mL
1/4 cup	chutney (if coarse, cut with kitchen scissors)	50 mL
2 tbsp	Worcestershire sauce	25 mL
2 tsp	each: granulated sugar, seasoned salt and lemon pepper	10 mL

1. *For rub:* Crack peppercorns, mustard and celery seeds to a coarse meal: place in a plastic bag and crush with bottom of a heavy skillet, or place in a spice grinder and pulse. Set aside.

2. Trim excess fat from beef and discard. Place in resealable plastic bag and reserve.

3. *For marinade:* In small bowl, combine pineapple and orange juice, steak sauce, chutney, Worcestershire sauce, sugar, seasoned salt and lemon pepper. Pour over roast, turn to coat and refrigerate for 6 hours or overnight; turn bag occasionally.

4. Preheat grill on high. Remove roast from marinade; reserve marinade. Press rub over roast. Place roast on spit: be careful to balance meat and follow spit manufacturer's directions. Adjust heat to medium-high and close lid. Cook (see Spit Roasting, pages 140–141) for about 1 1/2 hours.

5. Meanwhile, place marinade in small saucepan, bring to a boil, reduce heat and cook for 5 minutes; keep warm. Brush roast often with warm marinade. Remove from spit to carving board; cover loosely with foil for about 15 minutes before slicing. **Makes 6 to 8 servings.**

Tip: Remove roast from spit about 5°F (2°C) below desired doneness. Meat will continue cooking, covered with foil, during the 15 minute standing time.

 Wine: Serve with Merlot or Zinfandel.

Garlic Rotisserie Beef Tenderloin

Entertain with the stylish simplicity of spit-roasted beef tenderloin. Who could ask for anything more divine! Yet it's ever so easy on the chef.

WINE MARINADE

⅓ cup	port or dry red wine	75 mL
2 tbsp	sesame oil	25 mL
5	cloves garlic, crushed	5
1 tbsp	chopped gingerroot	15 mL
½ tsp	freshly ground pepper	2 mL
1½ to 2 lb	beef tenderloin (about 3 inches/7.5 cm thick)	750 g to 1 kg
	Fresh parsley	

1. *For marinade:* Combine wine, oil, garlic, gingerroot and pepper. Set aside.

2. *For beef:* Trim excess fat from beef and discard. Place beef in resealable plastic bag, pour wine mixture over and turn to coat. Close bag and refrigerate for 4 to 12 hours; turn bag occasionally.

3. Remove beef from marinade; reserve marinade. Place marinade in a small saucepan, bring to a boil, reduce heat and cook for 5 minutes; keep warm.

4. Preheat grill on high. Place meat on spit; be careful to balance meat and follow spit manufacturer's directions. Adjust heat to medium-high, close lid and grill (see Spit Roasting, pages 140–141) for about 30 minutes or until an instant-read thermometer inserted into beef registers desired temperature (see chart, page 141). Brush frequently with warm marinade. Remove beef from spit to carving board; cover loosely with foil for 10 to 15 minutes before slicing. **Makes 4 to 6 servings.**

 Wine: Any solid red will pair well — try a nice Meritage or Pinot Noir for a hot summer day.

Rotisserie Roast Beef on the Grill

Roasts such as sirloin tip, outside and inside round, and cross rib are best for fuss-free rotisserie grilling.

BALSAMIC SAUCE

¼ cup	butter or margarine	50 mL
4	cloves garlic, minced	4
¼ cup	balsamic vinegar	50 mL
1¼ cups	beef broth	300 mL
4 to 5 lb	beef roast	2 to 2.5 kg
8	cloves garlic, halved	8
	Freshly ground pepper	

1. *For sauce:* Melt butter in small saucepan over medium heat; add garlic and sauté for 1 minute. Add vinegar; cook for 3 minutes. Add broth; cook for 5 minutes; set aside.

2. *For beef:* Make small slits in beef; insert garlic halves into slits. Sprinkle beef generously with pepper.

3. Preheat grill on high. Place roast on spit; be careful to balance meat and follow manufacturer's directions. Adjust heat to medium-high, close lid and grill (see Spit Roasting, pages 140–141) for about 1½ hours or until an instant-read thermometer inserted into beef registers desired temperature (see chart, page 141). Remove beef from spit to carving board; cover loosely with foil for 10 to 15 minutes before slicing. Serve with warm Balsamic Sauce. **Makes 6 to 8 servings.**

SPIT-ROASTED LEG OF LAMB

The Soy Ginger Lemon Marinade and Baste lends a gentle taste of the Orient to the roasted lamb. This marinade can also be used for lamb chops.

4 to 5 lb	boneless leg of lamb	2 to 2.5 kg
¾ cup	Soy Ginger Lemon Marinade and Baste (page 226)	175 mL
2	large lemons, each cut into 4 slices	2

1. Trim excess fat from lamb and discard. Place roast in resealable plastic bag. Pour marinade over lamb, reseal and refrigerate for at least 4 hours or overnight; turn bag occasionally.

2. Remove roast from marinade; reserve marinade. Preheat grill on high. Place roast on spit; be careful to balance meat and follow the spit manufacturer's directions. Adjust heat to medium-high, close lid and cook (see Spit Roasting, pages 140–141) for about 1½ hours (see chart on page 141).

3. Meanwhile, place reserved marinade in small saucepan, bring to a boil, reduce heat and cook for 5 minutes. Brush roast occasionally with warm marinade. Place thick lemon slices on grill rack during last 10 minutes of grilling time.

4. Remove roast from spit to carving board; cover loosely with foil for about 10 minutes before slicing. Serve with grilled lemon slices. **Makes 6 to 8 servings.**

Suggested Menu: Start with Beet Borscht (page 31), then serve Szechwan Vegetable Salad (page 207) and brown rice with the lamb.

Wine: Opt for Pinot Noir.

Tip: Lamb is at its most tender and delicious when cooked until the meat is well browned on the outside but still pink in the center.

ROTISSERIE PORK LOIN WITH SALSA MARINADE

Spit-roast pork for tonight's dinner and have planned leftovers for tomorrow with this Mexican-oriented roast. The spiciness level is determined by your choice of salsa.

4 lb	boneless pork loin (center cut)	2 kg

SALSA MARINADE

2 tsp	canola or olive oil	10 mL
1	small onion, finely chopped	1
1/2 cup	each: ketchup and salsa (mild, medium or hot)	125 mL
1 tbsp	dry mustard	15 mL
2 tsp	red wine vinegar	10 mL
1/2 tsp	dried basil	2 mL
1/4 tsp	hot pepper sauce	1 mL

1. *For pork:* Trim excess fat from roast and discard. Place roast in resealable plastic bag.

2. *For marinade:* In nonstick skillet, heat oil on medium; cook onion for 5 minutes or until softened. Add ketchup, salsa, mustard, vinegar, basil and hot sauce. Bring to a boil, reduce heat and simmer for 10 minutes; cool before pouring over roast. Close bag and refrigerate for at least 4 hours or overnight; turn bag occasionally. Remove roast from marinade; reserve marinade. Place marinade in a small saucepan, bring to a boil, reduce heat and cook for 5 minutes; keep warm.

3. Preheat grill on high. Place meat on spit; be careful to balance meat and follow spit manufacturer's directions. Adjust heat to medium-high, close lid and grill (see Spit Roasting, pages 140–141) for about 2 hours or until an instant-read meat thermometer inserted into pork registers 160°F (71°C); brush frequently with warm marinade. Remove meat from spit to carving board; cover loosely with foil for about 10 minutes before slicing. **Makes 8 servings.**

Suggested Menu (tonight):
For a great south-of-the-border meal serve with a salad consisting of a variety of salad greens. Mexican Corn Salad (page 216) and warm tortillas complete this menu.

Suggested Menu (tomorrow):
Serve cold slivered pork in a main course salad with lots of fresh greens, mandarin orange sections, sliced cucumber and diced green pepper. Toss the salad with Poppy Seed Vinaigrette (page 220). It's an easy summertime meal.

Rotisserie Pork Loin with Salsa Marinade (recipe this page) and ▶ Rotisserie Country-style Ribs with Port Wine Marinade (page 171)

Spit-roasted Marinated Elk with Wine Mushroom Sauce

All the game meats are very lean and benefit from marinating and high-temperature short grilling time. They should never be cooked past medium-rare. Their roasts grill well on the spit. Regular basting during grilling helps to keep the meat moist. Bison, while not venison, has similar grilling characteristics.

2 to 4 lb	elk tenderloin roast	1 to 2 kg
1¼ cups	Basic Red Wine Marinade (page 225)	300 mL

WINE MUSHROOM SAUCE

½ cup	finely chopped onions	125 mL
1 tbsp	vegetable oil	15 mL
2	Portobello mushrooms, thinly sliced	2
½ cup	dry red wine	125 mL
1 tsp	dried thyme or 1 tbsp (15 mL) fresh	5 mL
	Salt and freshly ground pepper	

1. *For meat:* Place meat in a resealable plastic bag. Combine marinade ingredients and pour over meat. Close bag and refrigerate for 24 hours or up to two days; turn bag occasionally.

2. *For sauce:* In nonstick skillet, cook onions in oil on medium-high for 5 minutes or until softened. Add mushrooms, cook for 5 minutes or until liquid has evaporated. Add wine, thyme, salt and pepper. Simmer over medium heat for 10 minutes or until slightly thickened. Set aside and keep warm.

3. Remove meat from marinade; reserve marinade. Place marinade in a small saucepan, bring to a boil, reduce heat and cook for 5 minutes; keep warm.

4. Preheat grill on very high. Place meat on spit; be careful to balance meat and follow spit manufacturer's directions. Adjust heat to medium-high, close lid and grill (see Spit Roasting, pages 140–141) for about 20 minutes or until an instant-read meat thermometer inserted into meat registers no higher than 140°F (62°C); this will increase to 145°F (65°C) temperature while standing (see Grilling Tip below and chart on page 141). Brush frequently with warm marinade. Remove meat from spit to carving board; cover loosely with foil for 10 to 15 minutes before slicing. **Makes 4 to 6 servings.**

Suggested Menu: Wild Rice, Raisin and Apple Casserole (page 202) and a tossed green salad.

Grilling Tip: Remove roast from spit about 5°F (3°C) below desired doneness. The meat when covered with foil for 15 minutes will continue cooking. Elk or venison should not be cooked beyond the medium–rare stage, 145°F (65°C). Anything beyond that will tend to toughen the meat and it can develop a livery taste.

 Wine: Serve with either a Cabernet Sauvignon or a Meritage.

ROTISSERIE COUNTRY-STYLE RIBS WITH PORT WINE MARINADE

Spit roasting is the ideal way to grill ribs because they can be cooked slowly and evenly without scorching. The port marinade gives the ribs just the right blend of tanginess, heat and pungency that goes well with pork.

PORT WINE MARINADE

²⁄₃ cup	port wine	150 mL
¹⁄₂ cup	orange juice	125 mL
1	piece gingerroot (2 inch/5 cm), minced	1
2	cloves garlic, minced	2
1 tbsp	each: liquid honey and lime juice	15 mL
¹⁄₂ to 1 tsp	crushed chili peppers	2 to 5 mL
3 lb	country-style spareribs Orange slices	1.5 kg

1. In small saucepan, cook wine, orange juice, gingerroot, garlic, honey, lime juice and chili peppers until hot. Cool slightly and reserve.

2. Place ribs in shallow nonreactive dish large enough to allow ribs to lay flat in single layer. Pour marinade over ribs, turn to coat; cover and refrigerate for at least 4 hours or overnight. Remove ribs from marinade; reserve marinade. Place marinade in small saucepan, bring to a boil, reduce heat and cook for 5 minutes; keep warm.

3. Preheat grill on high. Lace ribs accordion style on spit rod; be careful to balance meat and follow spit manufacturer's directions. Adjust heat to medium-low, close lid and cook (see Spit Roasting, pages 140–141) for about 1¹⁄₂ hours. Brush frequently with warm marinade.

4. Remove ribs from spit, cover loosely with foil for about 10 minutes before cutting into serving-size pieces. Serve with sliced oranges. **Makes 6 servings.**

Suggested Menu: Serve with Grilled Corn on the Cob with Herb Butter (page 191), sliced tomatoes and potato salad. It makes a marvelous summertime meal.

 Wine: White Zinfandel or Shiraz are both excellent choices.

Apple-Stuffed Veal Roast with Mint Garlic Rub

Fresh from the garden, mint and rosemary, along with a juicy apple, contribute to the complex flavors in this recipe. The mint rub is suitable for both veal and lamb.

MINT GARLIC RUB

⅓ cup	each: granulated sugar and garlic powder	75 mL
⅓ cup	chopped fresh mint or 2 tbsp (25 mL) dried	75 mL
1 tbsp	chopped fresh rosemary or 1 tsp (5 mL) dried	15 mL
¼ tsp	freshly ground pepper	1 mL
4 lb	boneless veal loin roast	2 kg

APPLE STUFFING

1 tbsp	olive oil	15 mL
1 cup	sliced mushrooms	250 mL
1	large green apple, diced and peeled	1
1 tsp	lemon juice	5 mL
½ tsp	grated lemon peel	2 mL
	Salt and freshly ground pepper	

Suggested Menu: Serve with Leeks and Caramelized Onions (page 178) and a green vegetable. Flaming Blueberry Mango Crisp (page 243) is an easy dessert to finish this marvelous meal.

1. *For rub:* In plastic bag, combine sugar, garlic powder, mint, rosemary and pepper. Shake to blend. Place veal in bag; shake to coat thoroughly. Remove veal and set aside.

2. *For stuffing:* In nonstick skillet, heat oil on medium-high; cook mushrooms and apple for 10 minutes or until softened. Remove from heat, stir in lemon juice, peel, and salt and pepper to taste; set aside.

3. Cut a wide, deep pocket in side of roast; stuff apple mixture into pocket. Tie roast at 1-inch (2.5 cm) intervals with heavy string.

4. Preheat grill on high. Place roast on spit; be careful to balance meat and follow spit manufacturer's directions. Adjust heat to medium-high, close lid and cook (see Spit Roasting, pages 140–141) for about 1½ hours or until meat thermometer registers 160°F (70°C). Remove meat from spit to carving board; cover loosely with foil for about 10 minutes before slicing. **Makes 6 to 8 servings.**

CHAPTER 7
VEGETABLES ON THE GRILL

◀ *Grilled Red and White Onions (page 184) and Eggplant with Anchovy-Parsley Sauce (page 184)*

Just about everything tastes better on the grill. This is certainly true with vegetables. Putting them on the grill brings out their full flavor. Fresh produce offers bold, meal-enhancing flavors and colors that are perfect for grilling. Vegetables also provide a light approach to outdoor eating, a fitting accent to the current healthy eating trend. As well, grilling vegetables simplifies outdoor meal preparation as the cooking becomes part of the outside entertaining scene. And as long as the grill is on for your meat, why not add a few extras?

Grilling vegetables intensifies their flavor, making them delicious either hot or cold. The natural sugars in such vegetables as onions, garlic and sweet peppers caramelize when grilled. This imparts a depth and richness that no amount of pan sautéing could ever achieve. Other vegetables, such as eggplant and some of the exotic mushrooms like portobello, acquire the same woodsy smokiness as a good grilled steak.

You'll find exciting vegetable combinations like Sweet Potatoes with Carrots and Turnip (page 185) and new ways to grill vegetables such as Orange-sauced Roasted Beets (page 192) in this chapter's recipes.

Methods vary, but almost any vegetable can be cooked on the grill. Here are a few general guidelines. See pages 177–178 for detailed instructions for specific vegetables.

- If you want to see the grill marks, lay vegetables perpendicular to the spaces in the grill rack so they don't fall through. Otherwise use a grill basket. I still like to see the grill marks!
- Large vegetables should be sliced or cut into chunks so they grill to tenderness in a reasonable time, along with other smaller vegetables that may be on the grill at the same time.
- Foil pouches keep smaller vegetables from slipping through the grill rack. They also insulate delicate produce from direct heat. The vegetables steam in the pouches allowing the seasonings to mingle and intensify.
- To prevent vegetables from sticking to the grill rack, marinate them in an oil-based mixture or brush with oil (not butter, which burns at a relatively low temperature).
- To ensure even, thorough cooking, the grill chef should watch the temperature carefully and turn the vegetables regularly.
- Vegetables such as broccoli, carrots, beets, asparagus, cauliflower and potatoes require blanching or pre-cooking to prevent them from burning on the outside before softening within.
- Natural wrappers (such as corn husks) keep vegetables moist and tender.
- Unless specified otherwise, vegetables are grilled by the Direct Grilling (see page 6) method with the lid closed at medium-high heat.
- Finally, vegetables tend to absorb off-flavors more quickly than meat or poultry, so keep the grill rack as clean as possible.

ALL YOU NEED TO KNOW TO GRILL MOST VEGETABLES

HERB AND OIL BASTES FOR VEGETABLES

You'll find it handy to prepare seasoned mixtures ahead of time and keep them ready to brush on vegetables at the grill.

OIL AND VINEGAR BASTES

Combine ⅓ cup (75 mL) olive oil, 2 tbsp (25 mL) balsamic red or white vinegar; add 2 tbsp (25 mL) chopped fresh herbs. Use a combination of several herbs such as oregano, rosemary, basil, tarragon and thyme or a single herb. You can also replace fresh herbs with 2 tsp (10 mL) dried herbs. Store in tightly sealed container in the refrigerator for up to 5 days.

OIL AND GARLIC HERB BASTE

Combine in a plastic bag 1 tsp (5 mL) canola oil, 1 clove garlic, crushed, ½ tsp (2 mL) paprika, ¼ tsp (1 mL) each: salt and dried oregano or basil. Add vegetables to the bag and toss before grilling. This is best for small, sliced or cubed vegetables.

BALSAMIC BASTE

Combine in a plastic bag 2 tbsp (25 mL) each: canola or olive oil and balsamic vinegar, ½ tsp (2 mL) salt and freshly ground pepper. This is particularly great for carrots or other root vegetables.

PESTO BASTE

Combine 2 tbsp (25 mL) Broccoli Pesto (page 17) with 1 to 2 tbsp (15 to 25 mL) olive oil and freshly ground pepper.

HOW TO GRILL SPECIFIC VEGETABLES

ASPARAGUS

Snap off and discard tough stems of 1 bunch of asparagus; wash and pat dry. Microwave on high (100%) for 3 minutes. Brush lightly with one of the bastes. Grill for about 4 minutes or until tender and lightly charred; turn once. Sometimes it is nice to tie several stalks together before grilling, using cooked green onion tops. I also like to sprinkle grilled asparagus with grated Parmesan cheese.

CARROTS

Cut 5 medium carrots in half lengthwise; parboil or microwave for about 3 minutes. Brush with one of the bastes; grill for about 5 minutes or until tender and browned; turn occasionally.

CORN IN THE HUSK

Pull back husks and remove silk. Replace husks, tie at top with heavy twine or string. Soak in cold water for 1 hour. Remove from water; place on preheated oiled grill rack. Grill for about 20 minutes or until kernels are tender; turn frequently during grilling and brush occasionally with water.

EGGPLANT SLICES

Remove stem and blossom end from 1 medium eggplant and cut lengthwise into thin slices; do not precook. Brush slices lightly with 4 tsp (20 mL) olive oil or a mixture of 1 tbsp (15 mL) olive oil and 1 tsp (5 mL) sesame oil. Grill for about 8 minutes or until flesh is tender; turn once, and season lightly with salt and pepper after turning.

FENNEL

Snip off feathery leaves and remove stems; parboil whole bulb for about 8 minutes. Cut fennel lengthwise into 6 to 8 wedges. Brush lightly with one of the bastes. Grill for about 8 minutes; turn once.

LEEKS

Cut off green tops; trim bulb roots and remove 1 to 2 layers of white skin. Parboil for about 8 minutes, then halve lengthwise. Wash well and brush lightly with olive oil. Grill for about 8 minutes or until leeks are tender and golden brown.

MUSHROOMS

Clean mushrooms and pat dry; do not peel or precook. Brush lightly with one of the bastes. Grill for about 10 minutes or until golden brown; turn occasionally.

CARAMELIZED ONIONS

Place heavy skillet on grill rack for short time to preheat. Add 2 tbsp (25 mL) olive oil and heat for 3 minutes. Add 1 thickly sliced red or yellow onion. Sauté for about 12 minutes or until soft and caramelized; turn frequently.

SQUASH

Pierce the skin of acorn or pepper squash with a fork. Wrap securely with foil and grill for about 1 hour; turn once. Remove from grill, open foil carefully; cut squash in half and discard seeds.

SWEET PEPPERS

You can either cut peppers in half and remove seeds or grill them whole; do not precook. Grill for about 20 minutes or until skins are charred all over; turn often. Place peppers in paper bag until cool. Peel away black skin, brush with one of the bastes and serve.

NEW POTATOES OR SWEET POTATOES

Cut larger potatoes in half; parboil for 10 minutes or until almost tender. Remove from pan; peel sweet potatoes, if using. Cut potatoes into slices and brush with one of the bastes. Grill for about 12 minutes or until tender and golden brown; turn once. You can also grill sliced potatoes from the raw stage without parboiling; allow about 35 minutes grilling time.

WHITE TURNIP

Parboil peeled slices of turnip in boiling water for 5 minutes or until barely tender. Grill for about 12 minutes or until tender; turn often.

ZUCCHINI AND YELLOW SQUASH

Remove ends and cut lengthwise in quarters; do not precook. Brush lightly with one of the herb and oil bastes. Grill for about 6 minutes or until zucchini is tender; turn once. You can also cut zucchini or yellow squash diagonally into $1/2$-inch (1 cm) thick slices.

SAUCES FOR GRILLED VEGETABLES

Here are a few sauce ideas for grilled vegetables.

YOGURT CUCUMBER SAUCE

Combine $2/3$ cup (150 mL) finely chopped seedless cucumber, $1/2$ cup (125 mL) plain yogurt, and 2 tbsp (25 mL) chopped fresh mint, basil, chives or oregano. Season to taste with salt and freshly ground pepper. If desired, stir in a crushed small garlic clove. Makes 1 cup (250 mL). This sauce is excellent with asparagus, tomatoes and carrots.

CHÈVRE SAUCE

Combine $1/2$ cup (125 mL) chèvre with 2 tbsp (25 mL) sour cream in small saucepan; heat until cheese is almost melted. Stir in 1 chopped green onion and 1 small tomato, diced. Makes $1/2$ cup (125 mL). This is excellent with carrots, onions, leeks and zucchini.

MINT YOGURT SAUCE

Drain 1 cup (250 mL) plain yogurt for several hours. Stir thickened yogurt (sometimes called yogurt cheese) into chopped fresh mint and grated orange or lemon peel. Makes about $1/2$ cup (125 mL). Enjoy this sauce with carrots, asparagus, sweet peppers and fennel.

VEGETABLE KEBABS

Spit cooking of vegetables allows you to enjoy many different vegetables at one meal. In this recipe, the sauce supplies an interesting accent to summer vegetables.

VEGETABLES

1	large potato, cut into bite-size pieces	1
2	medium carrots, cut into bite-size pieces	2
1	medium onion, cut into wedges	1
1	medium zucchini, cut into bite-size pieces	1
1 cup	whole mushrooms	250 mL
4	metal or soaked wooden skewers	4

RUM SAUCE

3 tbsp	rum or 1 tsp (5 mL) rum extract	45 mL
2 tbsp	melted butter or margarine	25 mL
2	cloves garlic, crushed	2
¼ tsp	chili powder	1 mL
pinch	each: salt and freshly ground pepper	pinch

Tip: Wooden skewers are best soaked in water for at least 30 minutes before adding food to prevent them from scorching during grilling.

1. *For vegetables:* Partially cook potatoes, carrots and onion in boiling water for about 10 minutes or until barely tender; drain well. Cool slightly before arranging all vegetables alternately on soaked wooden skewers.

2. *For sauce:* Combine rum, butter, garlic and chili powder. Brush vegetables with mixture. Sprinkle lightly with salt and pepper.

3. Preheat grill on medium-high. Place skewers on oiled grill rack. Close lid and grill (use Direct Grilling, page 6) for about 20 minutes or until crisp and golden brown; turn several times. **Makes 4 servings.**

Thyme-scented Artichoke Kebabs

Grill bottled or canned artichokes on skewers for a vibrant vegetable accompaniment to many grilled meats. This way, all the "fuss and muss" of cooking raw artichokes is done for you.

2	cans (14 oz/398 mL) artichoke hearts, drained	2
2 tbsp	each: lemon juice and olive oil	25 mL
1 tbsp	minced fresh thyme or 1 tsp (5 mL) dried	15 mL
	Salt and freshly ground pepper	
	Fresh thyme sprigs	
18	cherry tomatoes (optional)	18
6	metal or soaked wooden skewers	6

1. Cut artichokes in half and place in a bowl. In a second bowl, combine lemon juice, oil, thyme and salt and pepper to taste. Pour over artichokes; toss well, cover and refrigerate for several hours to develop the flavors.

2. Drain artichokes; reserve marinade. Thread artichoke halves (alternating with tomatoes, if using) on metal or soaked wooden skewers; leave a small space between each piece.

3. Preheat grill on medium. Place kebabs on oiled grill rack. Close lid and cook (use Direct Grilling, page 6) for 12 minutes or until vegetables are lightly browned; turn and brush often with reserved marinade. **Makes 6 servings.**

Variation: If you choose to grill whole artichokes, I find it best to cook them beforehand (see directions on page 206). Then, lightly oil the artichoke and cook on preheated oiled grill rack (use Direct Grilling, page 6) until leaves have started to brown; turn frequently. (See photograph on page 34 of a whole artichoke grilled and served with Moroccan Lamb Chops, recipe on page 54.)

BASIL RATATOUILLE KEBABS

The flavors are similar to those of the traditional ratatouille of Provence, but this recipe takes some liberties by grilling the vegetables rather than cooking them in a skillet. Bon appétit!

1	small eggplant, halved lengthwise, peeled and cut into 1/2-inch (1 cm) slices	1
1	medium yellow squash, cut into thick slices	1
1	medium sweet red pepper, cut into square pieces	1
1	small onion, cut into 4 wedges	1
1/4 cup	loosely packed fresh basil leaves, chopped	50 mL
2 tbsp	lemon juice	25 mL
2 tsp	olive oil	10 mL
1/4 tsp	each: salt and freshly ground pepper	1 mL
2	medium tomatoes, quartered	2

1. In large resealable bag, place eggplant, squash, red pepper, onion, basil, lemon juice, oil, salt and pepper. Seal bag, shake contents to coat vegetables, and allow to marinate for about 1 hour. Remove vegetables from bag; reserve marinade. Thread vegetables alternately with tomatoes on metal or soaked wooden skewers.

2. Preheat grill on medium-high. Place kebabs on oiled grill rack. Close lid and cook (use Direct Grilling, page 6) for 7 minutes per side, basting occasionally with reserved marinade. **Makes 4 servings.**

ZUCCHINI FINGERS

Similar to French-fried zucchini, these fingers are easier to make and just as tasty. They're lower in fat too!

1/2 cup	unseasoned dried bread crumbs	125 mL
3 tbsp	grated Parmesan cheese	45 mL
2	medium zucchini, cut in 1- x 4-inch (2.5 x 10 cm) strips	2
1/2 cup	bottled creamy herb salad dressing	125 mL
	Fresh parsley sprigs	

1. In small bowl, combine bread crumbs with cheese. Dip zucchini strips into salad dressing, then coat with bread crumb mixture.

2. Preheat grill on medium. Place zucchini on oiled grill rack. Close lid and cook (use Direct Grilling, page 6) for about 10 minutes per side or until crisp and golden. **Makes 4 servings.**

Variation: Coat Zucchini Fingers beforehand and refrigerate until ready to grill. Yellow squash, thickly sliced onions and eggplant slices can also be grilled this way.

GARLIC AND LEMON BROCCOLI

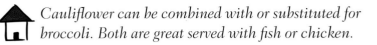

Cauliflower can be combined with or substituted for broccoli. Both are great served with fish or chicken.

1½ lb	broccoli, cut into spears	750 g
2	medium cloves garlic, minced	2
¼ cup	olive or canola oil	50 mL
8	lemon slices	8
	Salt and freshly ground pepper	

1. Bring a large amount of water to a boil. Add broccoli and blanch for 2 minutes or until bright green and almost tender. Drain and refresh broccoli in cold water to stop cooking; pat dry. Combine garlic and oil.

2. Preheat indoor grill on high for 5 minutes. Brush broccoli with some of the garlic oil. Place broccoli on lightly oiled grill rack. Grill for about 10 minutes or until broccoli is tender and lightly tinged with brown; turn occasionally and brush with oil. During last 2 minutes, add lemon slices to grill; brush with oil and cook until warm. Season to taste with salt and pepper. Serve lemon slices with broccoli. **Makes 4 servings.**

For Outdoor Grilling:

Follow procedure as above for Step 1.

Step 2: Preheat grill on medium–high. Place broccoli on lightly oiled grill rack or use a grill basket to keep vegetables from falling through the grill. Close lid and grill (use Direct Grilling page 6) for about 5 minutes or until broccoli is tender and lightly tinged with brown; turn occasionally and brush with oil. During last 2 minutes, add lemon slices to grill; brush with oil and cook until warm. Season to taste with salt and pepper. Serve lemon slices with broccoli.

EGGPLANT WITH ANCHOVY-PARSLEY SAUCE

Thin lengthwise slices of eggplant are grilled, rolled and served with a fabulous anchovy sauce.

2	large eggplants	2
	Salt	
2 tbsp	olive oil, divided	25 mL

ANCHOVY-PARSLEY SAUCE

1/4 cup	finely chopped onion	50 mL
6	large cloves garlic, diced	6
1/2 cup	red wine	125 mL
2 tbsp	each: anchovy paste and drained, washed capers	25 mL
1/4 cup	chopped fresh parsley	50 mL
1/4 tsp	freshly ground pepper	1 mL

1. Trim eggplants; slice lengthwise into 1/2-inch (1 cm) thick strips. Lightly sprinkle with salt, let stand for 30 minutes. Remove resulting moisture with paper toweling.

2. Preheat grill on medium-high. Place eggplant on oiled grill rack and brush lightly with olive oil. Close lid and cook (use Direct Grilling, page 6) for several minutes per side or until golden brown. Remove and roll each slice into a cylinder; keep warm.

3. *For sauce:* Meanwhile, in nonstick skillet, heat remaining oil on medium heat. Cook onion and garlic for 1 minute; add wine, anchovy paste and capers. Cook until heated and slightly thickened. Stir in parsley and pepper.

4. Serve several slices of eggplant on each plate with a small amount of sauce. **Makes 4 servings.**

GRILLED RED AND WHITE ONIONS

The aromatic pine flavors of rosemary and the sweet pungency of balsamic vinegar blend with the humble onion to create a rather exotic vegetable — excellent with grilled meats and poultry.

2 tbsp	balsamic vinegar	25 mL
2 tsp	chopped fresh rosemary or 1/2 tsp (2 mL) dried	10 mL
2	large red onions	2
2	large Vidalia or Spanish onions	2
1 tbsp	olive oil	15 mL
1/2 cup	chopped fresh parsley	125 mL
	Salt and freshly ground pepper	

1. In small saucepan, heat vinegar and rosemary over low heat until warm (do not boil). Remove pan from heat, cover and let mixture stand for 20 minutes.

2. Peel onions and slice crosswise into 3/4-inch (2 cm) thick slices.

3. Preheat grill on medium-high. Brush both sides of onions lightly with oil. Place onions in single layer on oiled grill rack, keeping slices intact. Cook onions in batches on uncovered grill (use Direct Grilling, page 6) for about 5 minutes on each side, or until softened and grill marks appear. Transfer onions when tender to large bowl; separate into rings.

4. Toss onions with vinegar mixture, parsley and salt and pepper to taste. Serve warm or at room temperature. **Makes 6 servings.**

SWEET POTATOES WITH CARROTS AND TURNIP

What could be more delectable than caramelized vegetables — sweet potatoes, carrots, turnips and chopped onion, flavored with orange. This recipe is a "gourmet" choice to cook, and so very easy.

2	medium sweet potatoes, peeled and thickly sliced	2
2	large carrots, sliced lengthwise	2
2	small white turnips, sliced	2
¼ cup	finely chopped onion	50 mL

ORANGE MARINADE

2	oranges: juice and long shreds of zest	2
3 tbsp	each: liquid honey and dark rum	45 mL
1 tsp	dried thyme or 1 tbsp (15 mL) chopped fresh	5 mL
	Salt and freshly ground pepper	
12	pitted prunes	12

Suggested Menu: Chicken on a Spit with Chardonnay Glaze (page 163) is an excellent choice to serve with these vegetables.

1. In large saucepan, bring water to a boil. Cook sweet potatoes, carrots, turnip and onion just until tender; drain well and place in large bowl.

2. *For marinade:* In small dish, combine orange juice and zest, honey, rum and thyme. Pour over vegetables and toss to coat.

3. Preheat grill on medium-high. Place vegetables on oiled grill rack or in grill basket; sprinkle with salt and pepper. Close lid and cook (use Direct Grilling, page 6) for about 12 minutes or until vegetables are starting to become golden; brush occasionally with orange mixture and turn once. Top with prunes when vegetables are turned. **Makes 6 servings.**

HERB-STUFFED MUSHROOMS

Herbes de Provence enhance the flavor of grilled mushrooms in this unique stuffed treatment of mushrooms.

¼ cup	dry white wine or sherry	50 mL
1 tbsp	chicken bouillon granules	15 mL
24	large mushrooms	24
¼ cup	finely chopped onion	50 mL
2 tbsp	olive oil, divided	25 mL
⅓ cup	fine dried bread crumbs	75 mL
½ to 1 tsp	herbes de Provence (see page 50)	2 to 5 mL
	Fresh parsley sprigs	
	Metal or soaked wooden skewers	

1. In microwaveable container, heat wine and bouillon on high (100%) until bouillon dissolves.

2. Remove mushroom stems; chop finely. In nonstick skillet, sauté stems and onion in 1 tbsp (15 mL) oil. Remove from heat; add wine mixture, bread crumbs and herbs; mix well.

3. Fit two mushroom caps together with some stuffing between them. Place 2 or 3 pairs on short soaked wooden or metal skewers.

4. Preheat grill on medium. Place kebabs on oiled grill rack; close lid and cook (use Direct Grilling, page 6) for 3 to 5 minutes, brushing with remaining olive oil. **Makes 12 double mushrooms, 4 to 6 side servings.**

Suggested Menu: Serve these mushrooms with any grilled beef, pork, poultry, venison or fish.

Tip: Assemble beforehand, refrigerate, then grill just before serving.

TARRAGON GRILLED SHIITAKE MUSHROOMS

The size, meaty flesh and full-bodied flavor of shiitake mushrooms make them ideal for grilling. Tahini, a thick paste made of ground sesame seeds, is frequently used in Middle Eastern cooking and is readily available at most supermarkets. Add the sesame taste of tahini for mushroom magic!

TAHINI BASTE

2 tbsp	each: water and tahini	25 mL
1 tbsp	each: lemon juice and soy sauce	15 mL
1 tbsp	chopped fresh gingerroot	15 mL
2 tsp	granulated sugar	10 mL
1	clove garlic, crushed	1
pinch	crushed red pepper flakes	pinch
8	large shiitake mushrooms	8
3 tbsp	dry sherry	45 mL
1 tsp	sesame oil	5 mL
	Fresh tarragon	

1. *For baste:* In bowl, combine water, tahini, lemon juice, soy sauce, gingerroot, sugar, garlic and pepper flakes; reserve.

2. Clean mushrooms (do not peel) and pat dry. In medium bowl, toss mushrooms with sherry and sesame oil. Cover and let stand for 30 minutes.

3. Preheat grill on medium. Place mushrooms on lightly oiled grill rack; close lid and cook (use Direct Grilling, page 6) for about 10 minutes or until golden brown; turn and brush often with reserved baste. Garnish with tarragon and serve. **Makes 4 servings.**

CORN-STUFFED RAINBOW PEPPERS

These pepper halves can be made beforehand, refrigerated and then grilled with the meat course. Since sweet peppers welcome almost any savory stuffing, rice or even couscous can be used instead of corn for a great alternative.

2	medium red, yellow, green or orange sweet peppers	2
	Canola oil	
1	small onion, finely chopped	1
2 tbsp	butter or margarine	25 mL
1 cup	fresh or frozen corn kernels	250 mL
½ cup	shredded Monterey Jack cheese	125 mL
1 tbsp	each: finely chopped fresh parsley, chives and basil or 1 tsp (5 mL) dried	15 mL
	Salt and freshly ground pepper	
	Fresh parsley, chives or basil	

1. Remove stem end from peppers, halve lengthwise and remove seeds. Lightly brush peppers with oil; set aside.

2. In small skillet, sauté onion in butter for 5 minutes. Remove to bowl; stir in corn, cheese, herbs and salt and pepper to taste. Divide mixture between pepper halves.

3. Preheat grill on medium. Place pepper halves, filling side up, on oiled grill rack. Close lid and cook (use Direct Grilling, page 6) for about 12 minutes or until peppers are softened and cheese is melted. Serve warm or at room temperature with a garnish of fresh herbs. **Makes 4 servings, ½ pepper per serving.**

GRILLED MEDITERRANEAN VEGETABLES

Reminiscent of Spain, southern France or Italy, this vegetable assortment is ideal for a North American backyard dinner. Grilling the vegetables in a grilling basket saves the trouble of turning each piece individually. The result is a perfectly cooked assortment of the garden's best. Any leftovers make a great veggie sandwich.

3	small Italian eggplants or 1 large eggplant, sliced diagonally ½-inch (1 cm) thick	3
2	small sweet red, green or yellow peppers, seeded and sliced into wide strips	2
3	small green or yellow zucchini, sliced ¾-inch (2 cm) thick	3
6	large mushrooms, halved	6
¼ cup	chopped fresh basil	50 mL
¼ cup	each: olive oil and lemon juice	50 mL
2	cloves garlic, minced	2
	Salt and freshly ground pepper	
	Chopped fresh basil	

1. Combine prepared vegetables in a large resealable plastic bag or shallow container.

2. Whisk together basil, oil, lemon juice, garlic, salt and pepper. Pour over vegetables; mix well. Cover and refrigerate for at least one hour.

3. Preheat grill on medium-high 400°F (200°C). Place vegetables directly on grill rack or in basket. Close lid and grill (use Direct Grilling, page 6) for 2 to 3 minutes per side or until vegetables reach desired doneness. Brush occasionally with extra marinade. Each vegetable will vary in amount of time needed.

4. Arrange on large serving plate, sprinkle with fresh basil just before serving. **Makes about 6 servings.**

GRILLED CORN ON THE COB WITH HERB BUTTER

It's summer, and the eating is great! Succulent corn every night of the week. That's what many people want. Place foil-wrapped corn alongside when grilling other foods.

8	fresh cobs of corn, husked and silk removed	8
2 tbsp	finely chopped fresh herbs — tarragon, thyme, basil and cilantro or chives	25 mL
1/8 tsp	salt and freshly ground pepper	0.5 mL
1/4 cup	melted butter or margarine	50 mL

Tip: Since steam builds up inside the foil packages, they will be very hot. Take care when opening.

1. Place each cob of corn on a piece of heavy-duty foil. In small bowl, combine fresh herbs, salt, pepper and melted butter. Brush lightly over each cob. Wrap corn securely in foil.

2. Preheat grill on medium. Place corn on grill rack; close lid and cook (use Direct Grilling, page 6) for about 20 minutes or until corn is tender; turn often. **Makes 8 servings, 1 cob each, or 4 servings, 2 cobs each.**

ORANGE-SAUCED ROASTED BEETS

Roasted beets develop a much mellower flavor than when boiled. Try this one in the oven when the weather is cold, and on the grill in grilling season. These citrus roasted beets are wonderful served with Pungent Pork Tenderloin Medallions (page 62).

8	medium beets, peeled and sliced	8
1 tbsp	olive oil	15 mL
2 tsp	red wine vinegar	10 mL
	Salt and freshly ground pepper	
1/3 cup	light sour cream	75 mL
	Zest and juice of 1 orange	

1. Place beet slices in overlapping layers on large square of heavy aluminum foil. Drizzle with oil and vinegar; sprinkle with salt and pepper to taste.

2. Preheat grill on medium-high 400°F (200°C). Place foil package on grill rack and cook (use Indirect Grilling, page 6) for about 1 hour or until beets are tender; turn occasionally. Open package and turn into serving bowl.

3. Combine sour cream, orange juice and zest. Serve with roasted beets. **Makes 6 servings.**

Grilling Tip: If one foil package is too bulky, divide beets into 2 or more packages. They will also cook faster.

GRILLED BEETS IN BALSAMIC VINEGAR

Beets marinated in this wonderful sauce are divine. They are a colorful and flavorful alternative to your usual veggies. Because they cook slowly on the grill, they can cook on one side of the grill rack while any large cut of meat is being grilled by indirect grilling on the other side.

4–6	medium beets	4–6
2 tbsp	balsamic vinegar	25 mL
2 tbsp	canola or olive oil	25 mL
1	clove garlic, crushed	1
1/4 tsp	salt	1 mL
pinch	freshly ground pepper	pinch

1. Precook beets in boiling water for about 10 minutes. Drain and cool under cold water. Peel and cut into wedges or slices; place in a shallow foil or metal pan.

2. Combine vinegar, oil, garlic, salt and pepper. Pour over beets; cover pan tightly with aluminum foil.

3. Preheat grill to medium-low (about 300°F/160°C). Place pan on grill (use Indirect Grilling, see page 6). Close lid and cook for about 1 1/2 hours, keeping temperature as close to medium-low as possible. Check every 30 minutes for tenderness and that sufficient liquid remains, adding a small amount of water if necessary. **Makes 6 servings.**

GRILLED BASIL TOMATOES

When summer's vast multitude of "the star of the garden" appears, we find as many ways as possible to eat them. This recipe is a favorite. Serve it as a vegetable side dish or as a quick appetizer while guests or family are waiting for slower-cooking grilled meat dishes.

4	large ripe tomatoes	4
2 tbsp	chopped fresh basil or 2 tsp (10 mL) dried	25 mL
1	small clove garlic, minced	1
1 to 2 tsp	olive oil	5 to 10 mL
1 tsp	lemon juice	5 mL
	Salt and freshly ground pepper	
1 cup	plain (4% M.F.) or Greek-style yogurt (optional)	250 mL

1. Cut ½ inch (1 cm) off stem end of tomatoes and remove core. Sprinkle with basil, garlic, oil, lemon juice, and salt and pepper to taste.

2. Preheat grill on high. Place tomatoes on oiled grill rack. Close lid and cook (use Direct Grilling, page 6) for about 10 minutes or until tender and warm throughout.

3. Serve with yogurt, if using. **Makes 4 servings.**

SLOW-ROASTED TOMATOES

When you yield to temptation at the farmers' market, or have far too many tomatoes ripening at the same time in your garden, remember how wonderful roasted tomatoes taste during the winter. They are always ideal for bruschetta, over cooked pasta or served at room temperature directly from the grill.

4 lb	plum tomatoes, halved lengthwise (9 to 10 large)	2 kg
6	garlic cloves, thinly sliced	6
⅓ cup	olive oil	75 mL
½ to 1 tsp	salt	2 to 5 mL
	Freshly ground pepper	

1. Slice tomatoes lengthwise in half (or if large, in quarters). Toss tomatoes with oil and garlic. Place cut side up on shallow baking pan. Sprinkle with salt and pepper.

2. Preheat grill on medium-low (about 300°F/160°C). Place tomatoes on one side of grill. Close lid and slow-roast them at about 250°F (120°C) (use Indirect Grilling, page 6) for 2 to 3 hours or until tomatoes have reached that mellow, soft texture but have not lost their shape. **Makes about 20 halved or 40 quartered tomatoes.**

CHAPTER 8

SIDES AND ALL THOSE EXTRAS

◄ *Black Olive, Rice and Spinach Salad (page 203)*

Smoky-sweet salads, pasta possibilities and greens galore, all make wonderful accompaniments to the book's many grilled entrées. Some are hot, some are cold, and all are delicious!

I am sure you'll love the elegant Grilled Beet and Minted Orange Salad (page 202). Grilled red onions in combination with Belgian endive, mixed salad greens and olive oil, with pungently sweet balsamic vinegar (page 204) will, I trust, become as popular in your home as mine. However, not all of the recipes in this chapter are grilled and hence can be made ahead to simplify the final meal assembly. In fact, it's nice for the chef to have a few stovetop and refrigerator dishes at the ready to arrive at the table. Leftover grilled vegetables from dinner will come in handy for an Open-face Grilled Vegetable Sandwich (page 221).

Two truly summer salads, Mexican Corn and Grilled Rosemary Potato Salad (pages 216 and 213) and a marvelous Barley Risotto with Vegetables (page 200), all provide the starch element so enjoyable served with grilled meat, poultry or fish.

Baking in foil comes into its own here when cooking potatoes on the grill. Foods baked in foil packages retain the maximum natural moisture and flavor. Prepared in advance, they once again assist with some of the last-minute work before dinnertime. When arranging foods in foil, arrange them so they do not overlap and they will cook more evenly.

And as an added bonus, I couldn't resist a few favorites: homemade salad dressings — a creamy buttermilk one and a poppy seed vinaigrette. Plus Classic Coleslaw (page 217) is absolutely essential to serve with Southern-style Pulled Pork (page 64). You would be hard-pressed to purchase better!

When it comes to preparing assorted green tossed salads, ever think of using some of the new leafy greens? For example, escarole, Belgian endive, romaine, radicchio and that wonderful peppery arugula which does so much to pep up an ordinary lettuce salad. Soft, crunchy, sweet or bitter — they all add their own delicious flavors.

Spicy Orange-stuffed Sweet Potatoes

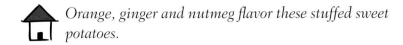

Orange, ginger and nutmeg flavor these stuffed sweet potatoes.

6	unpeeled medium sweet potatoes	6
1/2 cup	orange juice	125 mL
3 tbsp	butter or margarine	45 mL
1 tsp	each: grated orange peel and salt	5 mL
1/2 tsp	each: ground ginger and nutmeg	2 mL
pinch	freshly ground pepper	pinch
1/2 cup	chopped pecans	125 mL

1. In a medium saucepan, parboil potatoes in boiling water until almost tender. When cool enough to handle, cut each potato in half; carefully remove pulp from shell. Mash pulp and combine with orange juice, butter, orange peel, salt, ginger, nutmeg and pepper. Stuff potato shells with mixture; divide pecans evenly over the top.

2. Preheat indoor grill on high for 5 minutes. Place potatoes on lightly oiled grill rack; reduce heat to medium. Cover loosely with foil and cook for about 15 minutes or until potatoes are hot. **Makes 6 servings.**

For Outdoor Grilling:

Follow procedure as above for Step 1.

Step 2: Preheat grill on medium. Place potatoes on lightly oiled grill rack. Close lid and grill (use Direct Grilling, page 6) for about 15 minutes or until potatoes are hot.

Tip: A cover of aluminum foil resembles the closing of the outdoor grill lid and helps to cook the food faster. In the case of the indoor grill, it also helps keep the top of the food warm while the bottom is in direct contact with the hot grill.

Double Cheese-topped Potatoes

Chèvre and Stilton or Gorgonzola cheeses top grilled potatoes in this easy-to-do recipe.

6	small baking potatoes	6
1 tbsp	olive oil	15 mL
	Salt and freshly ground pepper	
1	roll (5 oz/140 g) creamy chèvre (about 1/2 cup/ 125 mL)	1
1/2 cup	crumbled Stilton or Gorgonzola cheese	125 mL
	Fresh parsley sprigs	

1. Cut each potato in half lengthwise. Brush cut side with olive oil; sprinkle lightly with salt and pepper.

2. Preheat grill on medium. Place potatoes, cut side down on oiled grill rack; close lid and cook (use Indirect Grilling, page 6) for about 45 minutes or until potatoes are tender; turn once.

3. Meanwhile, stir cheeses together until almost smooth. Turn potatoes, cut side up, during last 5 minutes; top with a small amount of cheese mixture; close lid and cook briefly until cheese has started to melt. Remove from grill, garnish with parsley and serve. **Makes 6 servings.**

ORZO SPINACH PILAF

Orzo, a rice shaped pasta, is an interesting replacement for rice in this spinach pilaf.

1	bag (10 oz/300 g) spinach, trimmed and washed or 1 pkg (10 oz/300 g) frozen chopped spinach, thawed	1
	Salt and freshly ground pepper	
2 cups	orzo	500 mL
1 tbsp	olive oil	15 mL
3	cloves garlic, thinly sliced	3
½ cup	finely chopped onion	125 mL
1 cup	sliced mushrooms	250 mL
1	medium zucchini, diagonally sliced into 12 pieces	1
1	medium sweet red pepper, seeded and cut into large dice	1
	Freshly grated Parmesan cheese	

1. In large saucepan, cook spinach with water that remains on leaves after washing, until wilted but bright green; or, cook frozen spinach according to package directions; drain well. Season to taste with salt and pepper.

2. In food processor or blender, purée spinach until almost smooth. Spoon ½ cup (125 mL) spinach purée into large bowl; reserve remaining purée for another use (one package of spinach provides enough purée to double this recipe or to make it again).

3. In large saucepan, cook orzo in boiling water for about 10 minutes or until al dente (tender but still firm). Drain well and stir into spinach.

4. Meanwhile, in large nonstick skillet, heat oil on medium-high. Add garlic and onion; cook for 5 minutes. Add mushrooms, zucchini and red pepper; cook, stirring often, for 10 minutes or until vegetables are tender. Stir into orzo-spinach mixture and toss to combine.

5. Serve sprinkled with Parmesan cheese. **Makes 6 servings.**

Suggested Menu: Serve with Grouper with Gazpacho Sauce (page 129).

Variation: Toss orzo pasta with olive oil and some chopped sun–dried tomatoes for an excellent side dish with grilled chicken or beef.

PINE NUT COUSCOUS

Couscous comes to us from Morocco, Tunisia and Algeria. It is made from 100% natural durum wheat semolina. Easy as instant rice to prepare, and versatile either hot or cold, it's a wonderful alternative to rice, potatoes and pastas.

2	green onions, sliced	2
2	cloves garlic, minced	2
1 tbsp	olive oil	15 mL
1 cup	boiling water	250 mL
1 tsp	instant chicken bouillon granules (1 small pouch)	5 mL
1 cup	dry couscous	250 mL
¼ tsp	freshly ground pepper	1 mL
¼ cup	toasted pine nuts	50 mL

1. In medium saucepan, sauté onions and garlic in oil for 5 minutes. Add boiling water and bouillon granules; return to boil. Remove from heat; stir in couscous, cover and let stand for 5 minutes. Season to taste with pepper and fluff with a fork. Sprinkle with pine nuts and serve. **Makes 4 servings.**

Suggested Menu: Middle Eastern Lamb Kebabs (page 151) with Pine Nut Couscous make excellent dining, and Cucumber Raita (page 85) adds a special touch.

Tip: To heat couscous when other foods are being grilled, place prepared couscous on a large piece of heavy-duty foil; do not add nuts when cooking couscous on the grill. Close foil to make a secure package. Place foil package on grill rack for 8 to 10 minutes on medium–high; turn frequently. Open package and sprinkle with pine nuts before serving.

Variation: Turn this recipe into a marvelous salad by replacing the pine nuts with halved grapes and tossing cold couscous with a small amount of mayonnaise.

BARLEY RISOTTO WITH VEGETABLES

Barley stands in for rice in this excellent version of risotto.

1 tbsp	canola or olive oil	15 mL
3	green onions, finely chopped	3
1	clove garlic, sliced	1
½ cup	grated carrot	125 mL
½ cup	chopped sweet red pepper	125 mL
½ cup	pearl barley	125 mL
2 cups	chicken broth	500 mL
pinch	freshly ground black pepper	pinch

1. Heat oil over medium heat in saucepan. Reserve 2 tbsp (25 mL) onion as a garnish. Add remaining onion and garlic to oil; sauté for 5 minutes or until soft. Add carrot and red pepper; sauté for 3 minutes. Add barley and cook for 1 minute; stir well.

2. Add broth, bring to a boil, reduce heat to low, cover and cook for 40 minutes or until barley is tender. Check to make sure there is still liquid. If necessary, add a small amount of water. Season with pepper, garnish with green onion and serve. **Makes 3 cups (750 mL).**

GRILLED PORTOBELLO MUSHROOMS

This recipe makes a perfect accompaniment to many grilled meats. Our daughter-in-law, Rachel, served this as a side dish for Spit-roasted Marinated Elk to everyone's enjoyment.

4	portobello mushroom caps	4
2 tbsp	each: balsamic vinegar and olive or canola oil	25 mL
1	clove garlic, minced	1
¼ tsp	each: salt and freshly ground pepper	1 mL
½ cup	crumbled blue cheese	125 mL

EXTRAS

Balsamic Onion Confit (page 18) and apricot chutney, optional

1. Place mushroom caps in a shallow dish. Combine vinegar, oil and garlic. Drizzle over caps; let stand for about 15 minutes. Sprinkle lightly with salt and pepper. Divide cheese over each mushroom.

2. If using, top the mushrooms with a dab each of: Balsamic Onion Confit and chutney.

3. Preheat grill on medium-high. Place mushrooms on lightly oiled grill rack and grill (use Direct Grilling, page 6) for 12 minutes or until hot and cheese is melted. **Makes 4 servings.**

 Wine: A red Gamay will offer a superb flavor combination with mushrooms.

POTATOES & ONIONS IN A POUCH

Grilling potatoes and onions together in a foil package gives us an interesting two-vegetable accompaniment for beef or poultry dishes.

1	large Vidalia onion, peeled and thickly sliced	1
2	medium white or sweet potatoes, peeled and thickly sliced	2
2	cloves garlic, minced	2
	Salt and freshly ground pepper	
2 tbsp	melted butter or margarine	25 mL
	Chopped fresh parsley	

1. Place overlapping slices of onion and potato on a large sheet of heavy-duty foil. Sprinkle with minced garlic and season lightly with salt and pepper; drizzle with melted butter. Fold foil edges together to form tight seal.

2. Preheat grill on medium. Place foil package on grill rack; close lid and cook (use Direct Grilling, page 6) for about 30 minutes, or until vegetables are tender and starting to turn golden brown; turn often.

3. Open package, sprinkle with chopped parsley and serve. **Makes 3 to 4 servings.**

LINGUINE, ARUGULA AND ROMANO CHEESE

Arugula, briefly sautéed to tame its peppery bite, is tossed with cooked pasta and grated cheese to create this exciting pasta dish.

1	pkg (1 lb/454 g) whole wheat linguine	1
3 tbsp	olive oil, divided	45 mL
3	large cloves garlic, minced	3
¼ tsp	hot red chili pepper	1 mL
8 cups	torn arugula	2 L
¼ cup	grated Romano cheese	50 mL
	Salt and freshly ground pepper to taste	

1. In large saucepan, cook linguine in boiling water for 9 minutes or until al dente (tender, but still firm). Drain well and return to saucepan to keep warm.

2. Meanwhile, heat 2 tbsp (25 mL) oil in large nonstick skillet. Add garlic and chili pepper; sauté for about 15 seconds or until fragrant. Add arugula; sauté for about 2 minutes or until wilted.

3. Add arugula, cheese and remaining oil to the pasta; toss to combine. Season to taste with salt and pepper. **Makes 4 servings.**

GRILLED BEET AND MINTED ORANGE SALAD

This colorful salad is the perfect accompaniment to a grilled lamb or chicken recipe.

2	large oranges	2
1½ cups	Grilled Beets in Balsamic Vinegar (page 192)	375 mL
½	medium red onion, thinly sliced	½

VINAIGRETTE

¼ cup	fresh orange juice	50 mL
2 tbsp	olive oil	25 mL
¼ tsp	salt	1 mL
pinch	freshly ground pepper	pinch
2 tbsp	chopped fresh mint	25 mL

1. Grate a small amount of orange peel; set aside. Remove skin and white pith from oranges. Thinly slice each orange.

2. On a serving platter, alternately arrange orange slices, beets and onion.

3. *For vinaigrette:* Whisk together orange juice, oil, reserved orange peel, salt and pepper. Drizzle salad with vinaigrette and sprinkle with chopped mint. **Makes 6 servings.**

WILD RICE, RAISIN AND APPLE CASSEROLE

The unique nutty flavor of wild rice makes this casserole the perfectly elegant accompaniment to Venison Kebabs with Cranberry Gravy (page 156) or any grilled poultry.

¾ cup	uncooked wild rice	175 mL
2	bay leaves	2
3 tbsp	butter or margarine	45 mL
½ cup	each: chopped celery and onion	125 mL
2	medium unpeeled tart apples, cored and chopped	2
½ cup	golden raisins	125 mL
1 tsp	each: dried sage, dried thyme and salt	5 mL
¼ tsp	freshly ground pepper	1 mL

1. Wash wild rice thoroughly under cold running water. In medium saucepan, bring 4 cups (1 L) water to a boil. Add wild rice and bay leaves, reduce heat, cover and cook gently for 45 minutes or until rice is tender; drain and discard bay leaves.

2. In large nonstick skillet, melt butter on medium-high; cook celery and onion for 5 minutes or until softened; stir into rice. Add apples, raisins, sage, thyme, salt and pepper. Heat to serving temperature. **Makes 6 servings.**

BLACK OLIVE, RICE AND SPINACH SALAD

Rice with bits of red peppers and green onions on a bed of spinach, garnished with black olives, makes a handsome salad. A generous splash of fresh lemon juice gives it a fresh and vibrant taste.

LEMON-DIJON VINAIGRETTE

3 tbsp	fresh lemon juice	45 mL
1 tbsp	Dijon mustard	15 mL
1 tsp	each: grated lemon peel and minced garlic	5 mL
¼ cup	extra virgin olive oil	50 mL

SALAD

1½ cups	cooked white or brown rice (about ½ cup/125 mL raw)	375 mL
½ cup	diced sweet red pepper	125 mL
2	green onions, thinly sliced	2
1	bunch fresh spinach, trimmed and torn into bite size pieces	1
½ cup	pitted kalamata olives	125 mL
	Paprika, salt and freshly ground pepper	

1. *For vinaigrette:* In a large bowl, whisk together lemon juice, mustard, peel, garlic and olive oil until thick and smooth.

2. *For salad:* Stir rice, red pepper and onions into vinaigrette; cover and refrigerate until ready to serve.

3. At serving time, slice 1 cup (250 mL) packed spinach into long shreds, stir into rice mixture. Arrange remaining spinach on a large serving platter. Top with rice mixture and olives; sprinkle with paprika, salt and pepper and serve. **Makes 6 servings.**

Suggested Menu: Serve with grilled chicken, Chicken on a Spit with Chardonnay Glaze (page 163) or grilled pork or beef.

GRILLED RED ONION ENDIVE SALAD

Onions are cooked on the grill and then combined with chilled salad greens to toss with this splendid balsamic vinaigrette.

ONIONS

3	large red onions, thickly sliced in rounds	3
1 tbsp	extra virgin olive oil	15 mL

SALAD

3	large Belgian endives, cut crosswise in ½-inch (1 cm) slices	3
2 cups	mixed salad greens or mesclun	500 mL
1	bunch arugula, torn	1
1	bunch watercress, stems removed	1

VINAIGRETTE

1 tsp	cumin seeds	5 mL
¼ cup	extra virgin olive oil	50 mL
3 tbsp	balsamic vinegar	45 mL
1 tsp	liquid honey	5 mL
	Salt and freshly ground pepper	

1. *For onions:* Toss onions with oil and place in a shallow foil or metal pan. Preheat grill on medium. Place pan on grill rack. Close lid and cook (use Direct Grilling, page 6) for about 15 minutes or until browned and crisp; stir occasionally. Remove and keep warm.

2. *For salad:* In a large bowl, toss endive with mixed greens, arugula and watercress. Cover and chill until serving time.

3. *For vinaigrette:* In a nonstick skillet, toast cumin seeds over medium-high heat until browned. Whisk together oil, vinegar, honey, salt and pepper to taste; add cumin seeds. Toss vinaigrette with salad greens. Serve salad on individual plates, topping each with reserved warm grilled onions. **Makes 8 servings.**

Suggested Menu: Always a favorite salad with Stuffed Rainbow Trout with Dill Sauce (page 118).

GREENS WITH PORT VINAIGRETTE

Port Wine Vinaigrette is especially versatile. While it is used as a salad vinaigrette here, it also doubles as a beef marinade.

PORT WINE VINAIGRETTE

1/3 cup	port wine	75 mL
3 tbsp	extra virgin olive oil	45 mL
2 tbsp	balsamic vinegar	25 mL
1 tbsp	Dijon mustard	15 mL
1 1/2 tsp	dried basil or 2 tbsp (25 mL) chopped fresh	7 mL
1/2 tsp	each: salt, freshly ground pepper and granulated sugar	2 mL

SALAD

8 cups	assorted greens — arugula, red leaf lettuce, romaine	2 L
2 cups	mesclun	500 mL
	Red onion slices, strips of sweet green and red pepper and bean sprouts	

1. *For vinaigrette:* Combine port, oil, vinegar, mustard, basil, salt, pepper and sugar; set aside.

2. *For salad:* Place assorted greens in large salad bowl. Toss gently with enough vinaigrette to lightly dress them.

3. Arrange dressed greens on 6 to 8 salad plates. Top each with mesclun, red onion, green and red pepper and bean sprouts. **Makes 6 to 8 servings.**

Variation: Here's how to prepare the recipe if you decide to use the vinaigrette as a marinade for beef.

1. Trim and discard excess fat from 2 to 3 lb (1 to 1.5 kg) beef tenderloin. Place beef in resealable plastic bag; pour vinaigrette over. Cover and refrigerate for 6 hours or overnight; turn beef occasionally. Remove beef from vinaigrette; place vinaigrette in small saucepan, bring to a boil, reduce heat and cook for 5 minutes; keep warm.

2. Preheat grill on high. Place beef in center of oiled grill rack; sear all sides until grill marks appear. Close lid, reduce heat to medium–low and grill (use Indirect Grilling, page 6) to desired stage of doneness (see chart on page 8); baste occasionally with warm marinade.

3. Remove meat to cutting board and cover with foil; allow to stand for 10 minutes before carving. Cut strings, carve meat and serve slices with salad.

 Wines: Pair with a big Grenache Syrah Mourvedre or an Amarone.

ARTICHOKE SALAD

Artichokes, peppers, tomatoes and an olive oil vinaigrette make an irresistibly easy salad to accompany a grilled meal. Olive oil, one of the world's most ancient foods, is enjoying a renaissance.

2	cans (14 oz/398 mL) artichoke hearts or 4 fresh medium artichokes	2

OLIVE OIL HERB VINAIGRETTE

1 cup	packed fresh parsley leaves	250 mL
½ cup	thinly sliced green onions or chives	125 mL
¼ cup	extra virgin olive oil	50 mL
2 tbsp	red wine vinegar	25 mL
1 tbsp	Dijon mustard	15 mL
4 tsp	lemon juice	20 mL
	Salt and freshly ground pepper	
	Red leaf lettuce	
½	sweet yellow pepper, cubed	½
1	large tomato, sliced	1

1. Drain artichoke hearts and cut into quarters. (If using fresh artichokes, see below.)

2. *For vinaigrette:* In food processor or blender container, process parsley and onions until finely chopped. Add oil, vinegar, mustard and lemon juice. Process until all ingredients are smooth. Season to taste with salt and pepper.

3. Arrange lettuce on serving plate; place artichoke hearts on lettuce. Add yellow pepper and tomato. Drizzle some of the vinaigrette over everything. Chill until serving time or serve at room temperature if desired. **Makes 6 servings and ¾ cup (175 mL) vinaigrette.**

Tip: Here's how to prepare fresh artichokes.

1. Bring a large saucepan with water to a boil. Remove and discard tough lower layers of leaves from artichokes until pale inner leaves are reached. Slice one-third off the top. Using scissors, snip off the sharp, thorny end of the remaining leaves. Cut stem to about 1 inch (2.5 cm).

2. Drop artichokes into boiling water to cover. Add 2 tsp (10 mL) olive oil, 4 tsp (20 mL) red wine vinegar, 2 large cloves garlic, 1 bay leaf and 10 peppercorns. Bring to a boil, cover and cook gently for about 20 minutes or until tender and a leaf will pull away easily. (Depending on the season and the size, artichokes may require as long as 40 minutes of cooking to become tender.) Place artichokes upside down to drain.

3. When artichokes are cool enough to handle easily, slice vertically. With a spoon, scoop out the inedible fuzzy choke. Allow to cool; then cut into quarters to use in salad.

Tip: Store extra vinaigrette in refrigerator to serve at a later time with a green salad.

Szechwan Vegetable Salad

This exotic salad with an Oriental influence requires only a quick steaming of the broccoli and snow peas. Calorie counters will love this salad.

VINAIGRETTE

1	large clove garlic, crushed	1
2 tbsp	white wine vinegar	25 mL
1 tbsp	each: canola and sesame oil	15 mL
2 tsp	soy sauce	10 mL
1	piece gingerroot (1 inch/2.5 cm), minced	1
1 tsp	granulated sugar	5 mL
¼ to ½ tsp	hot red chili peppers	1 to 2 mL
⅛ tsp	hot pepper sauce	0.5 mL

VEGETABLES

1 cup	snow peas, trimmed	250 mL
1 cup	broccoli florets	250 mL
6	medium mushrooms, thinly sliced	6
1 cup	bean sprouts	250 mL
2	green onions, white part only cut in thin strips	2

Suggested Menu: This salad is an excellent accompaniment for grilled fish, chicken breasts or lamb served with fluffy rice.

1. *For vinaigrette:* In small bowl, combine garlic, vinegar, oils, soy sauce, gingerroot, sugar, chili peppers, hot sauce and 2 tbsp (25 mL) water. Stir well and reserve.

2. *For vegetables:* Place snow peas in steamer basket over boiling water. Cover and cook for about 3 minutes or until just tender; drain and chill. Repeat for broccoli.

3. Arrange mushroom slices in circle on large shallow serving platter. Top with broccoli and bean sprouts. Tuck snow peas in around outer part of circle. Chill until serving time.

4. Drizzle with reserved dressing and top with onion strips. **Makes 6 servings.**

SPRING GREENS WITH STRAWBERRIES

This attractive and yet simple salad with strawberries can be combined with any variety of greens.

DRESSING

3 tbsp	each: white wine vinegar and water	45 mL
1 tbsp	each: liquid honey and extra virgin olive oil	15 mL
2 tsp	chopped fresh mint	10 mL
½ tsp	salt	2 mL
⅛ tsp	white pepper	0.5 mL

SALAD

3 cups	sliced strawberries	750 mL
6 cups	mesclun or mixed greens including spinach, arugula, leaf lettuce, watercress and radicchio	1.5 L
2 tbsp	toasted pine nuts	25 mL

1. *For dressing:* In small bowl, whisk together vinegar, water, honey, oil, mint, salt and pepper until well blended; set aside.

2. *For salad:* In large bowl, combine strawberries and ¼ cup (50 mL) dressing. Cover and refrigerate until serving time.

3. In salad bowl, toss mixed greens with marinated strawberries and remaining dressing. Sprinkle with pine nuts and serve. **Makes 6 servings.**

How to Toast Pine Nuts: place nuts in shallow pan; bake in low oven for 3 to 5 minutes or until toasted.

INSALATA CAPRESE

Insalata Caprese is served widely in Italy either as an antipasto course or at lunch as a single course. It's the perfect salad to accompany Grilled Steak, Arugula and Shaved Parmesan (page 39).

3	firm but not overripe tomatoes	3
1	pkg (300 g) buffalo mozzarella or bocconcini cheese	1
	Extra virgin olive oil	
	Salt, freshly ground pepper and oregano, to taste	
6	basil leaves	6
12	pitted green or black olives	12

1. Wash and slice tomatoes evenly. Slice mozzarella into evenly thick slices.

2. Drizzle the bottom of a shallow serving dish with some oil; sprinkle with salt, pepper and oregano. Alternately arrange tomato and cheese slices. Sprinkle again with salt, pepper, oregano and oil. Garnish with basil leaves and olives. **Makes 6 servings.**

Warm Pear Salad with Stilton

Grilled pears and Stilton tossed with assorted greens make a unique salad. You can prepare it year-round by substituting a stove-top skillet for the outdoor grill. Apples can be used instead of pears.

2	ripe, but firm Bartlett pears	2
½	medium red onion, peeled and thinly sliced into rings	½
5 tsp	olive oil, divided	25 mL
1 tsp	liquid honey	5 mL
½ tsp	each: dry mustard and salt	2 mL
⅛ tsp	freshly ground pepper	0.5 mL
2	Belgian endives, cut crosswise in 1-inch (2.5 cm) slices	2
1	bunch watercress, tough stems removed	1
½ cup	crumbled Stilton cheese	125 mL
2 tsp	red wine vinegar or sherry	10 mL
1 tsp	Worcestershire sauce	5 mL
	Salt and freshly ground pepper	

1. Cut pears lengthwise into quarters, core and cut each quarter into 1-inch (2.5 cm) chunks; place in small bowl. Add onion.

2. In another bowl, combine 4 tsp (20 mL) oil, honey, mustard, salt and pepper. Pour over pears and onions and toss well; set aside.

3. Preheat grill on medium-high. Remove pears and onions from honey mixture; reserve liquid. Place pears and onions on oiled grill rack or in grill basket. Close lid and cook (use Direct Grilling, page 6) for 10 minutes or until pears and onions are softened and golden brown; brush occasionally with reserved liquid.

4. In large salad bowl, place endive, watercress, cheese, remaining oil, vinegar and Worcestershire sauce. Toss in warm pears and onions. Season to taste with salt and pepper and serve warm. **Makes 4 servings.**

GRILLED PEPPER GAZPACHO SALAD

Bring the wonderful flavors and colors of gazpacho soup to a salad. The roasted peppers add their own sweet smoky signature.

VEGETABLES

2	medium sweet red or orange peppers	2
2	large tomatoes, peeled and chopped	2
½ cup	chopped seedless cucumber	125 mL
¼ cup	finely chopped red onion	50 mL
1	small clove garlic, minced	1

VINAIGRETTE

3 tbsp	olive or canola oil	45 mL
2 tbsp	red wine vinegar	25 mL
2 tbsp	chopped fresh basil or 1 tsp (5 mL) dried	25 mL
3–4	drops hot pepper sauce	3–4
	Salt and freshly ground pepper	
	Leaf lettuce	

1. *For vegetables:* Preheat grill on medium-high. Place whole peppers on lightly oiled grill rack. Close lid and grill (use Direct Grilling, page 6) for about 20 minutes or until peppers are streaked with brown and tender when pierced; turn frequently. Place peppers in a paper bag to cool for about 15 minutes. Peel away the blackened skin; remove and discard stems and seeds. Slice into thin julienne pieces.

2. Meanwhile, in a large bowl, combine tomatoes, cucumber, onion and garlic.

3. *For vinaigrette:* Whisk together oil, vinegar, basil, hot pepper sauce, salt and pepper. Pour over tomato mixture. Add roasted pepper slices and stir gently to combine. Chill briefly and serve on lettuce. **Makes 6 servings.**

WATERCRESS AND BEAN SPROUT SALAD

This salad is simple to prepare, and the crunchy texture is a change from tossed greens. A light version of a Roquefort dressing adds a special flavor statement.

BUTTERMILK ROQUEFORT DRESSING

⅓ cup	buttermilk	75 mL
2 tbsp	crumbled Roquefort cheese	25 mL
1 tsp	red wine vinegar	5 mL
½ tsp	each: Dijon mustard and Worcestershire sauce	2 mL
	Salt and freshly ground pepper	

SALAD

8 cups	bean sprouts	2 L
1	bunch watercress, trimmed of coarse stems	1
½ cup	thinly sliced radish (optional)	125 mL

1. *For dressing:* In food processor or blender, process buttermilk, cheese, vinegar, mustard and Worcestershire sauce until smooth; season to taste with salt and pepper.

2. *For salad:* In large salad bowl, toss bean sprouts, watercress and radish, if using. Drizzle with dressing and toss. **Makes 6 servings and about ⅓ cup (75 mL) dressing.**

Suggested Menu: This salad is a delicious accompaniment to Orange-spiced Pork Chops (page 67) and either Grilled Sweet Potatoes (page 178) or Grilled Rosemary Potato Salad (page 213).

Tip: Dressing can be made 3 days ahead and stored in a tightly sealed container in the refrigerator. Stilton or blue cheese can replace Roquefort.

PANZANELLA SALAD

This most famous of Italian salads is usually associated with Tuscany. Summer field tomatoes provide great eye appeal and wonderful flavors. This salad is best served at room temperature.

4	medium tomatoes, cubed	4
1 cup	diced cucumber	250 mL
2	cloves garlic, crushed	2
½ cup	chopped red onion	125 mL
2	green onions, sliced	2
⅓ cup	extra virgin olive oil	75 mL
¼ cup	chopped fresh basil	50 mL
2 tbsp	red wine vinegar	25 mL
¼ cup	grated Parmesan cheese	50 mL
¼ tsp	each: salt and freshly ground pepper	1 mL
1 cup	bread croutons	250 mL
1 cup	kalamata olives, pitted and sliced	250 mL

1. In large salad bowl, gently stir together tomatoes, cucumber, garlic, onions, oil, basil, vinegar, cheese, salt and pepper. Cover and let stand at room temperature for up to 2 hours.

2. Sprinkle with croutons and olives and serve. **Makes 6 to 8 servings.**

Variation: For a lighter salad to serve more people, toss mixture with one head of torn romaine lettuce.

How to Make Croutons: If you have stale bread, cube it and dry in the oven to make your own low-fat croutons. Store in an airtight container. Alternatively stir together 1 tbsp (15 mL) olive oil and 2 crushed garlic cloves, and brush over both sides of 3 thick slices of Italian bread. Place bread on preheated grill rack, close lid and toast, turning once, until bread is crisp and browned. Allow to cool, then cut into cubes.

GRILLED ROSEMARY POTATO SALAD

This simple summer salad with rosemary overtones is a perfect accompaniment to grilled pork chops, steaks, chicken, ribs or lamb.

12	small new potatoes, unpeeled and halved	12

ROSEMARY OIL

2 tbsp	extra virgin olive oil	25 mL
4 tsp	minced fresh rosemary or 1¼ tsp (6 mL) dried	20 mL
2	cloves garlic, minced (optional)	2

DRESSING

3 tbsp	light mayonnaise	45 mL
2 tbsp	white wine	25 mL
1 tbsp	white wine vinegar	15 mL
1 tsp	Dijon mustard	5 mL
	Salt and freshly ground pepper	
2	green onions, sliced	2
½ cup	sliced celery	125 mL
¼ cup	chopped fresh parsley	50 mL

1. In saucepan of boiling water, cook potatoes until barely tender; drain.

2. *For oil:* In small bowl, combine oil, rosemary and garlic; set aside.

3. *For dressing:* In second bowl, combine mayonnaise, wine, vinegar, mustard, salt and pepper to taste, onions, celery and parsley; stir well and set aside.

4. Preheat grill on medium-high. Drizzle rosemary oil on potatoes; toss well. Place potatoes on grill rack, cut side down. Close lid and cook (use Direct Grilling, page 6) for about 10 minutes or until tender and golden brown; turn frequently. To serve, transfer potatoes to bowl with dressing; toss and serve warm. **Makes 6 servings.**

BULGUR TABBOULEH

Tabbouleh is a salad of Middle Eastern origin made with bulgur wheat, chopped tomatoes, onions, and parsley or mint. This version is served at room temperature and will be a great addition to any Mediterranean or grilled menu.

SALAD

1 cup	bulgur wheat	250 mL
¾ cup	lightly packed fresh parsley or mint, or a combination of both, chopped	175 mL
1	large tomato, chopped	1
3	green onions, sliced	3

VINAIGRETTE

3 to 4 tbsp	red wine vinegar or lemon juice	45 to 60 mL
2 tbsp	extra virgin olive oil	25 mL
¼ tsp	each: salt and freshly ground pepper	1 mL

1. *For salad:* In bowl, pour 3 cups (750 mL) boiling water over bulgur; allow to stand for 10 minutes. Drain and cool. (The fully cooked grains are chewy but never crunchy.) Stir in parsley (and/or mint), tomato and onions.

2. *For vinaigrette:* Whisk together 3 tbsp (45 mL) vinegar, oil, pepper and salt. Pour over bulgur; stir lightly. Cover and let stand for 4 hours at room temperature to allow flavors to blend. Taste and add extra vinegar if needed. **Makes 6 servings.**

Suggested Menu: Tabbouleh is ideal served with another Mediterranean-type recipe such as Moroccan Lamb Chops (page 54).

Variation: You can replace the bulgur with ½ cup (125 mL) uncooked converted long grain brown rice. Cook the rice in ¾ cup (175 mL) boiling water, covered, for 5 minutes; drain. Combine all ingredients and proceed as above.

WARM SPINACH AND RADICCHIO SALAD

No lettuce! Cooked greens! This is certainly a different approach to a salad, and the first taste signals that it has more than novelty going for it!

1 tbsp	extra virgin olive oil	15 mL
1	clove garlic, minced	1
1½ cups	chopped spinach	375 mL
1 cup	chopped arugula	250 mL
1 cup	sliced radicchio	250 mL
1 tbsp	chopped Italian or regular parsley	15 mL
	Salt and freshly ground pepper	

1. In large nonstick skillet, warm oil over medium heat. Sauté garlic for 30 seconds; add spinach, arugula and radicchio and cook just until wilted, stirring often. Add parsley and season to taste with salt and pepper. Toss well and serve. **Makes 4 servings.**

Suggested Menu: This warm salad makes a wonderful bed for Quails with Lemon Marinade (page 110). Round out the menu with brown rice or wild rice. You might even try a combination of the two; since wild rice takes slightly longer to cook, add it to the water in the pan first, and give it a head start of about five minutes.

Mexican Corn Salad

Fresh, colorful and simple, this salad is the essence of summer. It is best made a few hours ahead of time. Plan burgers, steak or chicken on the grill to keep the rest of dinner preparation simple.

SALAD

8	ears of corn, husked and blanched or 1 pkg (1 kg) frozen corn niblets	8
2	large firm field tomatoes, cubed	2
½	each: small sweet green and red pepper, diced	½
½	ripe avocado, diced	½
3	green onions, sliced	3
2	medium cloves garlic, minced	2

DRESSING

⅓ cup	cider vinegar	75 mL
¼ cup	extra virgin olive oil	50 mL
1½ tsp	ground cumin	7 mL
½ tsp	each: chili powder, salt and freshly ground pepper	2 mL
¼ cup	chopped fresh cilantro	50 mL

1. With sharp knife, cut kernels from cobs to make 4 cups (1 L). In large saucepan, cook corn, covered, over medium heat in lightly salted water for 10 minutes or until tender or cook frozen corn according to package directions. Drain and cool slightly.

2. Gently stir in tomatoes, green and red pepper, avocado, onions and garlic.

3. *For dressing:* Whisk together vinegar, oil and seasonings. Pour over corn mixture. Stir in cilantro; toss to combine. Cover and refrigerate for several hours to allow flavors to develop. **Makes 6 servings.**

Tip: The best way to remove corn from the cob when you want whole kernels is with a very sharp knife. First, dip the ear in boiling water for a minute or two; then hold it under cold running water to "set" the milk so it does not spurt when you are cutting off the kernels. Hold the ear, tip end up in a bowl. Cut down the ear, removing a few rows at a time. You will get about ½ cup (125 mL) kernels from each ear of corn.

CLASSIC COLESLAW

This coleslaw, or as some call it pickled cabbage, was originally a German preparation for cabbage.

VINEGAR MIXTURE

½ cup	cider vinegar	125 mL
½ cup	granulated sugar	125 mL
¼ cup	water	50 mL
½ tsp	each: celery seeds and salt	2 mL
¼ tsp	freshly ground pepper	1 mL

SALAD

4 cups	shredded cabbage, green or red or a mixture	1 L
1 cup	grated carrots	250 mL
1 cup	grated cucumber	250 mL
¼ cup	finely chopped onion	50 mL

1. *For vinegar:* Combine vinegar, sugar, water, celery seeds, salt and pepper. Stir to dissolve the sugar (do not heat).

2. *For salad:* In a large container, combine cabbage, carrots, cucumber and onion. Pour vinegar mixture over; stir well to combine.

3. Cover and refrigerate for up to 24 hours before serving, but it keeps much longer. **Makes 6 cups (1.5 L), about 10 servings.**

Creamy Variation: If you prefer a mayonnaise-based cabbage salad, combine 1 tbsp (15 mL) each: fresh lemon juice and white vinegar, ⅔ cup (150 mL) mayonnaise, few drops hot sauce, salt and freshly ground pepper to taste. Toss with salad ingredients above. I usually do not add cucumber to this version.

CREAMY BUTTERMILK DRESSING

This is our choice whenever a light, creamy dressing is needed. It also makes a good dip.

⅔ cup	light mayonnaise	150 mL
½ cup	buttermilk	125 mL
1 tbsp	cider vinegar	15 mL
2 tsp	liquid honey	10 mL
1 tsp	each: lemon juice and Dijon mustard	5 mL
¼ tsp	each: salt, paprika and freshly ground pepper	1 mL

1. In small bowl, whisk together mayonnaise, buttermilk, vinegar, honey, lemon juice, mustard, salt, paprika and pepper until dressing becomes quite thick. Transfer to a tightly sealed container and refrigerate for up to 1 week. **Makes about 1 cup (250 mL).**

BASIL VINAIGRETTE OVER TOSSED GREENS WITH WARMED CHÈVRE

The warm creamy tartness of chèvre and the memorable aroma of basil distinguish this European-style salad.

BASIL VINAIGRETTE AND SALAD

2 tbsp	red wine vinegar	25 mL
2 tbsp	chopped fresh basil leaves or 2 tsp (10 mL) dried	25 mL
⅛ tsp	each: dry mustard, salt and freshly ground pepper	0.5 mL
⅓ cup	extra virgin olive oil	75 mL
6 cups	assorted salad greens or mesclun	1.5 L

TOAST AND CHEESE

6	thin slices French baguette, lightly brushed with olive oil and toasted	6
6	thick slices chèvre (125 g pkg)	6
	Chopped fresh parsley or tarragon	

1. *For vinaigrette:* In small bowl, whisk together vinegar, basil, mustard, salt and pepper. Slowly whisk in oil until dressing is creamy and thick. Set aside.

2. *For salad:* In large salad bowl, arrange greens, cover and refrigerate.

3. *For toast:* Preheat grill on medium. Place toasted bread on baking sheet; top each slice with cheese. Heat toasts on grill rack or in a 300°F (150°C) oven until cheese is softened and just beginning to melt.

4. Toss salad greens with prepared vinaigrette. Divide onto 6 serving plates. Top each with toasted bread and melted cheese. Sprinkle with parsley and serve. **Makes 6 servings.**

POPPY SEED VINAIGRETTE

You can choose either an apricot or an orange flavor for this poppy seed vinaigrette. Both are superb.

½ cup	orange juice or apricot nectar	125 mL
¼ cup	lemon juice	50 mL
3 tbsp	finely chopped onion	45 mL
3 tbsp	poppy seeds	45 mL
1 tbsp	granulated sugar	15 mL
½ tsp	each: dry mustard and salt	2 mL
⅓ cup	canola oil	75 mL

1. In blender or food processor, process juices, onion, poppy seeds, sugar, mustard and salt until blended. Slowly add oil while processor is running. Transfer to a tightly sealed container and refrigerate for several hours before using. Keeps refrigerated for about 1 week. Whisk at serving time. **Makes about 1 cup (250 mL).**

FRESH TOMATO VINAIGRETTE

This fresh-tasting vinaigrette is best with hearty greens, such as romaine lettuce or spinach. It is also excellent for marinating chicken, veal and beef and can be used as a baste for fish and chicken.

3	plum tomatoes, quartered	3
1½ tbsp	extra virgin olive oil	22 mL
1 tbsp	sherry wine vinegar	15 mL
1 tsp	Dijon mustard	5 mL
1 tbsp	chopped fresh oregano or marjoram	15 mL
	Salt and freshly ground pepper	

1. In food processor, purée tomatoes until smooth. Press through a sieve to remove seeds; discard seeds.
2. In small bowl, whisk together tomato pulp, oil, vinegar and mustard. Stir in oregano, salt and pepper to taste. **Makes about 1 cup (250 mL).**

RED PEPPER BASIL MAYONNAISE

The subtle smoky aroma of the roasted red peppers goes well with fish. It keeps the fish moist but adds fewer calories than if the fish were fried in oil.

½ cup	drained bottled roasted red peppers	125 mL
⅓ cup	light mayonnaise	75 mL
4 tsp	Dijon mustard	20 mL
1	clove garlic, crushed	1
1 tsp	lemon juice	5 mL
	Salt and freshly ground pepper	
½ cup	chopped fresh basil	125 mL

1. In blender or food processor, process red peppers, mayonnaise, mustard, garlic, lemon juice, and salt and pepper to taste. Spread 2 tbsp (25 mL) on one side of 4 fish fillets or steaks and grill.

2. Add ½ cup (125 mL) basil to remaining mixture and serve as a sauce with the grilled fish. **Makes about ¾ cup (175 mL).**

OPEN-FACE GRILLED VEGGIE SANDWICH

 Many meat lovers will also enjoy this vegetarian recipe.

MAYONNAISE SAUCE

¼ cup	mayonnaise	50 mL
2	cloves garlic, minced	2
1 tbsp	each: fresh lemon juice and olive oil	15 mL

VEGETABLES

1 cup	sliced sweet red peppers	250 mL
1	small green zucchini, sliced	1
1	small yellow zucchini, sliced	1
1	red onion, sliced	1
2 tbsp	olive oil	25 mL
1	focaccia loaf, cut into long fingers	1
½ cup	crumbled feta cheese	125 mL

1. *For sauce:* Combine mayonnaise, garlic, lemon juice and oil. Set aside.

2. *For vegetables:* Place vegetables in a resealable plastic bag; add oil and toss until well coated.

3. Preheat grill on medium-high. Remove vegetables from bag; place on grill rack or in basket. Close lid and grill (use Direct Grilling, page 6) for 2 to 3 minutes per side or until vegetables reach desired doneness. Each vegetable will vary in amount of time needed. Remove from grill; set aside.

4. Spread some Mayonnaise Sauce on bread slices, sprinkle with cheese, place on grill and heat just until bread is toasted and cheese starts to melt. Remove from grill and top with grilled vegetables. Serve as open-face sandwich. **Makes 4 servings.**

CHAPTER 9
MARINADES, BASTES, PASTES, RUBS AND SAUCES

◀ *Basil and Mustard Sauce (page 230), Pineapple, Soy and Honey Sauce (page 230) and Yogurt-Dill Sauce (page 230)*

All of the mixtures in this section enhance the flavors of meats, poultry, fish and sometimes vegetables before, during or after the grilling process of these foods. Much of the art of grilling lies in these additions. There are liquid marinades, dry rubs, pastes somewhat similar to rubs but with a liquid added, bastes added during the grilling process and, of course, sauces which are poured over the foods at serving time.

Marinades: These are seasoned liquids in which poultry, fish, meat and sometimes vegetables are marinated before cooking to enhance their flavors. As well, marinades can be brushed on foods during the grilling process. These mixtures of herbs, spices, sometimes oil and an acidic liquid, allow foods to develop the marinade flavor throughout. Marinades are frequently used to tenderize less-tender cuts of meat. The acid ingredient (vinegar, citrus juice, wine or yogurt) is essential to tenderizing because it penetrates meat fibers. The intensity of the flavor developed and extent of tenderizing depends on the length of time in the marinade. Generally, vegetables and fish require minimal time — just 20 minutes — as they do not require tenderizing. Poultry is marinated for no longer than 2 hours in strong, flavored marinades and about 4 in the milder ones. Beef, pork, lamb and turkey can marinate from 2 to 24 hours. Balsamic Marinade with Herbs (page 225) is an excellent example of a tenderizing marinade.

Quick Marinating Tips
A heavy resealable plastic bag is a great mess-free choice for marinating. Turn the bag occasionally to evenly distribute the marinade.

Always marinate meats, poultry and fish in the refrigerator.
If you use remaining marinade as a sauce or to brush on food as it grills, be sure to bring it to a boil, reduce heat and cook for 5 minutes to kill any harmful bacteria left from marinating raw food.
Leftover marinades should never be kept for using at a later date.

Rubs: There are two reasons to use rubs: Blends of herbs and spices are pressed (or rubbed) on meats before cooking to flavor their surface, and also to protect the surface of the meat during grilling. They are a shortcut to achieving robust flavors in larger cuts of meats like whole beef brisket roasts, pork and lamb shoulders and legs, whole chickens, turkeys and pulled pork. Chimichurri Rub (page 227) and All-purpose Salt-free Rub (page 227) are two excellent examples of rubs.

Pastes: These are similar to rubs except they get their consistency from the addition of a liquid such as honey, juice, oil or vinegar. Mustard Beef Paste, (page 229) is one you might like to try.

Bastes: They are like marinades, but are applied during the cooking process, usually toward the end. We love the Maple Cranberry Chicken Quarters (page 102), which is an excellent example of how to use a baste.

Sauces: Sauces are liquid seasonings served on the food or with the food to enhance its flavor.

BASIC RED WINE MARINADE

This is our basic beef and game marinade. It is superb for all beef cuts as well as venison. I especially like it for the Mushroom Dressed Beef Tenderloin (page 48).

1 cup	dry red wine	250 mL
4	cloves garlic, crushed	4
1	shallot, finely chopped (about ¼ cup/50 mL)	1
3	sprigs fresh thyme or 1 tbsp (15 mL) dried	3
1 tbsp	each: red wine vinegar and vegetable oil	15 mL
	Freshly ground pepper	

1. Combine wine, garlic, shallots, thyme, vinegar, oil and a generous amount of pepper. Place whatever meat you wish to marinade in a shallow pan or resealable plastic bag; pour marinade over. Cover and refrigerate for several hours or overnight. Turn meat occasionally. **Makes 1¼ cups (300 mL) marinade.**

Tip: I have also used this marinade for farm-raised venison or elk. But if you do, please add 2 tbsp (25 mL) vegetable oil and 1 tbsp (15 mL) coarsely ground juniper berries to the recipe for Spit-roasted Marinated Elk with Wine Mushroom Sauce (page 170).

BALSAMIC MARINADE WITH HERBS

This marinade adds lots of zip to any meat it meets, especially the less tender cuts.

¼ cup	balsamic vinegar	50 mL
1	green onion, finely chopped	1
2 tbsp	finely chopped fresh parsley	25 mL
1 tbsp	minced fresh tarragon or 1 tsp (5 mL) dried	15 mL
1 tbsp	each: Dijon mustard, water and olive oil	15 mL
	Salt and freshly ground pepper	

1. In small bowl, whisk together vinegar, onion, parsley, tarragon, mustard, water, oil, and salt and pepper to taste. **Makes about ½ cup (125 mL).**

CITRUS MARINADE

The fresh lemon and orange flavors of this easy-to-make marinade lend themselves to both shrimp and chicken.

2	large cloves garlic, thinly sliced	2
3 tbsp	olive oil	45 mL
3 tbsp	each: lemon and orange juice	45 mL
2 tbsp	dark brown sugar	25 mL
4 tsp	balsamic vinegar	20 mL
1 tsp	each: lemon and orange zest	5 mL
	Freshly ground pepper	

1. In small skillet, cook garlic in oil for 5 minutes or until it just starts to turn brown. Remove from heat and discard garlic; cool.

2. Add lemon and orange juice, sugar, vinegar and zests. Stir to blend. Add pepper to taste. **Makes about ²/₃ cup (150 mL).**

SOY GINGER LEMON MARINADE AND BASTE

This simple marinade with Oriental overtones is perfect with meat or poultry. It is used as a marinade for Spit-Roasted Leg of Lamb (page 167).

½ cup	each: lemon juice and soy sauce	125 mL
¼ cup	canola or olive oil	50 mL
1	piece gingerroot (2 inch/5 cm), grated	1
2 tbsp	ketchup	25 mL
4	cloves garlic, crushed	4
¼ tsp	freshly ground pepper	1 mL

1. In small bowl, combine lemon juice, soy sauce, oil, gingerroot, ketchup, garlic and pepper. Shake well. Store in tightly sealed jar in the refrigerator.

2. When ready to use, place meat, poultry or fish in shallow nonreactive dish or resealable plastic bag. Pour about ½ cup (125 mL) marinade over meat. Turn to coat, cover and refrigerate for up to 2 hours or overnight (depending on the meat being used and depth of flavor desired); turn meat occasionally.

3. Remove meat from marinade; reserve marinade. Place marinade in small saucepan, bring to a boil, reduce heat and cook for 5 minutes; keep warm. Grill meat as desired, basting often with warm marinade. **Makes about 1½ cups (375 mL), sufficient for about three uses (depending on the amount of meat being marinated).**

ALL-PURPOSE SALT-FREE RUB

Here's a rub for meat or poultry. The rub helps develop that crisp crust essential to true barbecue.

½ cup	granulated sugar	125 mL
2 tbsp	chili powder	25 mL
2 tsp	each: dried parsley, garlic powder and onion powder	10 mL
1 tsp	each: celery seed and paprika	5 mL
1 tsp	freshly ground pepper	5 mL
½ tsp	each: dried basil, marjoram, sage, cumin, dry mustard and dill seed	2 mL

1. In bowl, combine sugar, chili powder, parsley, garlic and onion powder, celery seed, paprika, pepper, basil, marjoram, sage, cumin, mustard and dill seed; mix well. Store in tightly sealed container. **Makes about ¾ cup (175 mL).**

Tip: Use about ¼ cup (50 mL) of the mixture for every 1 to 2 lb (500 g to 1 kg) of meat. Press the mixture over the meat surface before grilling to help develop the crust.

CHIMICHURRI RUB

This rub is especially wonderful on porterhouse and T-bone steak.

1 cup	loosely packed fresh parsley	250 mL
2 tbsp	each: red wine vinegar and canola oil	25 mL
2 tbsp	chopped fresh oregano or 2 tsp (10 mL) dried	25 mL
½ tsp	each: salt and freshly ground pepper	2 mL
3 to 4	cloves garlic	3 to 4

1. In food processor or blender, process parsley, vinegar, oil, oregano, salt, pepper and garlic until coarsely chopped.

2. *To use:* Press mixture over all sides of meat. Cover with plastic wrap and refrigerate for up to 6 hours.

3. *To grill:* Preheat grill on medium-high. Remove plastic wrap from meat, place meat on lightly oiled grill rack, retaining as much of the rub as possible. Close lid and grill (use Direct Grilling, page 6) to desired stage of doneness (see chart on page 10); turn meat once. **Makes enough rub for 2 steaks.**

 Wine: Serve with a Chianti when this rub is used on a steak.

BEEF 'N' STEAK RUB

Use this rub when you are not marinating beef. It gives the meat a wonderful, full-bodied "beefy" flavor. We start with our All-purpose Salt-free Rub (page 227) and then make additions. You may wish to make a quantity to keep on hand for future use.

¼ cup	All-purpose Salt-free Rub (page 227)	50 mL
1 tbsp	coarse or kosher salt	15 mL
¼ tsp	each: paprika, ground oregano, thyme, basil, freshly ground pepper	1 mL
pinch	cayenne pepper and ground cumin	pinch

1. Combine salt-free rub, kosher salt, paprika, oregano, thyme, basil, pepper, cayenne and cumin. Store in a tightly sealed container. **Makes about ⅓ cup (75 mL).**

To Use: 1 tbsp (15 mL) of the mixture is perfect for a steak and double that amount for a roast. Press the mixture over all sides of meat about 30 minutes before start of cooking.

PORK 'N' RIB RUB

Great on pork ribs, chops and roasts, this rub can be applied either a short time or a few hours before grilling. But the longer the time, the more intense will be the result. The rub stores well in a tightly sealed container.

½ cup	sweet paprika	125 mL
½ cup	coarse or kosher salt	125 mL
¼ cup	granulated sugar	50 mL
2 tbsp	each: freshly ground pepper and celery seed	25 mL
2 tbsp	each: dry mustard powder, garlic powder and oregano	25 mL

1. Combine paprika, salt, sugar, pepper, celery seed, mustard, garlic powder and oregano; stir well. **Makes about 1½ cups (375 mL).**

POULTRY RUB

Applied before grilling, this rub adds spice to chicken, duck, geese, turkeys, Cornish hens and quail.

1 tbsp	each: granulated sugar and salt	15 mL
2 tsp	lemon pepper	10 mL
1½ tsp	ground allspice	7 mL
1 tsp	each: grated orange, lime and lemon peel	5 mL
½ tsp	paprika	2 mL
¼ tsp	cayenne pepper	1 mL

1. In small bowl, combine sugar, salt, lemon pepper, allspice, orange, lime and lemon peel, paprika and cayenne; stir well. **Makes about 3 tbsp (45 mL).**

MUSTARD BEEF PASTE

Give your beef roast a marvelous all-over flavor boost with this mustard paste.

2 tbsp	grainy Dijon mustard	25 mL
2 tsp	horseradish	10 mL
2 tsp	dried basil	10 mL
1 tsp	olive oil	5 mL
½ tsp	each: freshly ground pepper, cayenne and chili powder	2 mL

1. In small bowl, combine mustard, horseradish, basil, oil, pepper, cayenne and chili powder; mix well.

2. Pat this mixture over all surfaces of a beef roast before placing on the grill or spit. **Makes about ¼ cup (50 mL), sufficient for a 4 lb (2 kg) roast.**

HORSERADISH SAUCE

Serve this zesty sauce with grilled beef dishes. Whisk in a small amount of plain yogurt or light mayonnaise to turn it into a creamy dressing for a beef salad.

¼ cup	each: canola oil and red wine vinegar	50 mL
2 tsp	Dijon mustard	10 mL
1 to 2 tsp	prepared horseradish	5 to 10 mL
½ tsp	salt	2 mL
¼ tsp	each: freshly ground pepper and ground thyme	1 mL

1. In bowl, whisk together oil, vinegar, mustard, horseradish, salt, pepper and thyme. Cover and refrigerate for up to one week; whisk before using. **Makes about ½ cup (125 mL).**

BASIL AND MUSTARD SAUCE

Use as a dip for raw vegetables, or as a sauce for cooked vegetables or plain grilled fish.

½ cup	light sour cream	125 mL
2 tbsp	finely chopped green onion or chives	25 mL
2 tbsp	chopped fresh basil	25 mL
1 tsp	Dijon mustard	5 mL
⅛ tsp	freshly ground pepper	0.5 mL

1. In small bowl, stir together sour cream, onion, basil, mustard and pepper. Cover and refrigerate for up to 3 days. **Makes ⅔ cup (150 mL).**

PINEAPPLE, SOY AND HONEY SAUCE

This is a favorite for dipping seafood kebabs and chicken nuggets and for drizzling over cooked rice.

¼ cup	pineapple juice	50 mL
3 tbsp	sherry vinegar	45 mL
2 tbsp	soy sauce	25 mL
4 tsp	liquid honey	20 mL
1 tbsp	each: olive oil, water and chopped gingerroot	15 mL
1	large clove garlic, crushed	1
	Salt and ground pepper	

1. In small bowl, whisk together juice, vinegar, soy sauce, honey, oil, water, gingerroot, garlic, and salt and pepper to taste. Heat before serving. **Makes about ⅔ cup (150 mL).**

YOGURT-DILL SAUCE

The tangy flavor of yogurt in this marinade is very effective with lamb, chicken and fish.

¾ cup	plain yogurt	175 mL
1 tbsp	liquid honey	15 mL
1 tbsp	white wine vinegar	15 mL
	Salt and freshly ground pepper	
1 tbsp	chopped fresh dill or 1 tsp (5 mL) dried	15 mL
2 tsp	finely chopped onion	10 mL

1. In small bowl, whisk together yogurt, honey, vinegar, and salt and pepper to taste. Stir in dill and onion. Cover and refrigerate for up to 1 week. **Makes about 1 cup (250 mL).**

CLASSIC TOMATO BARBECUE SAUCE

Many people prefer less-sweet barbecue sauces like this one. In addition to personal taste considerations, a less sweet sauce is not as likely to char during grilling and allows a more versatile selection of accompanying foods.

2	large onions, chopped	2
1	sweet red pepper, seeded and chopped	1
3	cloves garlic, crushed	3
2 tbsp	canola oil	25 mL
4 tsp	chili powder	20 mL
1 tsp	each: hot pepper sauce, prepared mustard and Worcestershire sauce	5 mL
1	can (7½ oz/213 mL) tomato sauce	1
½ cup	chili sauce	125 mL
3 tbsp	red wine vinegar	45 mL
1 tbsp	granulated sugar	15 mL

1. In large heavy saucepan, cook onion, red pepper and garlic in hot oil over medium-high heat for 5 minutes or until softened; stir often. Stir in chili powder, pepper sauce, mustard, Worcestershire sauce, tomato and chili sauce, vinegar and sugar. Bring to a boil, reduce heat, cover and cook gently for 20 minutes or until sauce has thickened. Stir often, especially as the sauce begins to thicken.

2. Store sauce in tightly sealed container in the refrigerator for up to 2 weeks. For longer storage, freeze or process in 2-cup (500 mL) mason jars using a boiling water canner for 35 minutes. **Makes 2 cups (500 mL).**

TOMATO-HERB SAUCE

The fresh tomato and herb flavors go well with grilled beef or veal. You can also use this sauce with pasta, or brush it on grilling chicken or fish. Serve either cold or warm.

1 tbsp	olive oil	15 mL
1 to 2	large cloves garlic, minced	1 to 2
4	large ripe tomatoes, peeled and diced	4
2 tbsp	each: finely chopped fresh oregano, basil and thyme or 1½ tsp (7 mL) dried	25 mL
½ tsp	each: salt and freshly ground pepper	2 mL
2 tbsp	chopped fresh Italian parsley	25 mL

1. In large saucepan, heat oil over medium heat. Add garlic; sauté for 1 minute. Add tomatoes, oregano, basil, thyme, salt and pepper. Bring to a boil, reduce heat and cook gently for 30 minutes or until sauce is thickened. Stir in parsley, cool and refrigerate. **Makes 1½ cups (375 mL).**

LIGHT NO-FAIL HOLLANDAISE SAUCE

Serve this low-fat, low-calorie, speedy-to-make version of a classic sauce with grilled vegetables.

½ cup	light sour cream or plain yogurt	125 mL
2 tbsp	light mayonnaise	25 mL
1 tsp	lemon juice	5 mL
½ tsp	each: dried tarragon and chervil	2 mL
	Lemon zest (optional)	

1. In small saucepan, combine sour cream, mayonnaise, lemon juice and seasonings. Cook, stirring occasionally, over low heat or until warm. Alternatively, microwave in glass dish on low (30%) for 2 minutes or until warm; stir once.

2. Spoon sauce over grilled vegetables. Garnish with lemon zest if desired. **Makes about ⅔ cup (150 mL), sufficient for 4 servings.**

Variations:

Mustard Sauce: Add 1 tbsp (15 mL) Dijon mustard to the cooked sauce.

Choron Sauce: Add 2 tsp (10 mL) tomato paste to sauce ingredients before cooking.

LIGHT BÉARNAISE SAUCE

While it is particularly good with grilled beef, this marvelous sauce also does amazing things for fish and vegetables. It is quick and easy to prepare with the help of a microwave oven.

1 cup	plain yogurt	250 mL
2 tsp	all-purpose flour	10 mL
1	egg white	1
2 tsp	white wine vinegar	10 mL
1 tsp	Dijon mustard	5 mL
1 tbsp	each: chopped fresh parsley and tarragon	15 mL
1	green onion, finely chopped	1
⅛ tsp	each: garlic powder and white pepper	0.5 mL

1. In small microwaveable bowl, whisk together yogurt, flour, egg white, vinegar and mustard. Microwave at medium-high (70%) for 2 to 3 minutes or until sauce is thickened and bubbly; stir several times. Stir in parsley, tarragon, onion, garlic powder and pepper. **Makes 1¼ cups (300 mL).**

GRILLED RED PEPPER SAUCE

The smoky-sweet grilled pepper flavor of this sauce goes so well with so many foods. Make large quantities when peppers are in season and freeze for future use. You can also make the sauce with green, orange or yellow peppers.

6	sweet red peppers, grilled (see page 178) and seeded	6
2	cloves garlic, minced	2
1 tbsp	balsamic or herb vinegar	15 mL
1/4 to 1/2 tsp	hot pepper sauce	1 to 2 mL
1/4 cup	chopped fresh cilantro or Italian parsley	50 mL
	Salt and freshly ground pepper	

1. In food processor, process peppers, garlic and vinegar until almost smooth. Remove to bowl, stir in pepper sauce, cilantro, and salt and pepper to taste. Store in refrigerator for up to 3 days or freeze for longer storage. **Makes 1 1/2 cups (375 mL).**

SESAME-ORANGE DIPPING SAUCE

Serve this dipping sauce with meat, chicken or fish kebabs. The plainer the meat and fish flavors, the more appropriate the sauce. It is also wonderful drizzled over cooked rice.

1/3 cup	chicken broth	75 mL
1/4 cup	orange juice	50 mL
1 tbsp	each: rice vinegar and soy sauce	50 mL
2 tsp	finely chopped gingerroot	10 mL
1 tsp	sesame oil	5 mL
1/4 cup	thinly sliced green onions (optional)	50 mL

1. In small bowl, combine broth, juice, vinegar, soy sauce, gingerroot and oil; stir well. Add green onions, if using, just before serving. **Makes 3/4 cup (175 mL); about 6 servings.**

CHAPTER 10
SWEET ENDINGS

◀ *Decadent Chocolate Fondue Sauce (page 238) and Warm Sabayon Sauce (page 238)*

Since the entrée is finished and the grill is still warm, why not grill a "sweet ending" just right for the end of the meal.

Anna's Cherry Upside Down Johnnycake (page 239) makes an easy cake when you are at a cottage and may not have an oven. Or try Cedar-planked Brie Cheese which accompanies Strawberry Brochettes (page 244).

Want something really simple? Slices of lightly grilled fresh fruit make a wonderful dessert.

Strawberries: Warm large strawberries slowly, turning a few times, until slightly soft. They are wonderful over ice cream — much like a fresh strawberry sauce.

Bananas: Under-ripe bananas are best. Remove peel from one side and place bananas, skin side down, on the grill. Cook for 5 minutes, sprinkle with a teaspoon of brown sugar, cook 5 minutes longer, then sprinkle them lightly with rum as you serve.

Apples: Peel a firm apple, a Granny Smith works well, cut into thick horizontal slices. Sprinkle with lemon juice and granulated sugar, grill for about 5 minutes, and dust with cinnamon just before serving.

Or one of the sauces found on pages 237–239: Decadent Chocolate Fondue, Coconut, Ginger Creamy Ricotta, all of them mouth watering, to accompany your choice of fruit. Generally fruit grills best at medium-low whether on a gas-fired grill or over the last glow of charcoal.

Too often the decision to grill dessert depends on how dirty the grill racks are. If you expect to grill a dessert, keep one grill rack clean by grilling the entrée on the remaining racks.

COCONUT SAUCE

This sauce is superb with Grilled Fruit Kebabs (see page 240).

1	can (14 oz/398 mL) coconut milk	1
1 tbsp	packed brown sugar	15 mL
1 tsp	vanilla extract	5 mL
1 to 2 tbsp	dark rum, optional	15 to 25 mL
pinch	ground nutmeg	pinch
½ cup	toasted coconut	125 mL

1. Combine coconut milk and sugar in small saucepan over medium heat. Bring to a boil, reduce heat and simmer, stirring occasionally, for 12 minutes or until mixture is reduced by half. Remove from heat; add vanilla, rum (if using) and nutmeg. Cool and refrigerate until mixture thickens. Serve over kebabs with a sprinkle of coconut. **Makes 1½ cups (375 mL) sauce.**

LIME RUM SAUCE

This sauce highlights the tropical in any tropical fruit, like papayas, pineapple or mangoes. It's also great over frozen yogurt or ice cream.

	Juice of 2 limes	
½ cup	water	125 mL
¼ cup	dark rum	50 mL
2 tsp	vanilla extract	10 mL
1 tsp	ground cinnamon	5 mL
¼ tsp	ground cloves	1 mL
½ cup	packed brown sugar	125 mL

1. Combine lime juice, water, rum, vanilla, cinnamon and cloves. Pour over fruit and refrigerate for several hours. Remove fruit from marinade; reserve marinade. Bring marinade and brown sugar to a boil in small saucepan; reduce heat and simmer for about 10 minutes or until sugar is dissolved and sauce is golden. Remove from heat and cool. **Makes 6 servings.**

GINGER CREAMY RICOTTA SAUCE

Use this sauce when a fast dessert is needed with whatever fruit is on hand to grill.

1	pkg (17 oz/475 g) smooth ricotta cheese	1
¼ cup	icing sugar	50 mL
3 tbsp	finely chopped crystallized ginger	45 mL
1 tsp	each: grated lemon peel and vanilla extract	5 mL

1. Cream together ricotta cheese and sugar until smooth. Stir in ginger, vanilla and lemon peel. Store in tightly sealed container in refrigerator for up to 2 weeks. **Makes about 2 cups (500 mL) sauce.**

WARM SABAYON SAUCE

Sabayon is a rich French custard dessert frequently served as a sauce.

6	egg yolks	6
1/3 cup	granulated sugar	75 mL
2/3 cup	sweet white wine	150 mL

1. Beat egg yolks and sugar with an electric mixer until thick and light colored in a double boiler or heavy saucepan; beat in wine. Place over simmering water; cook, beating constantly, until thick and fluffy. Serve over fresh fruit. **Makes about 1 1/2 cups (375 mL).**

Variation: For an Italian zabaglione, use Marsala, Madeira or sherry.

Tip: Leftover sauce is best kept refrigerated.

DECADENT CHOCOLATE FONDUE SAUCE

Most agree that chocolate is the perfect finish for a meal. Satisfy your yearning with this luscious chocolate sauce over cake, ice cream, frozen yogurt or fresh fruit.

1/2 cup	chocolate chips	125 mL
1/4 cup	butter or margarine	50 mL
1/2 cup	corn syrup	125 mL
1/2 cup	granulated sugar	125 mL
13 oz	can low-fat evaporated milk	385 mL
4 tsp	cornstarch	20 mL
2 tsp	vanilla or rum extract	10 mL

1. Melt chocolate chips and butter over medium-low heat in small saucepan. Stir in corn syrup and sugar. Gradually stir in milk and cornstarch. Cook gently on low heat for 5 minutes or until bubbly and smooth; stir frequently. Remove from heat and stir in vanilla. Cool before storing in covered container in refrigerator. Serve either cold or warm. **Makes 2 cups (500 mL).**

Banana Boats: Another use for the sauce is with grilled bananas. Open banana peel to form a pocket. Drizzle with some sauce, add a few marshmallows, seal bananas in foil pouches and grill for about 10 minutes. Yummy!

Grilling Tip: If you are eating outdoors, this sauce may be prepared at the grill just before dessert.

To add a Mexican flavor touch, stir in some ground cinnamon.

CARAMEL SAUCE

A drizzle of caramel sauce adds fame to the simplest of desserts. The perfect sauce for Soused Dessert Kebabs (page 242).

1 cup	caramel candies	250 mL
¼ cup	butter or margarine	50 mL
½ cup	packed brown sugar	125 mL
½ cup	evaporated milk	125 mL
1 tsp	vanilla extract	5 mL

1. Heat candies and butter on low heat in heavy saucepan until melted. Stir in sugar and milk. Simmer until smooth and thickened; stir frequently. Remove from heat, stir in vanilla and reserve. **Makes about 1 cup (250 mL) sauce.**

ANNA'S CHERRY UPSIDE DOWN JOHNNYCAKE

You might well ask, why bake a cake on the grill? Well, if you are without an oven, maybe at a cottage, or camping, or you just want to stay outside with the crowd, you can still come up with a great baked dessert. And who is Anna? She is my 11-year-old granddaughter who helped me develop this recipe while visiting from Calgary. The name "johnnycake" is thought to be the precursor of the pancake and dates back to the 1700s.

½ cup	butter or margarine, divided	125 mL
¾ cup	lightly packed brown sugar	175 mL
3 cups	drained pitted sour cherries	750 mL
1 cup	all purpose flour	250 mL
¾ cup	cornmeal	175 mL
1½ tsp	baking powder	7 mL
½ tsp	baking soda	2 mL
½ tsp	each: salt and ground ginger	2 mL
¾ cup	buttermilk	175 mL
1	large egg	1
	Ground cinnamon	

1. Melt ¼ cup (50 mL) butter and brown sugar over medium heat in an 8-inch (2L) square baking pan for about 3 minutes or until sugar is dissolved; stir occasionally. Add drained cherries.

2. Combine flour, cornmeal, baking powder and soda, salt and ginger. Melt remaining butter; stir in butter, buttermilk and egg. Stir into dry ingredients just until mixed. Spoon batter evenly over cherries in pan. Sprinkle with cinnamon.

3. Preheat grill on medium (about 350°F/180°C). Using Indirect Grilling (page 6), place baking pan on rack over the cold burner. Close lid and cook for about 35 minutes or until top springs back when lightly touched. Let cool in pan for about 10 minutes before inverting onto a serving platter. Cool completely before cutting. **Makes 8 to 10 servings.**

Suggestion: Naturally, the cake can be baked in any oven at 350°F (180°C).

Variation: Follow same procedure as above using drained pineapple tidbits, sliced peaches, apples or pears.

GRILLED FRUIT KEBABS

Choose any combination of fresh fruits in season to grill on individual bamboo skewers, one for each guest. In season, strawberries are a marvelous replacement for apricots or plums. And apricots can replace sliced peaches. Coconut Sauce (page 237) becomes the perfect sauce to serve with the kebabs.

½	fresh pineapple, peeled and cut into small wedges	½
2	bananas, peeled and cut into 4 pieces	2
3	peaches, peeled and sliced	3
6	plums, halved and pitted	6
3	pears, cut into large pieces	3
2	oranges	2
½	lemon	½
¾ cup	granulated sugar	175 mL
¼ cup	dark rum	50 mL
1 tsp	ground nutmeg	5 mL
	Soaked wooden skewers	

Tip: To easily peel peaches, lower peaches, a few at a time, into boiling water for about 30 seconds or until skins start to separate from the fruit. Remove and plunge into cold water until cool enough to handle before removing the skin.

Serving Suggestion: Serve with assorted flavors of ice cream.

1. Combine prepared fruits in large bowl. Remove zest from oranges and lemon and squeeze juice. Combine zest, juice, sugar, rum and nutmeg; stir into fruit mixture. Allow fruit and liquid to blend at room temperature for at least 30 minutes.

2. Drain fruit; reserve liquid. Thread fruit alternately on soaked wooden skewers. Preheat grill on medium; spray with nonstick coating. Place kebabs on grill rack; close lid and grill (use Direct Grilling, page 6) for about 10 minutes; brush occasionally with drained liquid. Turn skewers frequently. **Makes 10 to 12 servings.**

SOUSED DESSERT KEBABS

Wonderful things happen when day-old pound cake is made part of these fruit kebabs. Add a drizzle of a favorite spirit at serving time along with a dab of Caramel Sauce (page 239) and we have a new dessert dimension.

1	medium banana	1
1	pear	1
12	whole strawberries	12
12	small mango wedges	12
½	pound cake, cubed	½
6	skewers	6
	Brandy, optional	

1. Cut banana into 12 pieces. Core and slice pear into 12 wedges. Stem strawberries. On 6 metal or soaked wooden skewers, alternately thread banana, pear, strawberries, mango and cake cubes.

2. Preheat grill on medium; spray with nonstick coating. Place kebabs on grill rack. Close lid and grill (use Direct Grilling, page 6) for about 5 minutes or until cake is toasted and fruit is warm; turn once.

3. For each serving, remove fruit and cake from skewers to 6 serving plates, drizzle lightly with brandy, if using. **Makes 6 servings.**

GRILLED FRUITS AND PINEAPPLE

Fresh fruits suitable for grilling are halved and cored pears, peaches, papayas, apples, nectarines, strawberries and — why not? — a whole pineapple (see below).

2 tbsp	melted butter or margarine	25 mL
2 tbsp	fresh lemon juice	25 mL
1 tbsp	liquid honey	15 mL
	Fresh mint sprigs	
	Assortment of fresh fruits	

1. *Prepare fruits:* Place prepared fruits in bowl. Add butter, lemon juice and honey. Toss well to coat; let stand at room temperature for 30 minutes or up to 3 hours.

2. Preheat grill on medium-high; spray rack with nonstick coating. Place fruit, skin side down, on rack. Close lid and grill (use Direct Grilling, page 6) for 10 minutes or until skin starts to turn golden brown. Turn and cook for 5 minutes or until tender. Place fruits on individual dessert plates; serve with a spoonful of Ginger Creamy Ricotta Sauce (page 237) and garnish with a mint sprig.

Grilled Whole Pineapple: Now that you are in the swing of grilling your desserts, it's time to try grilling a whole pineapple. Cut off crown and remove skin from pineapple. Place fruit on metal barbecue spit. Follow manufacturer's directions, taking care that the fruit is well secured by the prongs at each end of the spit.

Lime Rum Sauce (page 237) makes a great basting sauce. During grilling, brush the fruit often with the sauce. Sprinkle generously with nutmeg. To serve, slice the fruit crosswise into ½-inch (1 cm) thick slices and accompany with plain cake and ice cream, frozen yogurt or gelato. What a delicious ending for a meal!

FLAMING BLUEBERRY MANGO CRISP

Flaming adds a dramatic touch to this wildly delicious dessert.

TOPPING

¾ cup	dried, crumbled macaroon cookies	175 mL
¼ cup	ground almonds	50 mL
2 tbsp	finely chopped candied ginger	25 mL
2 tbsp	melted butter or margarine	25 mL

FRUIT

2	large mangoes, peeled and cut into thick slices	2
1 cup	blueberries	250 mL
¼ cup	granulated sugar	50 mL
2 tbsp	each: orange liqueur and rum	25 mL

1. *For topping:* Combine macaroons, almonds, ginger and melted butter; mix well.

2. *For fruit:* Arrange mango slices and blueberries in shallow foil pan; sprinkle with sugar and topping mixture.

3. Preheat grill on high (about 400°F/200°C). Using Direct Grilling (page 6), place baking pan on grill rack. Close lid and cook for about 8 minutes or until fruit is warmed throughout. Heat liqueur and rum and ignite. Drizzle, flaming, over the fruit. **Makes 6 servings.**

APPLE STRAWBERRY CRUMBLE

A favorite dessert that is normally baked in the oven! This time it is grilled outdoors so we can continue enjoying the summer and keep heat out of the kitchen.

TOPPING

⅔ cup	lightly packed brown sugar	150 mL
½ cup	large-flake rolled oats	125 mL
¼ cup	all purpose flour	50 mL
½ tsp	ground cinnamon	2 mL
¼ cup	butter or margarine	50 mL

FRUIT

4	medium apples, peeled and sliced	4
1½ cups	sliced strawberries	375 mL

1. *For topping:* Combine sugar, rolled oats, flour and cinnamon; cut in butter until coarse crumbs form.

2. *For fruit:* Arrange apples and strawberries in an 8-inch (2 L) lightly greased foil baking pan. Sprinkle rolled oat mixture over top.

3. Preheat grill on medium (about 350°F/180°C). Using Indirect Grilling (page 6), place baking pan on the rack over the cold burner. Close lid and cook for about 45 minutes or until topping is golden brown and fruit is bubbly. Turn pan part way through cooking. **Makes 6 servings.**

MAPLE FRUIT PIZZA

Gourmet flatbreads, so readily available in stores, make excellent pizza bases. Here we use them to carry a grilled maple fruit topping.

¼ cup	softened butter or margarine	50 mL
¼ cup	pure maple syrup	50 mL
½ tsp	ground cinnamon	2 mL
1	round plain Italian-style regular or thin flatbread (14 oz/400 g)	1
1	pear, cored and sliced	1
1	red-skinned apple, cored and sliced	1
1 cup	halved grapes or sliced peaches	250 mL
1 cup	halved strawberries	250 mL
	Fresh mint leaves	

1. Cream butter, maple syrup and cinnamon until smooth. Spoon onto flatbread and spread almost to the edge. Spray flat baking pan with nonstick coating. Place flatbread on pan and arrange fruit in an attractive design covering the base of the pizza.

2. Preheat grill on medium. Place baking pan on grill rack; close lid and grill (use Direct Grilling, page 6) for 10 minutes or until fruit is almost tender and butter mixture is melted. Remove to cutting board and cut into wedges to serve. **Makes 6 to 8 servings.**

STRAWBERRY BROCHETTES

Plump, juicy and full of flavor, early summer strawberries gently kissed on the grill along with Cedar-planked Brie Cheese (recipe below), what more could you ask for!

¼ cup	brown sugar	50 mL
¼ cup	Grand Marnier or Cointreau liqueur	50 mL
	Sweetened whipped cream	
6	metal or soaked wooden skewers	6

1. Wash and hull strawberries; dip while still moist into sugar. Thread onto 6 small metal or soaked wooden skewers. Place each skewer on double thickness of foil. Drizzle liqueur over fruit; seal edges of foil securely.

2. Preheat grill on high. Place packages on grill rack. Close lid and cook (use Direct Grilling, page 6) for about 4 minutes or until fruit is warm. Remove from grill and serve in the packages. Pass a bowl of sweetened whipped cream. **Makes 6 servings.**

Variation:

Strawberry Brochettes with Cedar-planked Brie Cheese:
Place wheel or wedge of brie on soaked wooden plank. Preheat grill on medium-high. Place plank on grill rack, close lid and cook for 5 minutes or until cheese starts to melt. The cheese is ready when the sides are bulging and it becomes golden brown. Remove from grill and serve with strawberries and fresh baguette slices.

APPENDIX

How to Plank

Grilling planks must be of untreated wood (woods used in construction can contain toxic preservation chemicals). They can be any size that fits the barbecue, but purchased planks are commonly 15 x 5½ x ⅜ inches. Different woods produce different smoke flavors. See the table below for suggested matching of foods to wood varieties.

Before use, soak the plank in water for at least an hour, but overnight is ideal. Start with hot water to open the wood pores. Be sure to place a weight on the plank to ensure complete immersion.

After soaking, dry the excess moisture from the plank and lightly coat the smooth finished side of the plank with olive, canola or any other vegetable oil.

After preheating the grill with the lid down, place the plank on a grill rack over a lit burner (or charcoal). Preheat the plank for five minutes so it starts to smoke when the food starts to grill, thus maximizing exposure to smoke. Then load the plank with the food to be grilled, including any enhancements placed under or over the food.

Grill the planked food according to the recipe. Check briefly (say every five minutes) for flare-ups, and extinguish them with just enough water from a spray bottle kept at hand. We don't want to stop the plank from smoking. Otherwise keep the lid down to maximize the smoke effect. Food on a plank will take approximately twice as long to grill as food directly on top of the grill rack.

Having checked for doneness, remove food from the plank. Remove the plank after extinguishing any flames with the water spray.

Make sure the plank is completely cooled. Placing it in a pail of water works well before discarding or storing it.

PLANK AND WOOD CHIP VARIETIES

WOOD TYPE	CHARACTERISTICS	GOOD FOOD MATCHES
Hickory	Pungent, smoky, bacon-like flavor	Pork, chicken, beef, wild game, cheeses
Pecan	Rich, more subtle than hickory but similar taste; burns cooler for low-heat smoking	Pork, chicken, lamb, fish, cheeses
Mesquite	Sweeter, more delicate flavor than hickory; burns hot	Most meats, especially beef; vegetables
Alder	Delicate flavor to enhance lighter meats	Salmon, swordfish, sturgeon, other fish, chicken, pork
Oak	Forthright, pleasant flavor; blends well with a variety of textures and flavors	Beef (particularly brisket), poultry, pork
Maple	Mildly smoky, somewhat sweet	Poultry, vegetables, ham
Cherry	Slightly sweet, fruity smoke	Poultry, game birds, pork
Apple	Slightly sweet but denser, fruity smoke flavor	Beef, poultry, game birds, pork (particularly ham)
Cedar	Pungent cedar aroma	Classic for planked salmon

A well-charred plank is of no further use as a cooking plank. However if it is only lightly used or was used for indirect grilling, it can be reused after washing the cooking surface. (Some recipes place the planked food on the indirect side of the grill so smoke is not generated and the food is flavored only by the wood.)

How to Use Wood Chips

Wood chips must be from untreated wood. They can be readily obtained from most stores selling grilling supplies. See the table on page 245 for suggested matching of foods to wood varieties.

Before use, chips must be soaked in hot water or a liquid such as beer, wine, whiskey, fruit juices, etc. Soaking time should be at least an hour for water but less for stronger-flavored liquids.

On a gas grill, wood chips need to be contained while they smoke. Some grills are equipped with containers for that purpose with instructions for their use. Failing such devices, a smoke box can be purchased for a reasonable cost. It is a rectangular steel or cast iron box with holes in the lid. As well, wood chips can be loosely wrapped in aluminum foil with holes made in the top.

Do not stuff the smoke box. There must be room for the chips to breathe. One-half cup of wood chips should be the starting quantity for a 6 x 10 inch smoke box.

For gas grills, the smoke box should be placed under the cooking grate and above the burner, unless otherwise directed by the manufacturer of your barbecue. The smoke box can also be placed on top of the cooking grate if it does not fit below it. Food is then placed on an adjacent grate to be grilled by indirect heat.

A smoke box can be recharged with fresh chips by removing it from the hot grill with tongs while wearing gloves and plunging it into a pail of water. It quickly cools sufficiently to be handled with bare hands, recharged with chips and returned to the hot grill.

Be sure chips are extinguished before disposal.

For charcoal grills, soaked wood chips or wood chunks can be placed directly on the burning charcoal when the coals are ready for cooking. They can be replaced as needed.

Equipment

Grills come in all shapes, sizes, configurations and prices. As with any other purchase it is a matter of what we feel is useful for our needs and what we are willing to pay. Here are some considerations:

- What fuel will you use? Your choices are charcoal, natural gas, propane, or electricity.
- Charcoal is for traditionalists who believe a truer barbecue flavor comes from burning charcoal than with any other fuel. These traditionalists are ready to put up with a time-consuming start up, and a somewhat dirty fuel to handle that can be difficult to keep at a constant temperature. Longer grilling periods require refueling.
- Natural and propane gas give instant starts without the dirt and fuss of charcoal. Constant temperatures are easily maintained throughout the grilling period. Most of us are quite happy with the barbecue flavor achieved with gas. Natural gas piped directly to the grill involves higher installation costs, but eliminates the bother of changing and refueling propane tanks, sometimes in the middle of grilling that special meal for guests!
- Electricity has all the advantages of natural gas except it does not typically provide as high heat levels, resulting in longer grill times. It is the only option for people living where neither gas nor charcoal grills are allowed. Only electric grills can be used indoors.
- What about quality? Grills tend to lead a hard life. Although they can be covered when not

in use, they still live outside, exposed to the elements most or all of the year. They are also exposed to high heats when in use. Solid construction of frame, lid and grill racks is a sign of potential longevity. Burners and fuel lines in gas grills are often the first components to fail, so initial quality is important, as is easy replacement and availability of parts. Screening of fuel lines to prevent entry of insects is both an operational and safety issue.

- How many burners? Two burners are typically the smallest number included in gas grills. This allows sufficient space for indirect grilling and room to direct grill for a modest party. Three burners allows for two active burners for indirect grilling for better heat distribution. As well, three burners provide more flexibility in dealing with larger groups. An infrared back burner is nice for spit roasting and an infrared burner under the grill racks is handy for the fast searing of meats. Side burners are handy if the grill is located a distance from the kitchen. If it is close by, the kitchen stove may very well be a better option. From there, the choice of how many burners to have will depend on how many mouths you want to feed at a time and the size of your pocketbook!

- What about infrared burners? Infrared energy is a form of electro-magnetic energy as is energy from the sun or radio waves. Infrared burners focus a gas flame on a ceramic tile that has thousands of microscopic holes in it. This converts the heat of the gas flame into infrared energy capable of achieving temperatures in the order of 1800°F (985°C). Such intense heat produces cooking times that can be 2 to 4 times faster than with gas. Meat is quickly seared, locking in moisture and flavor. Preheating over an infrared burner is almost instantaneous. Flare-ups are virtually eliminated since drippings instantly vaporize. However, high

temperatures and short cooking times can easily lead to burnt food. Infrared technology is not well-suited to lower temperature, longer cooking times required by some foods. Some grillers use an infrared burner to sear meats and then finish on a gas burner. Thus it would seem that a griller planning to use infrared burners should do so in combination with gas burners. Infrared is commonly used in back burners for spit roasting. This application works well because of the constant rotating of the cooking meat.

- Is it easy to clean? The better grills tend to be easier to clean and can turn this important maintenance function from a dirty and difficult job to a quick and easy one. Removable non-stick trays are particularly helpful in this regard. Regular cleaning is a safety consideration, as build-up of grease can easily catch fire and ruin a good meal.

Tools

The right tools are important to a griller's enjoyment and well-being from the time the food hits the grill until it is removed and placed on the diner's plate.

- Barbecue gloves (or mitts) are the griller's protection from burns. They should be waterproof (water turns to steam when heated) and fireproof. They should come well up the arm. Good to have them at hand when grilling. The neoprene ones do the job quite nicely.

- An instant-read meat thermometer eliminates guesswork when establishing doneness. The digital ones are easier to read and give a more accurate reading.

- Spatula and tongs are the food handler's tools. Don't go for wimpy ones. You can't afford to drop an expensive piece of meat. They should be of stainless steel to stand the heat of the grill as well as being easy to keep clean. They should have long enough handles to keep the griller a safe distance from the heat source. The spatula should be big enough to hold a delicate cooked salmon fillet. Its stainless steel blade should be strong, but also thin enough to allow the separation of skin from the meat of fish cooked "on skin." Tongs must provide sufficient grip to ensure the safe transport of food. A fork should never be part of the tools inventory. It pierces meat, allowing precious juices to be lost. Use the tongs instead.

- Skewers keep pieces of food together for cooking. They can be bamboo presoaked in water for appetizers and larger steel skewers for kebabs. The nicest steel skewers I have seen are from Turkey. Mine are from the Grand Bazaar in Istanbul. The flat (so they don't roll on the grill) stainless steel blades are 14-inches long with decorative brass handles. They work very well and are a joy to behold loaded with kebabs.
- Brushes are used for basting, marinating, etc. The best are made of silicon. They can withstand the heat of the grill and are easy to wash. Have a few at hand as you don't want to use the same brush for basting as was used to brush the marinade on raw meat.
- Grill Topper is a tray that goes on the grill rack to keep small food items from falling through. Its nonstick perforated bottom allows drippings to fall through the grill rack to produce the barbecue taste.
- Baskets of various sizes and shapes allow easy grilling of smaller food items that would otherwise fall through the grill rack. Others are for such tasks as grilling fish or grilling and flipping a quantity of hamburgers all at once. Still others are designed to attach to a spit to allow spit roasting of kebabs and ribs or to "tumble" smaller food items. These are not "must have" tools, but can provide satisfaction.
- Apron, as grilling can be very messy at times.

Safety Tips

- For propane gas cylinders, whether full or empty, and fire starter fluid, provide safe storage outside and away from heat sources.
- Make sure gas hoses and connectors are in good condition and hooked up according to the manufacturer's directions. Compressed gas is a dangerous commodity, and the hardware that controls it must always be treated with respect.
- Periodically clean your grill of fat accumulations that could lead to flare-ups. Occasionally fire up the empty grill on high temperature for 10 minutes or so to burn off excess accumulation.
- Charcoal grillers should use only fire starters certified for use with outdoor grills. Never spray fire starter on hot coals. You don't want to set fire to more than the charcoal!
- Always keep the grill cover open when igniting gas burners. You don't want to blow the cover off the grill. Make sure to follow the manufacturer's instructions for turning your grill on and off.
- Never line the bottom of a gas or charcoal grill with aluminum foil. It obstructs airflow.
- Never use a charcoal or gas grill indoors or in any other enclosed area. Gas and charcoal combustion produces carbon monoxide and carbon dioxide gases. Both are lethal in confined areas.
- Never grill too close to trees, deck railings or house overhangs for fire safety.
- Never leave a grill unattended or in the care of a child. The unforeseen must always be expected.
- Use the proper tools for the job — see previous section.
- Keep a water-filled spray bottle at hand to extinguish minor flare-ups as well as a supply of baking soda for more serious flare-ups. You can also move food to another part of the grill, close the lid and let the flare-up burn off. Closing the lid reduces the oxygen supply to smother the fire. Do have a fire extinguisher readily available

in case the situation escalates out of hand.

- Eliminating as much excess fat as is feasible mitigates the flare-up problem before it happens.
- Never baste food on the grill with used marinade unless it has been boiled for at least 5 minutes to kill bacteria. Discard any leftover marinade.
- Remove cooked food from the grill to a clean plate to prevent cross-contamination from the plate the raw meat was on. This can prevent food poisoning.

Health Concerns

Grilling and broiling do not present any more health risks than other methods of high-temperature cooking such as broiling or pan-frying. Furthermore, grilling is a low-fat cooking method because some of the fat in meat drains off during cooking. However, there are still three principal health risks associated with grilling:

- Risk of food contamination leading to food poisoning is probably the highest health risk because grilling is performed out of doors where the level of sanitation practiced may be less than in the family kitchen. The solution of course is to think and practice sanitation as you grill. Wash your hands, guard against bacteria cross-contamination from dishes, tools and counter surfaces exposure to raw meat.
- Risk of cancer from eating charred food is well-recognized by cancer authorities. Fortunately, the answer is very simple: Don't eat charred food. Trim it off. Better still, don't char the meat when you grill it by avoiding flare-ups (see Safety Tips, previous page) and overcooking.
- Cancer specialists also recognize risk from cancer-causing chemicals deposited on grilling foods from the smoke from burning fat. The cure is to use leaner cuts of meat and trim fat from meat before grilling.

And in closing, I found this little phrase very appropriate "Gentlemen, in the little moment that remains to us between crisis and catastrophe, we may as well drink a glass of champagne" — Paul Claudel (1868–1955).

It goes without saying that a glass is raised to all, gentlemen or ladies, who find this book helpful, fun to use and also a good read.

ACKNOWLEDGMENTS

We wish to thank and acknowledge the many interested and helpful people who have assisted me with this revision of *All Fired Up!* There are always certain challenges that are encountered in a revision, as newer recipes must replace old favorites. It has been great fun to be "back at the grill." The new, and we hope helpful information, as well as greatly improved meat cooking charts will assist when you are "at the grill" — beef, pork, lamb, veal, game meats and poultry, be they spit-roasted or done as kebabs, indirect or direct grilled. The many new and tasty recipes, I hope will inspire you to grill for a longer time period, but remember most recipes that use direct grilling can also be broiled in the oven or grilled on an indoor grill on your stove. Most recipes that use indirect grilling can be roasted in the kitchen oven. Thus *All Fired Up!* need not be placed on the bookshelf during the colder weather.

To Michael Worek, Associate Publisher, and Nicole Caldarelli, Editor, from Firefly Books for all their guidance and support.

To my husband John, who dug into this revision with such enthusiasm that he quickly became official Director of Research. While I typed recipes, tested recipes and tasted recipes (along with many other tasters), John looked up everything new on grilling that has been developed over the past 12 years since the original *All Fired Up!* was written. But John also was the key player in all grilling activities. And when he was not grilling, he used his considerable writing and editing skills to help me complete the manuscript.

Family members, daughters Martha and Janice, granddaughter Anna, sons Paul, wife Margie, son Andrew and his wife Rachael and their families as well as many friends who helped eat (and comment) their way through many grilled dinners over the revising and testing summer of 2009.

Del Rollo, National Director of Hospitality, Vincor Canada, a Constellation Company, who advised us on wine pairings, was like having a personal sommelier at my side. Plus he was invited to become another member of the Howard clan when he conducted an amazing wine tour for all of us in British Columbia Vincor wine country.

Bonnie J. Lacroix, PhD, RD, PHEc, who reviewed and commented on the meat temperature cooking charts.

Jake Doherty, a good friend and journalist, for his considerable editing skills.

I acknowledge the following, whose expertise I found invaluable. Web sites are provided:
Beef Information Centre — www.beefinfo.org
Canadian Pork Council — www.cpc-ccp.com
Chicken Farmers of Canada — www.chicken.ca
Turkey Farmers of Canada — www.turkeyfarmersofcanada.ca
Ontario Veal Association — www.ontariovealappeal.ca
Fresh Canadian Lamb — www.freshcanadianlamb.ca
Canadian Sheep Federation — www.cansheep.ca
Saskatchewan Sheep Development Board — www.sksheep.com
USDA Food Safety and Inspection Service — www.fsis.usda.gov/FactSheets
Vincor Canada — www.vincorinternational.com
Constellation Foods — www.cbrands.com
University of California at Berkeley Wellness Newsletter, July 2008

Welcome to the wonderful world of barbecuing!

Index

S